STEAM Through the Year: MATHEMATICS

by

Gary Carnow ■ Beverly Ellman ■ Joyce Koff

Copyright © 2018 by Inventive Thinkers®

All rights reserved. No part of this book may be reproduced, scanned, or distributed in any form or by any means electronic or mechanical without permission in writing from the publisher. All trademarks, service marks, registered trademarks, and registered service marks mentioned in this book are the property of their respective owners. Educators and noncommercial or nonprofit entities that have purchased this book may make copies of worksheets for classroom use.

We are appreciative of the staff and students of the following schools for their enthusiastic participation in the making of this book:
Coeur d'Alene Elementary, Venice, CA
Grant Elementary, Santa Monica, CA
Paul Revere Middle School, Los Angeles, CA
Santa Monica High School, Santa Monica, CA

Other books by these authors:
STEM Through the Months: Back-to-School
STEM Through the Months: Fall
STEM Through the Months: Winter
STEM Through the Months: Winter Holidays
STEM Through the Months: Spring

For information about Inventive Thinkers® workshops write to:

Inventive Thinkers®
www.inventivethinkers.org

Some illustrations by Sian Bowman

Brainy Icons Free are licensed under the Creative Commons Attribution License
http://handdrawngoods.com/store/brainy-icons-free/

2016 ISTE Standards for Students, ©2016, ISTE®
(International Society for Technology in Education), iste.org. All rights reserved.

ISBN-13: 978-1537642024
ISBN-10: 1537642022

Table of Contents

Welcome to STEAM Through the Year: MATHEMATICS 8

January

January Monthly, Weekly, and Moveable Holidays and Celebrations 20
January Days for STEAM Makers and Poets 21
January Overview 24

Celebration of Life Month
Math Lesson: Times of Our Life 25
Poetry Lesson: from Song of Myself by Walt Whitman 27

New Year's Day
Math Lesson: Mathematics Calendar Challenge 31
Poetry Lesson: New Year by Ella Wheeler Wilcox 32

International Thank You Day
Math Lesson: Geometry Grid Art Thank You Note 35
Poetry Lesson: Thanksgiving by Ralph Waldo Emerson 37

Martin Luther King, Jr. Day
Math Lesson: Milestone Math 40
Poetry Lesson: Hold Fast to Dreams by Langston Hughes 41

February

February Monthly, Weekly, and Moveable Holidays and Celebrations 44
February Days for STEAM Makers and Poets 45
February Overview 49

Black History Month
Math Lesson: Mancala 50
Poetry Lesson: We Wear the Mask by Paul Laurence Dunbar 52

National Freedom Day
Math Lesson: 1860 Census Data and Slavery 55
Poetry Lesson: Bury Me in a Free Land by Frances Ellen Watkins Harper 58

Valentine's Day
Math Lesson: Memory Matching Game With Candy Kisses 61
Poetry Lesson: A Red, Red Rose by Robert Burns 62

Presidents' Day
Math Lesson: President's Birthday Day Data Crunch 65
Poetry Lesson: Excerpt from The People, Yes by Carl Sandburg 68

March

March Monthly, Weekly, and Moveable Holidays and Celebrations 71
March Days for STEAM Makers and Poets 73
March Overview 77

Women's History Month
Math Lesson: Women's Barrier-Breaking Years 78
Poetry Lesson: Praised Be Diana's Fair and Harmless Light by Sir Walter Raleigh 81
Music in Our Schools Month
Math Lesson: Fractionated Rhythms 84
Poetry Lesson: The Violin – A Little Bit Nervous by Vladimir Mayakovsky 86
St. Patrick's Day
Math Lesson: Charming Math 90
Poetry Lesson: Limericks by Edward Lear 92
Suddenly It's Spring
Math Lesson: Fractional Spring Words 95
Poetry Lesson: The Caterpillar by Robert Graves 96

April

April Monthly, Weekly, and Moveable Holidays and Celebrations 99
April Days for STEAM Makers and Poets 101
April Overview 105
Children and Nature Awareness Month
Math Lesson: Nature Mastermind 106
Poetry Lesson: The Gladness of Nature by William Cullen Bryant 107
National Poetry Month
Math Lesson: OuLiPo Snowball Poems 110
Poetry Lesson: Introduction to Songs of Innocence by William Blake 112
Math Awareness Month
Math Lesson: Math in the Real World Scavenger Hunt 115
Poetry Lesson: Arithmetic by Carl Sandburg 117
Earth Day
Math Lesson: May The Forest Be With You 120
Poetry Lesson: The Cloud by Percy Bysshe Shelley 122

May

May Monthly, Weekly, and Moveable Holidays and Celebrations 126
May Days for STEAM Makers and Poets 128
May Overview 132
Wildflower Month
Math Lesson: Wildflower Calculations 133
Poetry Lesson: I Wandered Lonely as a Cloud by Williams Wordsworth 136
May Day
Math Lesson: Hawaiian Lei Day 139
Poetry Lesson: In May by William Henry Davies 141
Mother's Day
Math Lesson: Flower Power Bar Graph 144
Poetry Lesson: Child and Mother by Eugene Field 145

Memorial Day
Math Lesson: Savings Bonds 148
Poetry Lesson: Decoration Day by Evaleen Stein 149

June

June Monthly, Weekly, and Moveable Holidays and Celebrations 152
June Days for STEAM Makers and Poets 154
June Overview 158
National Fresh Fruit and Vegetable Month
Math Lesson: Fruit Divide Game 159
Poetry Lesson: Ode to Tomatoes by Pablo Neruda 162
National Zoo and Aquarium Month
Math Lesson: Go Fish for Equivalent Fractions 165
Poetry Lesson: An Aquarium by Amy Lowell 168
Father's Day
Math Lesson: Geometric Art 171
Poetry Lesson: A Boy and His Dad by Edgar Guest 172
Finally It's Summer
Math Lesson: Summer Solstice 175
Poetry Lesson: I'll Tell You How the Sun Rose by Emily Dickinson 177

July

July Monthly, Weekly, and Moveable Holidays and Celebrations 180
July Days for STEAM Makers and Poets 182
July Overview 185
National Picnic Month
Math Lesson: Planning a Picnic 186
Poetry Lesson: Excerpt from Audley Court by Alfred Lord Tennyson 188
Fourth of July
Math Lesson: Hot Dog Eating Contest 191
Poetry Lesson: Fearless Flying Hot Dogs by Jack Prelutsky 193
Math 2.0 Day
Math Lesson: Website Round-Up 196
Poetry Lesson: Excerpt – The Hunting of the Snark by Lewis Carroll 198
Moon Day
Math Lesson: Moon Day Crossword 201
Poetry Lesson: First Men on the Moon by J. Patrick Lewis 203

August

August Monthly, Weekly, and Moveable Holidays and Celebrations 206
August Days for STEAM Makers and Poets 207
August Overview 211
National Back-to-School Month
Math Lesson: Figure Me Out 212

Poetry Lesson: The Village Schoolmaster by Oliver Goldsmith 213
National Sandwich Month
Math Lesson: Sandwich Shop 216
Poetry Lesson: Recipe for a Hippo Sandwich by Shel Silverstein 217
National Friendship Week
Math Lesson: Card Sharks 220
Poetry Lesson: Inviting a Friend to Supper by Ben Jonson 222
National Ride the Wind Day
Math Lesson: Diamond Kites 225
Poetry Lesson: The Wind by Amy Lowell 227

September

September Monthly, Weekly, and Moveable Holidays and Celebrations 230
September Days for STEAM Makers and Poets 231
September Overview 236
Hispanic Heritage Month
Math Lesson: Salsa Measure by Measure 237
Poetry Lesson: One Today by Richard Blanco 239
Let's Celebrate Fall
Math Lesson: Leaf Length Investigation 242
Poetry Lesson: In Autumn by Winifred Marshall Gales 244
Skyscraper Day
Math Lesson: Math Empire State Building Run-Up Race 247
Poetry Lesson: Skyscraper by Rachel Lyman Field 249
Grandparents Day
Math Lesson: Leaf Symmetry Cards 252
Poetry Lesson: Butterfly Laughter by Katherine Mansfield 253

October

October Monthly, Weekly, and Moveable Holidays and Celebrations 256
October Days for STEAM Makers and Poets 258
October Overview 262
Apple Month
Math Lesson: Apple Pie Graph 263
Poetry Lesson: The Old Apple-Tree by Paul Laurence Dunbar 265
United Nations Day
Math Lesson: Time Zones 268
Poetry Lesson: I Dream a World by Langston Hughes 269
Statue of Liberty Dedication Day
Math Lesson: Monumental Math 272
Poetry Lesson: The New Colossus by Emma Lazarus 274
Halloween
Math Lesson: Comparing Pumpkins 277
Poetry Lesson: Excerpt from The Raven by Edgar Allen Poe 278

November

November Monthly, Weekly, and Moveable Holidays and Celebrations 282
November Days for STEAM Makers and Poets 284
November Overview 288

National Aviation Month
Math Lesson: Cruising Altitude Rule of Thumb 289
Poetry Lesson: High Flight, by John Gillespie Magee, Jr. 291

Native American Heritage Month
Math Lesson: Throw Sticks Game 294
Poetry Lesson: The Thanksgivings translated by Harriet Maxwell Converse 296

Veteran's Day
Math Lesson: Honoring the Numbers 299
Poetry Lesson: In Flanders Fields by John McCrae 301

Thanksgiving Day
Math Lesson: Traveling to Medford 304
Poetry Lesson: Thanksgiving Day by Lydia Maria Child 306

December

December Monthly, Weekly, and Moveable Holidays and Celebrations 309
December Days for STEAM Makers and Poets 310
December Overview 313

National Write a Letter to a Friend Month
Math Lesson: Writing in Code 314
Poetry Lesson: O! why was I born with a different face? by William Blake 317

Winter
Math Lesson: Marshmallow Geometry 321
Poetry Lesson: Winter Haikus by Matsuo Basho 323

December Holidays
Math Lesson: Shopping for Holiday Parties 326
Poetry Lesson: little tree by e. e. cummings 327

New Year's Eve
Math Lesson: Minute to Win It 330
Poetry Lesson: A Song for New Year's Eve by William Cullen Bryant 333

About Us

About Us 338

WELCOME

Welcome to STEAM Through the Year: Mathematics. Designed for teachers and students, these mathematics-focused STEAM activities will carry your class throughout the calendar year. Using monthly-themed events as a springboard, poetry as a language arts component and the maker movement for inspiration, your students will gain strong and relevant skills as they build cross-curricular connections while integrating math with science, technology, engineering and the arts.

THIS BOOK IS DESIGNED FOR YOU

This book was designed for teachers, students and parents. The activities are primarily for students in grades two through six. We know you will find these engaging lessons and projects easy to adopt and adapt for learners of all ages. You will STEAM through the year as you select special days, weekly celebrations and monthly-themed events.

Need a creative STEAM math lesson idea? Simply turn to one of the selected days and you're off and running. The math and poetry lessons have been classroom-tested and provide enjoyable learning experiences in a variety of environments: a traditional classroom, home schooling, after-school programs, scouting, gifted and talented programs, extracurricular clubs and ESL classes. For families looking for weekend or rainy day activities, we think you will find this to be a useful resource.

WHAT'S INSIDE?

Inside you will find twelve months of STEAM lessons and projects. The math units will keep your students motivated and engaged every month of the year. Learning standards are correlated to those developed by the National Council of Teachers of Mathematics (NCTM). The poetry experiences are inspired by holidays, special days, traditional observances and wacky celebrations. Drawing on the inner poet in every child and the "let me do-it-myself" nature inherent in all learners, the activities and lessons will help your students earn an "A" for the Arts and will bring STEAM to your STEM initiatives.

We begin each month with monthly, weekly and movable holidays. Whether it's a silly celebration or a traditional holiday, you will find it listed here, ready to kick start the imaginations of your students. Next, Integrating Math Days provide you with make and do activities that highlight at least six days of the month with background information and STEM/STEAM mathematically-inspired projects. In each month, there are four math units of study that coincide with a special day or a holiday along with a poetry lesson. Learning standards are correlated to the NCTM standards to help you with your planning. You will find the standards with each monthly overview. Do not feel obliged to use these ideas and projects only in these specific months. The projects and activities are great with their calendar collaborations, but your math curriculum and schedule may vary. We encourage you to use the activities and projects on a day that fits into your classroom plans.

STEM GAINS AN "A" - STEAM

The national movement to provide STEM experiences (science, technology, engineering and mathematics) for students gains steam on a daily basis. This is why we have focused on the arts to integrate a big "A" into STEM. Each unit includes a poetry lesson complete with a poet biography along with a poem. Students write their own poems based on the work of famous poets as they master common core language arts standards. The poems they craft will enhance the thematic experience. By exposure to poets, their lives and their works, students extend their observational skills as they write their own poems. Then their secrets unfold. From our teaching experience, we have learned that some teachers are uncomfortable teaching poetry. You will be amazed how easily these classroom-tested activities will assist young poets in discovering the joy of reading and writing poetry.

ABOUT STEAM

Educators and parents have no doubt heard the STEAM acronym, but are often confused as to what it means or what it actually looks like. STEAM is an acronym for five disciplines: science, technology, engineering, the arts and mathematics. These five disciplines are related and overlap, but we tend not to think of STEAM as unique unto itself. STEM/STEAM has become the next big thing due to concerns that U.S. students are falling behind and will not be able to fill the void left by an aging workforce. As we become increasingly global dependent, we want our students to be on equal footing with other students worldwide.

As classrooms adopt STEAM activities, teachers and students quickly realize that design thinking and project-based learning are at the core of all STEAM disciplines. To be college and career ready, a firm foundation of mathematics is required. Science is also essential and is a part of modern life. Science includes a body of knowledge and the ability to follow methods and processes to construct understanding. There are many scientific disciplines taught in school (for example, life science, earth science, physical science) and they spiral and interlap. In K-12, engineering education has long been overlooked. Engineering brings design thinking to the classroom and students collaborate, communicate, and think creatively as they construct solutions to real-world problems. The practical applications of engineering in conjunction with science and math foundations are a necessity. Technology is a part of our everyday life and should be a part of daily school practice. Technology, particularly computing technology, be it handheld devices or desktop computers, is a tool that enhances learning. Technology can be an underlying support in all aspects of schooling, not just a tool for STEAM disciplines.

As STEAM education is adopted in state standards for mathematics and included in the Next Generation Science Standards (NGSS), schools are looking for innovative ways to integrate these highly engaging disciplines. We believe that STEM experiences are important for all students at all grade levels. We see STEAM as highly engaged learning and we know that you will find the projects and activities in this book helpful.

MATHEMATICS, POETRY AND STEAM CONNECTIONS

Albert Einstein said "Pure mathematics is, in its way, the poetry of logical ideas." Poetry and mathematics have much in common. Both poetry and mathematics contain patterns, symbolism, rhythms and beats. For example, a graph in math or a rainbow in poetry use symbolism. Symmetry is found in mathematical equations and in the structure of poetry. Additionally, balanced equations in mathematics are as orderly as the rhythm and harmony in poetry. Both are mysterious and need to be practiced and experienced to understand. Then their secrets unfold.

STEAM learning and teaching encourages students to observe their world through their senses. Students construct knowledge through observation and practice in science, technology, engineering, and math. This is also true for poetry.

Each monthly chapter includes the work of four famous poets. Each selected poet is presented along with a biography, a sample poem and a lesson guide. Most of the poems we have selected are in the public domain. Those that are not, are easily found. Your students will call upon their inner voices as they experience writing a poem in the style of the poet that they are studying. Students will also gain an appreciation for the life circumstances and the period of time in which the poet lived and worked. Each poet is presented in a thematic unit based upon a holiday or special day. The poets are the glue that binds each unit of study in the book and provides a unique language arts underpinning to STEAM education.

TECHNOLOGY

We hope that you have access to some classroom or school technology. As technology-using educators, we know that consistent involvement with technology enriches the classroom experience. For over thirty years, students and teachers have used technology tools to add exciting dimensions and high interest to classroom work. We have specifically designed these activities and projects to be enriched through the use of technology; however, it is not a pre-requisite. Paper, pencils and other common classroom supplies will suffice. If you have access to a few computers and a printer, great; we believe strongly in using what you have. There is no need to go out and buy the latest and greatest.

Handhelds including tablets, smartphones, watches and other devices utilize mobile apps that can enhance your learning environment. Students become engaged in their learning and build knowledge through hands-on experiences with various apps. Some schools have adopted BYOD (bring your own device) policies that enrich their technology opportunities for their students. You don't need a full classroom set of anything to integrate technology into your curriculum.

Many schools have employed Chromebooks for use in their classrooms. With a Chromebook, students use Google Docs, Sheets and Slides as their productivity applications.

Google also provides Chromebook Classroom, Picasa, Calendar, and Sites. New features and applications are enhanced and added on a regular basis. Third-party developers have also created essential tools and fun applications. With a Chromebook, students create their documents and presentations and store them in the cloud using Google Drive. Students can invite others to collaborate on their documents giving them the ability to edit, view and comment. You can also view a document's revision history and go back to previous versions. Google Docs plays well with Microsoft Word, OpenOffice, Pages and other word processing programs. Similarly, Google Sheets imports and converts from Excel and other spreadsheet file formats, including Numbers. Google Slides share formats with PowerPoint and Keynote.

Many of the projects in this book use word processing, spreadsheet and presentation software. Whether you have access to computers with that software on the drive or Chromebooks with the application in the cloud, you are set to go. For classrooms with laptops or desktop computers with a hard drive, you have the additional functionality of editing video and using music software. Many tablets and iPads with apps like iMovie and Garage Band will also give you this functionality.

IMPLEMENTING GREAT MATH LESSONS

We construct new knowledge by utilizing our existing knowledge, past experiences, motivations and learning styles. Integrating your content along with real-world problems, student mathematical skills develop. Use real-world objects and manipulatives (for example, commercially available attribute blocks, cubes or Cuisenaire® rods and/or classroom-made flash cards, play money and geometric shapes). If you have access to a 3D printer, you can even print out your own tangram and cube puzzle manipulatives. Along with manipulatives, we encourage students to work in cooperative groups and to document the process of mathematical thinking by writing, journaling or group charting their responses.

When implementing your math lessons, discuss and talk about the mathematics involved. Model the mathematical thinking and logic as you work with manipulatives appropriate to the content. Read and write in the symbolic language of mathematical equations. Work with students to connect spoken language with written and symbolic language. For example, if three very cool cats meet two other very cool cats, how many cool cats met at school? It's often helpful to diagram or draw a picture of the problem. Students can then tally and count, speak the words along with the number representations and finally create an equation along with a complete sentence.

TECHNOLOGY TOOLS AND APPS

Here are a few of our favorite technology tools and apps, divided into a series of categories. As programs and apps tend to come and go, what was initially free, may now be a paid app or require a subscription. In any event, hopefully you will find something new to try along with some of our long-standing favorites.

Art, Graphics and Photo Software
Blender (free and open source) – https://www.blender.org/
Corel Paint Shop
Kid Pix Deluxe 4 and Kid Pix 3D
Photoshop and Photoshop Elements
PIXLR (free) – https://pixlr.com
Turtle Art (free) – http://turtleart.org
Tux Paint (free) – http://tuxpaint.org
wpclipart (public domain clip art for schoolkids) – https://www.wpclipart.com/index.html

Education Suites
Adobe Creative Cloud (monthly subscription)
Apple Keynote, Numbers, and Pages (bundled with a Mac)
Google Apps (Classroom, Gmail, Drive, Calendar, Docs, Sheets, Slides, and Sites)
Microsoft Office Suite
Open Office (free) – http://openofficefreedownload.org

Design
Canva – https://www.canva.com/
PrintShop 3 for Mac – https://www.mackiev.com/printshop3/features/whatsnew.html

Interactive Applications
HyperStudio – http://www.mackiev.com/hyperstudio/
ThingLink – https://www.thinglink.com/

iPhone/iPad/Android Apps
Snapseed – available on iTunes or Google Play
Sock Puppets – https://itunes.apple.com/us/app/sock-puppets/id394504903?mt=8
Zoodle Comics – https://itunes.apple.com/us/app/zoodle-comics/id520954201?mt=8

Miscellaneous Applications
Chartgo (free) – http://www.chartgo.com/
Create A Graph (free) – https://nces.ed.gov/nceskids/createagraph/
Comic Life – https://plasq.com/apps/comiclife/macwin/
GarageBand (bundled with a Mac)
Timeliner – http://teacher.scholastic.com/products/tomsnyder.htm

Presentation (also see Screencasting)
Any of the education suites.
PowToon (basic version free) – https://www.powtoon.com/
Prezi (free trial available) – https://prezi.com/

Programming/Coding
Scratch (free) – https://scratch.mit.edu/
Tynker (free version available, subscription plans too) – https://www.tynker.com/
Hopscotch (free) – https://www.gethopscotch.com/
Tickle (free) – https://tickleapp.com/

Screencasting Tools
Snagit – https://www.techsmith.com/snagit.html
Screencast-O-Matic – https://screencast-o-matic.com/home
Screencastify – https://www.screencastify.com/
Movenote – https://www.movenote.com/
Explain Everything – http://explaineverything.com/

Search Engines
Duck Duck Go (free) – https://duckduckgo.com/
Google
Google Kiddle (free) – http://www.kiddle.co/

Video Editing
Adobe Premiere Elements
Adobe Premiere Pro (subscription)
Animoto (free trial available) – https://animoto.com/
iMovie (free with Mac purchase)
Loopster (web based, basic version free) – http://www.loopster.com/
WeVideo (web based, free trial available) – https://www.wevideo.com/

Writing
Inspiration, Kidspiration and Kidspiration Maps (lite version free) –
    http://www.inspiration.com/
Stationery Studio Writing Collection Deluxe – http://shop.fablevisionlearning.com
Storybird – https://storybird.com/

MATHEMATICS ON THE WEB
There are many great mathematic websites that are at no cost for you and your students. Here are a few worth checking out.

www.aaamath.com
A wide range of interactive arithmetic lessons translated into over one hundred languages.

www.hoodamath.com
Classroom math games with customizable content for your classroom.

illuminations.nctm.org
A website designed by the National Council of Teachers of Mathematics. Here you will find featured lessons, mobile games, interactive activities and brain teasers.

www.khamacademy.com
The site offers instructional videos, practice exercises, and a personalized learning dashboard to assist student learning inside and outside of the classroom.

https://kids.usa.gov/math/
Kids.gov is the official kids' portal for the U. S. government organized into K-5, 6-8, teachers and parents. Click on the math offerings.

www.mathabc.com
Dr. Genius provides free websites for math skills in grades K-6.

www.mathgametime.com
Free, fun and engaging math games, worksheets and videos.

www.mathplayground.com
Over 100 free educational games that can be played on any mobile device.

www.mathisfun.com
K to grade 12 curriculum providing fun math activities from the United Kingdom.

multiplication.com
Flashcards, worksheets, games, and quizzes for grades 1-8.

CLASSROOM PUBLISHING

Students use language arts to show others their thinking, compositions and creativity. Making work public validates the work. As early as the one-room schoolhouse, teachers have displayed student writing and drawings. Work is sent home and no doubt is still published on refrigerator doors. With appropriate technology your students can discover, invent and explore as they publish, illustrate and arrange their written work. These *STEAM Through the Year* projects and lessons will be enhanced if you have access to word processing software or classroom publishing software. Your students will enrich their STEAM content as they also develop skills in page layout, illustrations, color and typography. Students will also receive value from seeing their ideas in print, whether they are working on a report or a classroom newsletter. We encourage you to explore the use of a simple digital handheld device, for example, a camera or a tablet, so that students can publish their work to digital lockers, websites or social media.

"STEAM'ING" ACROSS THE CURRICULUM

You may be familiar with "writing across the curriculum." Today we challenge you to use "STEAM'ing" across the curriculum. The activities in this book follow monthly, weekly and daily celebrations across the academic spectrum, with a focus on mathematics as it integrates with the arts. Student participation is continuously encouraged through questioning, problem solving, collaboration and hands-on activities. Teacher facilitators guide students as they plan and design projects and work in groups to master content.

COMPUTER PROGRAMMING

Schools are looking at ways to add programming into their curriculum. The tools to do so are readily available and even young children are learning to code. Most of the block programming languages are related to Seymour Papert's Logo. Logo is more than just a programming language, it is also a philosophy of education. Logo employs discovery learning and is linked with constructivism, a learning theory. Constructivism relies on students experimenting and solving real-world problems. Students construct their knowledge and understanding through experiences and reflective thought.

A good place to get started with programming is with Scratch, designed for kids at the MIT Media Lab. Scratch is browser-based and is on the web. There are millions of projects created and ready for your students to explore, remix and customize to your liking. There are plenty of tutorials and educator websites for you to explore. Get started here at https://scratch.mit.edu/. Scratch works well with many of the projects in this book. Presentations and animations can be done in Scratch.

WHAT IS THE MAKER MOVEMENT?

The Maker Movement is a revolutionary global collaboration of people learning to solve problems with modern tools and technology. Children and adults are combining new technologies and timeless craft traditions to create exciting projects. The Maker and DIY (Do-It-Yourself) movements are fostering a new enthusiasm to work with your hands and see tangible results. In the 1990s, as we prepared a new generation of knowledge workers, the goal was to round up all warm bodies and send them off to college, then to a cubicle in a career to fuel the information economy. This vision has not materialized. Now, more than ever, we need people who know how to do things: build houses, fix cars and solve problems.

WHAT IS A MAKERSPACE?

The new buzz word is makerspace. These spaces are sometimes called STEM Labs, STEAM Labs and/or Fab Labs. As the Maker Movement continues to grow exponentially in local communities, makers in on-line spaces and physical spaces are coming together in meet-ups and hackerspaces to create, collaborate and share resources. These spaces are what we call makerspaces. They come in many shapes and sizes. Students use makerspaces to build and invent as they creatively engage. A makerspace is more than an art room, a woodshop, a computer lab or a science lab. A makerspace, however, may contain elements found in these traditional spaces.
A makerspace culture promotes student construction and prototyping. Students cross-pollinate their ideas and knowledge as they make products and solve problems. These activity hubs foster collaboration and a culture of creativity. The activities support design thinking, project-based learning and STEM/STEAM initiatives.

We encourage you to start with what you have. Your space might be a mini-space or a pop-up space. Your makerspace may initially, double as another space. Don't worry too much about the physical space, what is more important is the building of a maker and design thinking culture. A makerspace is not necessarily defined by what tools and materials are contained in the space, but is perhaps better defined by what happens in the space – *making*

WHAT GOES IN A MAKERSPACE?

Making is not a shopping list of products. With that said, there are categories of maker materials and tools that you may wish to consider.

- Arts and Crafts
  Materials (cardboard, paint, felt, etc.)
  Tools (glue gun, a Cricut®, silk screen, etc.)

- Building Systems
  Erector Sets®
  LEGO®
  K'NEX®
  Lincoln Logs®
  Tinkertoys®

- Computer Controlled Fabrication
  Additive Fabrication (3D printers)
  Subtractive Fabrication (mills, cutters)

- Computers
  Chromebooks
  Desktops
  iPhones and Android phones
  Laptops
  Tablets
  Watches

- Conductive Materials
  Traditional – wire, solder, brads, paper clips
  New – conductive thread, yarn, paint, fabric, yarn, graphite
  Future – electro conductive adhesive gel (Tac Gel) and biomaterials

- Electronics
  Batteries
  Displays
  LEDs
  Motors
  Sensors

- Interfaces
  MaKey MaKey
  Hummingbird

- Physical Computing
  Microcontrollers (Arduino, HyperDuino)
  Microcomputers (RaspberryPi)
  Robotics

- Programming
  Block programming (Scratch, SNAP)
  Text-based programming (C++, Python, Arduino)

- Textiles and Sewing
  e-textiles
  Wearables (Arduino, Lilypad, Flora)

MAKER TOOLS AND RESOURCES

Many of the lessons and projects in this book can be enhanced with maker tools and resources. The units and lesson extensions are starting points that can be enhanced with some of the exciting maker products now available. There are a variety of low-cost products that work with a computer and will challenge your students. Here are just a few of the many creative, open-ended products that your students can use to enhance your STEM/STEM curriculum with maker experiences. There is a growing list of materials and kits chock full of creative projects to try. Search Google for maker materials and supplies and you will find a wealth of choices. For example:

- littleBits – http://littlebits.cc/
  littleBits has a library of over sixty modules and each module works with every other. Begin with a power source, like a battery, and snap together (with magnets) to create a circuit. It's an easy way to learn how electronics work with or without programming skills. There is no soldering or use of breadboards. You can control the input and output with touch sensors and wires to create motion, light lights and create sounds. littleBits however, is not low-cost.

- MaKey Makey - http://www.makeymakey.com/
  MaKey MaKey is an invention kit. You turn everyday objects into touchpads and combine them with the Internet. The kit comes with an interface board, alligator clips, a USB cable and instructions. You can use any material that will conduct a bit of electricity to send your computer a keyboard or mouse input. Kids can devise games, mazes, musical instruments and much more.

- Makedo - https://mymakedo.com/
  Makedo are tools for cardboard construction. Using recycled cardboard you can build anything. If you can dream it, you can build it. Makedo are simple plastic parts, a safe-saw, plastic "scrus" and straps that become joints or hinges. Your projects will promote collaboration and problem solving.

- Hummingbird – www.humingbirdkit.com
  The Hummingbird Robotics Kit is a product of the Carnegie Mellon's CREATE Lab. Hummingbird's enable robotic and engineering activities. It is aimed at ages thirteen and up, but works well with ages eight and up with adult supervision. The kit parts along with crafting materials can make robots, animatronics and kinetic sculptures. Hummingbirds play well with Scratch and other programming languages.

- HyperDuino – www.hyperduino.com
  HyperDuino enables you to easily create your own interactive maker projects. The HyperDuino is a piggy-back board to an Arduino (a microcontroller) that connects to a Chromebook, a Macintosh and/or a Windows computer. The two-way hyperlink connects models in the physical world to the microcontroller. For example, you program the controller to play a video segment on a computer or light an LED on your physical model.

3D PRINTING

In this book there are many projects where you could incorporate a 3D printer and use the products you make in some of the activities. Besides the obvious technology and engineering aspects of 3D printing, students can design and prototype projects in a way they could have never done before. Kids have made musical instruments, jewelry and scale models of buildings and monuments and so much more.

Home hobbyists have enthusiastically used 3D printers to make and create a variety of prototypes and products and now your students can too. The cost of 3D printing has dramatically decreased and schools are beginning to purchase and use 3D printers. There are a variety of printers available and more are being introduced each year. Make magazine has an annual review of these printers. Currently, printers for schools and for home use cost anywhere from $400 to $2800.

What are kids doing with a 3D printer? Kids are using computer-aided design programs to create files in the needed stereolithography file format known as .stl. These files are loaded into a 3D printer from a computer. The software that comes with the printer slices these files into layers. The printer begins the additive process of printing an object, layer by layer.

There are many websites where you can get 3D .stl files. Some of these sites feature open source files, which let you modify and customize the files to your liking. You can get an idea of what is available by visiting sites like YouMagine (www.youmagine.com) and Thingiverse (www.thingiverse.com).

NOW LET'S GET STARTED

We think you will find the lessons and projects wonderful additions to your curriculum. We know that *STTEAM Through the Year: Mathematics* will jumpstart you to make, do and enjoy every month of the year.

January Monthly Holidays

Adopt a Rescued Bird Month • Bath Safety Month • Celebration of Life Month • Get Organized Month • International Creativity Month
Learn to Ski and Snowboard Month • National Braille Literacy Month
National Hot Tea Month • National Mail Order Gardening Month
National Mentoring Month • National Polka Music Month
Oatmeal Month • Walk Your Pet Month

January Weekly Holidays

First Week of January
Braille Literacy Week • National Lose Weight-Feel Great Week
New Year's Resolution Week

Second Week of January
Cuckoo Dancing Week • Elvis Presley Birthday Celebration Week
Healthy Weight Week • National Pizza Week • Universal Letter Writing Week

Third Week of January
Celebrity Read-a-Book Week • Fresh Squeezed Juice Week • Hunt for Happiness Week • International Printing Week • National Clean Out Your In-Box Week • National Thrift Week • No Name Calling Week

Fourth Week of January
Catholic Schools Week • Junior Achievement Week • National Handwriting Analysis Week • National School Choice Week

January Moveable Holidays

National Weigh-in Day ....first Monday

National Clean-Off-Your-Desk-Day .... second Monday

Martin Luther King Day of Service... third Monday

Bubble Wrap® Appreciation Day...last Monday

Fun-at-Work-Day .... last Friday

January Days for STEAM Makers and Poets

1. Ellis Island Day
2. National Science Fiction Day
3. National Drinking Straw Day
4. Trivia Day
5. National Bird Day
6. National Bean Day
7. International Programmer's Day
8. Bubble Bath Day
9. National Static Electricity Day
10. National Cut Your Energy Costs Day
11. International Thank You Day
12. National Pharmacist Day
13. Skeptics Day
14. National Dress Up Your Pet Day
15. National Hat Day
16. Appreciate a Dragon Day
17. Kid Inventors' Day
18. Thesaurus Day
19. National Popcorn Day
20. Camcorder Day
21. Granola Bar Day
22. National Answer Your Cat's Question Day
23. National Handwriting Day
24. National Peanut Butter Day
25. Observe the Weather Day
26. Disneyland Ground-Breaking Day
27. National Chocolate Cake Day
28. Christa McAuliffe Day
29. Puzzle Day
30. National Escape Day
31. Backwards Day

Integrating January Math Days

Science Technology Engineering Arts Math

	Day	Make and Do
1	Ellis Island Day	Twelve million immigrants passed through the halls of Ellis Island from 1892 to 1954. The National Park Service offers distance learning, curriculum materials and more through the Ellis Island website at www.nps.gov/elis/index.htm. Download the U.S. Immigration Statistics from: https://www.nps.gov/elis/learn/education/upload/statistics.pdf. Use the data to create math problems, graphs and charts using the data from 1892 to 1924.
4	Trivia Day	Create a math trivia board game to play with your friends. Choose an area of math that interests you. For example, if you select geometry create a set of game cards and a game board. Focus on shapes, lines and angles. If you want to make an interactive math trivia game, check out Kahoot. You can find it at getkahoot.com.
6	National Bean Day	Some believe that National Bean Day commemorates the death of geneticist Gregor Mendel in 1884 who famously used beans and pea plants to demonstrate his theories on inheritance. It's a great day to play Bean Nim. Nim is a math game where both payers have exactly the same information and chance plays no part. Start with a pile of dried beans. Alternate turns by taking up to three beans and you may not pass. The loser takes the last bean. What was your winning strategy? Try replaying the game, but this time the winner is the one who takes the last bean.

7	International Programmer's Day	Celebrate by exploring Scratch, a programming language and online community developed by Mitchel Resnick at the MIT Media Lab and launched in 2006. You can find Scratch at http://scratch.mit.edu. Scratch is a free programming platform that lets you create interactive stories, games and animations. Scratch users embrace their slogan: "Imagine, Program, Share." What will you program today? Begin by checking out the tutorial. Create an animated math problem.
8	Bubble Bath Day	For over 50 years, Mr. Bubble continues to be the best-selling bubble bath in the USA. Become a product engineer and make your own customized bubble bath. Start with ½ cup of shampoo, dish soap, hand soap or Castile soap. Add one tablespoon of honey as a moisturizer or choose from olive, almond or jojoba oil. Add an egg white to help keep your bubbles big and strong. Lastly, add five drops of the essential oil of your choice. Select lavender, lemon or sandalwood. Shake it up in a plastic container. What will you name your creation? Design a label for your bubble bath. Create a spreadsheet that shows how much of each ingredient you will need to make fifty bottles of bubble bath and determine the cost of your raw ingredients.
24	National Peanut Butter Day	Today is National Peanut Butter Day. Invent the best peanut butter sandwich ever. Write the recipe and list the ingredients and quantity. Using a spreadsheet, calculate the cost of making your peanut butter sandwich for everyone in your class. You will need to determine the cost of your ingredients by checking out serving sizes and prices on the Internet.
29	Puzzle Day	Be it crosswords, jumbles, jigsaws or sudoku, puzzles are lots of fun. Have a puzzle day party and set up a series of competitions. Logic puzzles are also fun to solve and to create. You can even plan your event online at www.logic-puzzles.org.

January Overview

Celebration of Life Month
Math Lesson: Times of Our Life
Poetry Lesson: from Song of Myself by Walt Whitman
With this month's theme, we reflect and appreciate each day of our life and recognize that life is precious. In this lesson students think about future celebrations. Students decide the age they will be for specific life events, determine how many years from now the events will take place and compute what year it will be accomplished. Using Whitman's Song of Myself as a model, students write a catalog poem celebrating life.
NCTM STANDARD 2: Algebra, Gr 3 – 2B-3; Gr 4 – 2B-4; Gr 5 – 2B4

New Year's Day
Math Lesson: Mathematics Calendar Challenge
Poetry Lesson: New Year by Ella Wheeler Wilcox
In the United States, we think of the New Year as a time to begin again with new hopes and dreams. Students use a calendar for the upcoming year as they work in groups to create mathematical word problems. In the poetry lesson, students speak to the "New Year" telling what they will do to make it a good one.
NCTM STANDARD 1: Numbers and Operations, Grade 3 – 1A-1
NCTM STANDARD 2: Algebra, Gr 3, 2B-3; Gr 4 – 2B-4; Gr 5 –2B-4; Gr 6 – 2B-4

International Thank You Day
Math Lesson: Geometry Grid Art Thank You Note
Poetry Lesson: Thanksgiving (A poem for everyday) by Ralph Waldo Emerson
We celebrate this day by taking the time to say thank you to the people in our lives and let them know they are appreciated. Students hone measurement, graphing and other math skills to create enlarged grid thank you cards for special school personnel. In the poetry lesson, students reflect upon and write about people and things for which they are thankful.
NCTM STANDARD 3: Geometry, Gr 6 – 2B-3

Martin Luther King, Jr. Day
Math Lesson: Milestone Math
Poetry Lesson: Hold Fast to Dreams by Langston Hughes
This day was established to remember and honor Martin Luther King, Jr. Using birthdates and milestone timelines, students practice creating and solving multi-step math problems. With Langston Hughes' poem as a model, students write about the importance of dreams.
NCTM STANDARD 4: Measurement, Gr 4 – 4B-11
NCTM STANDARD 2: Algebra, Gr 6 – 2B-4

Celebration of Life Month
Math Lesson: Times of Our Life

With this month's theme, we pause to reflect and appreciate each day of our life. In this lesson students think about future celebrations. Students decide the age they will be for specific life events, determine how many years from now the events will take place and compute what year it will be accomplished.

MATERIALS
- Pencil, paper
- Board, chart, marker
- Celebration of Life Worksheet

PLAN
- Talk about the Celebration of Life monthly theme with the class.
- Have students brainstorm to create a list of the events they hope to celebrate during the days of their lives. Some possible events are:
    - Getting a driver's license
    - High school graduation
    - Voting
    - College graduation
    - Starting a career
    - Renting an apartment
    - Getting married
    - Having a family
    - Buying a home
    - Traveling to another country
    - Becoming a grandparent
    - Retirement

DO
- Divide the class into small groups to discuss the events on the class list.
- Have the group members discuss what events they see themselves celebrating, at what age and how many years from now the events will occur.
- Distribute the Celebration of Life Worksheet to each student and have each complete his/her worksheet.
- Display the completed worksheets on a Celebration of Life bulletin board.

Celebration of Life Worksheet

Your Name_____   Current Year_____

Year You Were Born_____   Your Age_____

Life Event Selected	Age to Accomplish?	How Many Years From Now?	Year to Accomplish?

Celebration of Life Month
Poetry Lesson: Song of Myself

There couldn't be a more ideal poet to represent Celebration of Life Month than Walt Whitman. In his epic poem, *Song of Myself*, he celebrates himself by stating "the song of me rising from bed and meeting the sun." He includes in his celebration everything in creation that he experiences, starting with the smallest "spear of summer grass." The poem is Whitman's journey where he learns about himself through first-hand experiences and advises his readers that they must take their own journey to discover who they are, "You shall not look through my eyes either, nor take things from me, /You shall listen to all sides and filter them from your self." Whitman extols "The smoke of my own breath" to the entire universe and to all time. He is the universe – a part of all present and past as he makes his celebrated journey. Whitman uses a poetic technique known as catalog and he lists all people, animals and objects he meets on his journey. They become part of him just as he becomes part of them.

MATERIALS
- Walt Whitman Biography and his poem *Song of Myself*
- Word processing or desktop publishing software or pencils, pens and paper
- Board or chart

PLAN
- Read and discuss Walt Whitman's biography.
- Read and discuss *Song of Myself* using the following questions:
    - What does Whitman celebrate?
    - What does he mean when he states, "For every atom belonging to me, as good belongs to you?"
    - What kind of learning does he think is the most valuable?

DO
Getting Ready to Write
- During a brainstorming session, ask students to review the following questions and discussion points. As they give their responses, list them on the board or on a chart.
    - What things about yourself do you celebrate?
      For example: *your laughter, your smiling face, your great hugs*
    - What are the most memorable experiences that you celebrate?
      For example: *reading a book with your mother*
    - What are the most memorable things in nature that you celebrate?
- Have class expand each item on the list using metaphors, similes, descriptions and personification.

Writing the Poem
Students write a catalog poem. A catalog poem begins with a list. Have students write a poem with a minimum of ten lines.
- Suggest students title their poem "Song of My Life."
- Begin the first line with the words "I celebrate life."
- Begin the second line with something about their body. For example: *my beating heart*
- Continue the poem by listing other aspects of themselves, their experiences, and things in nature, each on a separate line.
  For example:
  the freckles that sit on my nose
  reading a book with my grandmother
  the shade of the oak tree.
- Students may expand and enhance each item on their list.

Editing and Publishing
- Have students read and edit poems with partners.
- Students compose or publish their poems in a word processing program.
- Students illustrate their final masterpieces.
- Extend the lesson by selecting some of the best poems to include in a class anthology.

Walt Whitman Biography
May 31, 1819 – March 26, 1892

Walt Whitman was born in Long Island, New York. His parents could not read or write very well. Walt lived part of his childhood on a farm on Long Island and part in the city of Brooklyn. He was very smart but seemed to be lazy and in a dream world.

He left school when he was eleven years old and worked at many different jobs. Although eleven seems very young to us now, it was not uncommon in the 1800s for a child to leave school at a young age.

After years of searching Whitman became a journalist. It was a perfect profession for him because he loved to write. After working for many newspapers, he was offered a job in New Orleans, Louisiana. In the 1800s, travelling from New York to Louisiana was a very long trip. On his travels to Louisiana he had the opportunity to see much of America. He traveled the open roads, down rough rivers and across the land.

As he traveled, Whitman saw much of this country and met many different people. He felt lucky for the kind of education he received through his travels. He believed the only way to understand something was to experience it first-hand. The cities and people he saw on his travels became subjects for much of his poetry.

Whitman's poetry sings with the freedom he felt as he travelled. He developed a form of poetry called free verse. Instead of restricting himself to accepted formulas for writing poetry, Whitman wrote as he spoke. His poetic lines were the natural flow and pauses of his own speech. His voice became a symbol of our country, where people have the freedom to express themselves, each in their own way.

Excerpt from Song of Myself
by Walt Whitman

I celebrate myself, and sing myself,
And what I assume you shall assume,
For every atom belonging to me, as good belongs to you.

...

I loafe and invite my soul;
I lean and loafe at my ease, observing a spear of summer grass.

...

The smoke of my own breath,
Echoes, ripples, buzz'd whispers, love-root, silk-thread, crotch and vine,
My respiration and inspiration, the beating of my heart, the passing of blood
    and air through my lungs,
The sniff of green leaves and dry leaves, and of the shore and dark-color'd sea-
    rocks, and of hay in the barn,
The sound of the belch'd words of my voice loos'd to the eddies of the wind,
A few light kisses, a few embraces, a reaching around of arms,
The play of shine and shade on the trees as the supple boughs wag,
The delight alone or in the rush of the streets, or along the fields and hill-sides,
The feeling of health, the full-noon trill, the song of me rising from bed and
    meeting the sun.

Have you reckon'd a thousand acres much? have you reckon'd the earth much?
Have you practis'd so long to learn to read?
Have you felt so proud to get at the meaning of poems?

Stop this day and night with me, and you shall possess the origin of all poems,
You shall possess the good of the earth and sun--(there are millions of suns
    left,)
You shall no longer take things at second or third hand, nor look through the
    eyes of the dead, nor feed on the spectres in books;
You shall not look through my eyes either, nor take things from me,
You shall listen to all sides, and filter them from your self.

New Year's Day
Math Lesson: Mathematics Calendar Challenge

In the New Year's Mathematics Calendar Challenge, students review math concepts to get ready for new learning. Student groups create word problems using the days and weeks of the month.

MATERIALS
- January calendar page
- Pencils
- Projector
- Chart paper

PLAN
- Project the calendar page for January on the board.
- Using calendar information, guide the class as they create one or two math questions about concepts they have learned. Write the problems and their solutions on the chart.
- The following are examples from the January 2017 calendar page:
  1. Multiply the date of the fourth Wednesday in January by the fraction created by using the date of the first Thursday in January as the numerator and the fourth Wednesday in January as the denominator.
     Answer: $25 \times 5/25 = 25 \times 1/5 = 5$
  2. Write the numerals for the first five days in the second week of January (beginning on Sunday) in sequential order. Place commas where they belong and write the word name of the created numeral.
     Answer: 89,101,112
     Eighty-nine million, one hundred one thousand, one hundred twelve

DO
- Divide the class into small groups.
- Distribute a January calendar page to each group.
- Using the calendar, have each group write several challenging math problems and their solutions.
- Have student volunteers from each group write one or two of the problems their group has created on chart paper for the rest of the class to solve.

New Year's Day
Poetry Lesson: New Year

In her poem, Ella Wheeler Wilcox personifies the New Year as she looks "straight into its eyes." Throughout the poem she tells the New Year that because of her positive perspective, strength and courage, she can help make it a good year.

MATERIALS
- Ella Wheeler Wilcox Biography and her poem *New Year*
- Word processing or desktop publishing software or pencils, pens, and paper

PLAN
Read and discuss Wilcox's biography and poem. Some sample guiding questions include:
- Where does Wilcox use personification?
- What does the New Year look like when she first sees it?
- Is she concerned about what this New Year will bring?
- How does she think she can make it a good New Year?

DO
Getting Ready to Write
During a brainstorming session, ask students the following questions:
- Using personification how would you begin talking to the New Year?
- What kind of person do you picture the New Year to be?
- What actions would you take to make the New Year a good one?

Writing the Poem
- Begin poems by greeting the New Year.
- Describe the New Year.
- Tell the New Year how you plan to make it a good year.
- Use powerful and descriptive parts of speech.

Editing and Publishing
- Have students read and edit poems with partners.
- Have students write their poems in a poetry book or enter them in a word processing program.
- Illustrate their final masterpiece.

Ella Wheeler Wilcox Biography
November 5, 1850 – October 30, 1919

Ella Wheeler Wilcox was born in Wisconsin. She was raised in an environment that nurtured her poetic talent. Her mother and many of her aunts and cousins wrote poetry and she was introduced to great works of literature. At a young age, she began to write poems. Her writing was well known in Wisconsin before she had even graduated from high school. She was an optimistic person and most of her poetry expresses that optimism. One of her most famous poems begins with the lines "Laugh, and the world laughs with you;/Weep, and you weep alone."

At age thirty-four she married Robert Wilcox. They loved to have gatherings in their home in Long Island where they entertained literary and artistic people. They had one son who died at a very young age. She and her husband were spiritual people. They remained married until his death.

One of her brothers said, "She wrote for the same reason that a bird sings. It was what she was made for." Wilcox became a well-known poet and a writer of quotes. In the opening of the movie JFK directed by Oliver Stone, she is quoted, "To sin by silence when we should protest makes cowards out of men." The first stanza of her poem *Worthwhile* can be seen in Disney's Hollywood Studios. The first four lines describe how Ella Wheeler Wilcox lived her life and how she encouraged others with her optimistic and brave view:

> "It is easy enough to be pleasant
> When life flows by like a song,
> But the man worthwhile is the one who will smile
> When everything goes dead wrong."

New Year
by Ella Wheeler Wilcox

New Year, I look straight in your eyes –
Our ways and our interests blend;
You may be a foe in disguise,
But I shall believe you a friend.
We get what we give in our measure,
We cannot give pain and get pleasure;
I give you good will and good cheer,
And you must return it, New Year.

We get what we give in this life,
Though often the giver indeed
Waits long upon doubting and strife
Ere proving the truth of my creed.
But somewhere, some way, and forever
Reward is the meed of endeavour;
And if I am really worth while,
New Year, you will give me your smile.

You hide in your mystical hand
No "luck" that I cannot control,
If I trust my own courage and stand
On the Infinite strength of my soul.
Man holds in his brain and his spirit
A power that is God-like, or near it,
And he who has measured his force
Can govern events and their course.

You come with a crown on your brow,
New Year, without blemish or spot;
Yet you, and not I, sir, must bow,
For time is the servant of thought
Whatever you bring me of trouble
Shall turn into good, and then double,
If my spirit looks up without fear
To the Source that you came from, New Year.

International Thank You Day
Math Lesson: Geometry Grid Art Thank You Note

We celebrate this day on January 11th by taking the time to say thank you to the people in our lives and let them know they are appreciated. Students work in pairs as they hone measurement, graphing and other math skills to create enlarged grid thank you cards for special school personnel on this day.

MATERIALS
- 5" x 7" standard greeting card pictures
- Cardstock or poster paper cut to 10" x 14"
- Paper or canvas
- Ruler
- Pencil
- Pen
- Eraser
- Board or chart
- Paints, markers, colored pencils

PLAN
- During the first week in January ask students to bring standard 5" x 7" greeting cards from home with pictures they would like copy and enlarge to create a large card to give on International Thank You Day.
- Discuss the purpose of International Thank You Day.
- Brainstorm a list of possible school personnel who will be recipients of the cards.
- Record the list on a board or chart.
- Divide the class into pairs and have each pair select a person for whom they will make a card.

DO
- Students select the 5" x 7" picture they want to enlarge for their thank you cards. Students may wish to use old greeting cards, pictures from magazines or a picture they found on the Internet.
- The partners decide whether they want to select a 1/2" grid spacing or a 1" grid spacing on their card.
- Students drawing grids for the first time might need to use a pencil with an eraser to erase mistakes. Experienced students may use a pen on the picture because each cell is then easier to see.
- Students draw the grid.

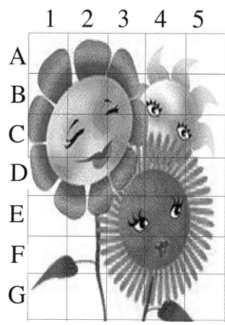

- Students use numbers to label the top boxes of the grid and letters on the left side as in the sample grid.
- Students create a reproduction of the gridded picture that is double the size of the original.
    - Draw a grid using a pencil on the 10" x 14" paper or cardstock as lightly as possible. The grid lines will be erased at the completion of the card.
    - The cardstock is double the size of the original 5" x 7" picture and students need to double the size of the grid. For example, a 1" grid space on their source pictures becomes a 2" grid space on the 10" x 14" cardstock. A 1/2" space becomes a 1" space.
    - Students draw the outline of each grid box on the cardstock by copying what they see in their gridded picture.
    - Remind students to pay attention to where the original drawing begins and ends in each grid box to achieve the most accurate reproduction of the original picture.
    - When the drawing is complete, students check the drawing to see that they have drawn each box accurately.
    - Color in the picture using paints, colored markers, colored pencils or an assortment of all three.
    - Students write a thank you message to the person of their choice on the enlarged card and deliver it on International Thank You Day.

International Thank You Day
Poetry Lesson: Thanksgiving

It may be January, but Ralph Waldo Emerson's poem *Thanksgiving* is truly a poem for all months. He reminds us to give thanks to people and to everything that enhances our lives, "For rest and shelter of the night,/For health and food,/For love and friends."

MATERIALS
- Ralph Waldo Emerson Biography and his poem *Thanksgiving*
- Word processing or desktop publishing software or pencils, pens and paper, fancy stationery or art materials to create stationery

PLAN
Read and discuss Emerson's biography and poem with sample guiding questions including:
- To what does Emerson think we should give thanks?
- Who is "thy"?

DO
Getting Ready to Write
During a brainstorming session, ask students the following questions. As the class gives their responses, list them on the board or on a chart.
- Emerson is thankful for "each new morning." What are you thankful for in your life?
- To whom would you give thanks?

Writing the Poem
- Suggest students title their poem *Thanksgiving*.
- Have them begin each line with "For" and to whatever and whomever in their everyday life they give thanks.
- Suggest they use line breaks just as Emerson did.

Editing and Publishing
- Students embellish their poem with a fancy border and print.
- Create a display of the finished poems.

International Thank You Day

Ralph Waldo Emerson Biography
May 25, 1803 – April 22, 1882

Ralph Waldo Emerson, who became one of the greatest of all American writers, was born in Concord, MA. By the time Ralph was a year old, he could talk. When he was three years old, he began working at jobs around the house. He was either in school or working. His father was very strict and never showed any affection or love for Ralph or his three brothers. He was a serious little boy, but his aunt thought that he was lazy, loving to read storybooks and recite poems rather than doing the lessons assigned to him. When his father died, his family became very poor. He and one of his brothers, having only one sweater between them, had to trade off wearing it. Other children would laugh at them.

By the time Ralph was nine, he began writing poetry and spent the little spare time he had writing. Ralph and one of his brothers went to live with their mother at their grandparents' home in Concord. He loved the farm in Concord where there was a river for swimming and boating. Climbing the hills and listening to the birds gave him great enjoyment. It was here that he developed a love of nature that would remain with him throughout his life. At Harvard College, Ralph was a mediocre student but loved literature. Rather than loving sports, he loved to write in a journal where he also played games with words. He graduated as class poet.

His passion was writing but he presented lectures to make a living. He traveled all over the United States and England. He always spoke to a full house, to both the very educated and the uneducated. The audience came away from his lectures uplifted.

When Ralph grew older, one of his greatest joys was showing love for his children and grandchildren, always remembering his hard childhood and being grateful that it was over. Emerson was a man with magical qualities. He spoke and wrote about the relationships of the spirit with nature and with man's goodness. The goodness that he wrote and lectured about was the goodness that comes from within. Those who knew him well and those that saw him speak considered him an angel.

Thanksgiving
by Ralph Waldo Emerson

For each new morning with its light,
For rest and shelter of the night,
For health and food,
For love and friends,
For everything Thy goodness sends.

For the stars that light the night sky
Noah – 2nd grade

For the last drop of water that we drink
Morgan – 2nd grade

Martin Luther King, Jr. Day
Math Lesson: Milestone Math

Using birthdates and milestone timelines, students practice creating and solving multi-step math problems.

MATERIALS
- Projector (optional)
- Pencils and paper
- MLK, Jr. Milestone Timeline and Children's Birthdates and Parent's Birthdates

MLK, Jr. Milestone Timeline

1/15/1929	1944	1946	1953	1956	1957	1963	1964	1968
Birth	Graduated High School	Graduated College	Married Coretta Scott	Win Bus Boycott	Formed Southern Christian Leadership Conference	Made "I have a Dream Speech"	Youngest recipient the Nobel Piece Prize	Assassinated

MLK's Children's Birthdates and Parent's Birthdates

Yolanda Denise .... November 17, 1955
Martin Luther III .... October 23, 1957
Dexter Scott .... January 30, 1961
Bernice Albertine .... March 28, 1963
Martin Luther "Daddy" King, Sr. .... December 19, 1897
Alberta Christine Williams .... September 13, 1903

PLAN
- Copy and distribute or project the above information.
- Write the following multi-step word problem for students to solve.
- How old was MLK and his father at the time MLK won the Nobel Peace Prize?
    - Step 1: Determine his father's age at the time Martin was born.
      1929 - 1897 = 32
    - Step 2: Determine Martin's age at the time he won the Nobel Peace Prize.
      1964 - 1929 = 34
    - Step 3: Add his father's age at Martin's birth plus his age when he won the prize.
      32 + 35 = 67
- Practice using the data to create and solve another multi-step problem.

DO
- Divide the class into small groups and have each group write word problems and their solutions.
- Each group presents their problems to the class and call on classmates to solve them.
- Culminate the lesson by discussing what students have learned about solving multi-step problems and about the life of Dr. Martin Luther King, Jr.

Martin Luther King, Jr. Day
Poetry Lesson: Hold Fast to Dreams

Like Martin Luther King, Jr., Langston Hughes also believed in the power of dreams. Hughes wrote about the importance of dreams and what happens "when dreams die." In his first stanza of the poem, Hughes describes the desperation of a life without dreams in the metaphor "Life is a broken-winged bird/That cannot fly."

MATERIALS
- Langston Hughes Biography and his poem *Hold Fast to Dreams*
- Word processing or desktop publishing software or pencils, pens, and paper

PLAN
- Read and discuss Langston Hughes's biography.
- Read the poem and explain a metaphor. For example: A metaphor compares two objects to each other without using the words like or as. Hughes compares life without dreams to both a "broken-winged bird" and "a barren field."
- Discuss the following questions:
    - What kind of dreams is Hughes writing about?
    - What does "hold fast" in the title mean?
    - How does he feel about life without dreams?

DO
Getting Ready to Write
During a brainstorming session, ask students to think of metaphors to describe life without dreams. For example, *Life without dreams is a clock that cannot tell time.*

Writing the Poem
- Students title their poem "Hold Fast to Dreams" or anything that has a similar meaning.
- For each stanza, students begin by copying the first two lines of Hughes' poem.
- Begin their third line with "Life is" and their own metaphor.
- Students add as many stanzas as they like.

Editing and Publishing
- Students read a stanza of their poem to the class.
- Students write their poems in a poetry book or enter them in a word processing program.
- Students illustrate their final masterpiece.

Langston Hughes Biography
February 1, 1902 - May 22, 1967

Langston Hughes began writing poetry in grammar school. When Hughes was growing up, he encountered prejudice not only because he was Black but also because he was part Indian and part white. He achieved recognition as a Black poet. His grandmother always had confidence in his ability to succeed and he did. From the time he was very young, she told him stories about slaves.

After his grandmother died, Hughes went to live with his mother and stepfather. He was elected class poet in grammar school and from that moment on he knew he wanted to be a poet.

Langston was involved in politics and continued to be a social activist throughout his life. He toured the Southern and Southwestern United States, doing readings at black and white universities. He was often upset by the lack of social activism on the part of educated Black people. Hughes continually called for an end to racism and segregation in America. He felt Blacks should not be "secondary Americans." He did not allow himself to be in that position and believed no one of any race should be.

Hughes often said that he wished to give Black children pride in themselves. Many of his poems are directed to children encouraging them to hold on to their dreams no matter what happens. Hughes knew the value of dreams, without which life is empty and nothing changes.

Hold Fast to Dreams
by Langston Hughes

The poem is available online. Search or go to the following website and find the poem where it is ready to print, copy, and share with your class.

http://www.poemhunter.com/poem/dreams-2/

With the use of metaphors, Hughes in his two-stanza poem, *Hold Fast to Dreams*, describes what life is like without dreams. Below are two consecutive lines from the first stanza illustrating one of these metaphors.

> Life is a broken-winged bird
> That cannot fly.

February Monthly Holidays

American Heart Month • Black History Month • National Canned Food Month • Celebration of Chocolate Month • Great American Pie Month International Embroidery Month • National Cherry Month • National Children's Dental Health Month • Potato Lover's Month • Return Shopping Carts to the Supermarket Month

February Weekly Holidays

First Week of February
African Heritage and Health Week • Burn Awareness Week • Children's Authors and Illustrators Week • National School Counseling Week • Pay Your Bills Week • Shape Up with Pickles Week • Women's Heart Week

Second Week of February
Boy Scouts Week • Celebration of Love Week • National Crime Prevention Week • Big Brothers/Big Sisters Week • Jell-O® Week Laughter Keeps Us from Getting Dizzy Week

Third Week of February
National Brotherhood Week • National Engineers Week

Fourth Week of February
National Pancake Week • Read to Me Week

February Moveable Holidays

Bubble Gum Day	first Friday
Ice Cream for Breakfast	first Saturday
Super Bowl Sunday	first Sunday
Clean Out Your Computer Day	second Monday
Race Relations Sunday	Sunday nearest February 12
President's Day	third Monday
Chinese New Year	second new moon after the Winter Solstice
Chinese Lantern Festival Day	fourteen days after Chinese New Year

February Days for STEAM Makers and Poets

1. Hula in the Coola Day
2. Groundhog Day
3. Elmo's Birthday
4. Winter's Midpoint Day
5. National Weatherperson's Day
6. Mary Leakey's Birthday
7. National Periodic Table Day
8. National Kite Flying Day
9. National Toothache Day
10. Plimsoll Day
11. National Inventor's Day
12. National Lost Penny Day
13. World Radio Day
14. Have a Heart Day
15. National Gumdrop Day
16. National Almond Day
17. The Volkswagen Beetle Beats Ford Day
18. National Battery Day
19. Birthday of Nicolaus Copernicus
20. Metropolitan Museum of Art Opening Day in 1880.
21. Introduce a Girl to Engineering Day
22. George Washington's Birthday
23. Curling is Cool Day
24. National Trading Card Day
25. Quiet Day
26. Levi Strauss Day
27. National Strawberry Day
28. International Tongue Twister Day
29. Leap Day

Integrating February Math Days

Science	Technology	Engineering	Arts	Math

	Day	Make and Do
1	Hula in the Coola Day	For those in cold climates, Hula in the Coola Day comes just in time to warm your chilly bones. Become a party planner. Your job is to plan a hula party with grass skirts, coconut shells and all things tropical. What games will you play? What tropical food will you serve? What will your party invitation look like? Develop a list of party items and figure how much the party will cost. Create an invoice for your prospective client.
2	Groundhog Day	Punxsutawney Phil may or may not see his shadow today, but if you have sunshine go outside and draw shadows. Measure and record a classmate's shadow with chalk in the morning and before lunch. What time was your shadow the longest and what time was it the shortest? Observe and record the position of the sun at each time.
4	Winter's Midpoint Day	Celebrate winter's midpoint today. We are halfway to spring. Make a list of ten midpoint questions with ten answers. For example, when is the midpoint of the school year? Be sure and answer in complete sentences.
5	Bubble Gum Day	Bubble Gum Day is a day of fun, learning and charitable giving. Sometimes the day is celebrated on the first Friday in February. At participating schools, everyone who donates 50 cents or more gets to chew gum in school. Incorporate bubblegum into your day. In science class, unwrap a piece of gum and weigh it. After chewing for five minutes, has the weight changed? Why? In math, practice estimation. How many gumballs will fill a container?

11	National Inventor's Day	In 1983, President Reagan designated February 11 as National Inventor's Day in honor of Thomas Edison's birthday and to recognize the enormous contribution made by inventors to the nation and the world. Create a "Gallery of Math Inventions." Have students work in teams to make a group oral presentation, a bulletin board, or a multimedia slideshow about a great math invention. For example, students might select one of the following math tools for their reports: abacus, calculator, computer, protractor, ruler, scale or slide rule. They learn as much as they can about the math tool they selected and the mathematicians that developed the tool. As a group, they decide how best to present their information and create visuals to go with the presentation style of their choice.
12	National Lost Penny Day	Lincoln, our 16th president, was born on this day in 1809. Lincoln is immortalized on the penny, so it is only fitting in honor of this great man that we celebrate Lost Penny Day. The first US penny was made of pure copper and minted in 1787. In 1909, to mark the 100th anniversary of Lincoln's birth, the U.S. mint debuted the first Lincoln penny. For one week, search, gather and count all the lost pennies you can find and donate them to a favorite charity. Did you know that it costs 1.67 cents to make a penny?
15	National Gumdrop Day	Gumdrops look great on gingerbread houses, but today is reserved for some tasty gumdrop engineering. With 25 toothpicks and 11 gumdrops, build a geodesic dome (just like EPCOT). You will find complete directions at the Scientific American website found at: http://www.scientificamerican.com/article/sphere-based-science-build-your-own-geodesic-dome/

19	Birthday of Nicolaus Copernicus	Born on this day in 1473, Copernicus revolutionized scientific thought with the heliocentric theory that the earth revolved around the sun and was not the center of the universe. Research the interesting life of Copernicus. Write a short biography and illustrate with pictures.
28	International Tongue Twister Day	Find ten tongue twisters and hold a tongue twister contest to see who can read the twisters the fastest without making any errors. Here's a famous one to get you started: Peter Piper picked a peck of pickled peppers. A peck of pickled peppers Peter Piper picked. If Peter Piper picked a peck of pickled peppers, where's the peck of pickled peppers Peter Piper picked? Have a contest to find out how many times you can repeat the tongue twister in ten seconds, twenty seconds, thirty seconds and so forth. Create a chart displaying the results.
29	Leap Day	Julius Caesar in 45 B.C.E. proposed changing the calendar to accommodate the fact that it takes 365 days, 5 hours, 48 minutes and 45 seconds to complete a trip around the sun. So every four years those extra hours add up to an extra day and an extra three days every 400 years. In 1582, Pope Gregory XIII abolished the Julian calendar and established the Gregorian calendar. Now the discrepancy is only 26 seconds a year and won't add up to a full day for another 3,323 years. How do you tell if it is a Leap Year? Leap Years are years that can be evenly divided by 4 (like 2016, 2020) or can be evenly divided by 400 (like 2000, 2400). Years that can be evenly divided by 100 (like 2000, 2100, etc.) are not. For Leap Year Day, find ten historical events and calculate if any of them occurred in a leap year. Was the year you were born a leap year?

February Overview

Black History Month
Math Lesson: Mancala
Poetry Lesson: We Wear the Mask by Paul Laurence Dunbar

February is the month that is set aside to remember and celebrate the contributions of African Americans. Students play Mancala, the ancient African game of counting and strategy. Students study a poem by Paul Laurence Dunbar that speaks metaphorically about those who wear a mask to cover their feelings as an inspiration for their own poetic work.
NCTM Process Standard – Problem Solving: Apply and adapt a variety of appropriate strategies to solve problems.

National Freedom Day
Math Lesson: 1860 Census Data and Slavery
Poetry Lesson: Bury Me in a Free Land by Frances Ellen Watkins Harper

This day observes the signing of the 13th Amendment by President Lincoln. Student mathematicians examine data from the 1860 Census referring to slaves in the confederate and border states to discover the underpinnings of the Civil War. After reading a poem about the cruelty of slavery, students write about actions they cannot accept and describe a world where both justice and tolerance prevails.
NCTM STANDARD 5: Data Analysis and Probability, Gr 3 – 5C-4, 5C-6; Gr 4, 5C-3; Gr 6, 5A-1

Valentine's Day
Math Lesson: Presidents' Day Data Crunch
Poetry Lesson: A Red, Red Rose by Robert Burns

Valentine's Day became popular in the United States in the 1800s when Esther Howland began mass-producing cards. Today, millions of people send and receive cards. Student mathematicians work together to create math concentration games using candy kisses. In the poetry lesson, students read a love poem written by Burns and write their own Valentine's Day poem to someone special.
NCTM STANDARD 1: Numbers and Operations, Gr 3 – 5C all; Gr 4 – 5C all; Gr 5 – 5C all; Gr 6 – 1A all.

Presidents' Day
Math Lesson: President's Birthday Day Graph
Poetry Lesson: Excerpt from The People, Yes by Carl Sandburg

Presidents' Day is celebrated on the third Monday in February to honor our presidents. Student mathematicians analyze and organize raw data about United States Presidents and complete a bar graph showing their birth months. In the poetry lesson, students write about issues they believe the president of their choice would or would not support.
NCTM STANDARD 5: Data Analysis and Probability, Gr 4 – 3A, 4A, 5A; Gr 5 – 3A, 4A, 5A5; Gr 6 – 4A, 5A

Black History Month Math Lesson: Mancala

During Black History Month students learn to play Mancala, a game of counting and strategy that originated in ancient Africa. The game is easily learned but requires a great deal of strategy to win. After creating the game boards, the class pairs up and proceeds to play.

MATERIALS
For one game board:
- Egg carton from a dozen eggs
- Two small bowls or boxes
- Playing pieces – 48 each of beans, pebbles, marbles, coins, jelly beans, etc.
- Paint and paintbrushes (optional)

PLAN
- Divide the class into pairs.
- Distribute materials to each group.
- Each group creates a Mancala game board as follows:
- The game board has two rows of six pockets known as pits.
- Take an empty egg carton and remove the top.
- Use the bottom half which has 12 pockets.
- If you wish, paint the egg carton.
- Put a small bowl or box to each side of the Mancala board as illustrated. These are known as the stores.
- Distribute 48 playing pieces evenly among the 12 pits (4 per pit).

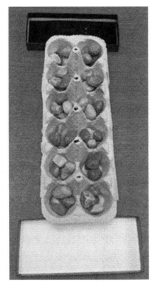

DO
The game Mancala is played all over the world and students who have played the game may have played it in a slightly modified way. Demonstrate how to play the game using the rules below. Suggest watching a video of game play on YouTube. To play, follow these directions:
- One player picks up all of the pieces in any of the pits on his side to begin.
- Moving counter-clockwise, the player deposits one of the stones in each pit until the stones run out.
- When the player runs into his/her own store, the player places one piece in it.
- If the player runs into the opponent's store, he/she skips it.
- The player gets a free turn if the last piece dropped is in the player's store.
- If the last piece dropped is in an empty pit on the player's side, the player captures that piece and any pieces in the pit directly opposite. All captured pieces are placed into the player's store.
- A turn is defined as depositing 4 stones and any implications as stated above. When the first player's turn is completed, the second player begins.
- The game ends when all six pits on one side of the board are empty.

- The player who still has pieces on his/her side of the board when the game ends captures all of those pieces.
- The player who has the most pieces in his/her store is the winner.

Note: in the game of Mancala, the person who goes first has an advantage. If possible, have the players repeat the game reversing playing order.

Students can continue to hone their Mancala strategies online. Some websites geared for student math play are: http://www.coolmath-games.com/0-mancala and http://www.mathplayground.com/mancala.html.

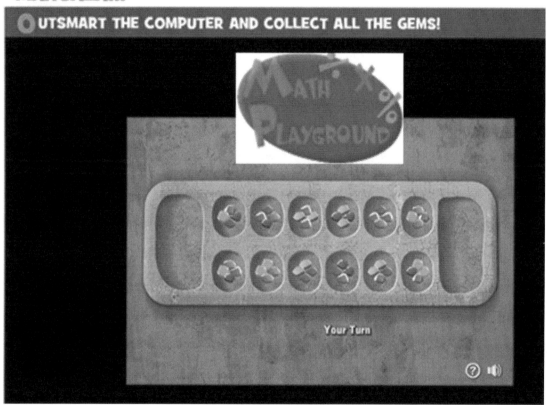

Black History Month
Poetry Lesson: We Wear the Mask

In his poem *We Wear the Mask*, Paul Laurence Dunbar speaks to African Americans who covered their anguish and agony by wearing a "mask that grins and lies." The mask is an extended metaphor used to show the need to hide "their torn and bleeding hearts." It was the armor used to hide their vulnerability from the prejudice they faced.

MATERIALS
- Paul Laurence Dunbar Biography and his poem *We Wear the Mask*
- Word processing or desktop publishing software or pencil, pens and paper
- Construction paper
- Digital camera

PLAN
Discuss Dunbar's biography and poem asking the following questions:
- Why and where does Dunbar use the mask as a metaphor?
- Why does Dunbar use "we" throughout the poem? Who does "we" represent?
- Ask students why it was necessary to wear a mask.

DO
Getting Ready to Write
During a brainstorming session, ask students the following questions. As the class gives their responses, encourage discussion.
- What experiences have you had where you wear a mask?
- In what ways do you or your friends mask true feelings?
- When have you or your friends felt the need to wear a mask?
- Were you or your friends able to mask those feelings?

Writing the Poem
- Students title their poems "I Wear a Mask."
- Suggest they start the body of their poem with, "I wear a mask that grins and lies."
- Students continue their poems describing several different experiences that have happened to make them wear a mask.
  For example: *When my friends laughed at my mistake*
  or *When someone told me my hair was too curly*

Editing and Publishing
- Students read and edit poems with partners.
- Students take a picture of themselves using the face they use when their mask is on and when their mask is off.
- Students mount their poems with photos on construction paper.
- The finished products are displayed around the room.

Paul Laurence Dunbar Biography
June 27, 1872 - February 9, 1906

Paul Laurence Dunbar was born in Dayton, Ohio. Both his mother and father had been slaves. His father escaped from slavery and served as a soldier in the Civil War. His mother became a freed slave. Although his family was poor, his mother provided him with a rich education filled with her love of storytelling and songs. She even learned to read to help him with his schooling. He was reading and writing poetry when he entered school as a six year old. In high school, he was part of the debate team, president of the literary society and editor of the school paper. He was a very successful student.

Dunbar was one of the first African-American poet to achieve fame as a writer. In much of his poems, short stories and novels, he wrote about the problems that faced his race. Dunbar's work is known for its colorful language and conversational tone.

After his first book of poetry was published, both writers and critics saw his great talent. His popularity grew. When his second book of poetry was published, he was asked to do a reading in London. At this point of Dunbar's career and at the age of twenty-five, he had achieved fame both nationally and internationally. President Theodore Roosevelt honored him with a ceremonial sword.

Dunbar died at the young age of thirty-three from tuberculosis. He was internationally respected and his renowned work will never be forgotten. In 1975 a 10-cent postage stamp was issued in his honor.

We Wear the Mask
by Paul Laurence Dunbar

We wear the mask that grins and lies,
It hides our cheeks and shades our eyes,
This debt we pay to human guile;
With torn and bleeding hearts we smile,
And mouth with myriad subtleties.

Why should the world be over-wise,
In counting all our tears and sighs?
Nay, let them only see us, while
We wear the mask.

We smile, but, O great Christ, our cries
To thee from tortured souls arise.
We sing, but oh the clay is vile
Beneath our feet, and long the mile;
But let the world dream otherwise,
We wear the mask.

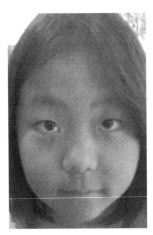

I wear a mask
When my friends laugh at my mistake
My mask laughs
And I cry
by Ashley – 4th Grade

National Freedom Day
Math Lesson: 1860 Census Data and Slavery

This day observes the signing of the 13th Amendment by President Lincoln. Student mathematicians examine data from the 1860 Census referring to slaves in the confederate and border states to discover the underpinnings of the Civil War.

MATERIALS
- Slavery Data Worksheet A – students compare data
- Slavery Data Worksheet B – requires students to compute percentages
- Map of the United States
- Projection device, colored pencils, pencils and paper

PLAN
- Discuss the observance of National Freedom Day that honors President Lincoln's signing of the resolution on June 1, 1865. The resolution outlawed slavery and became the thirteenth amendment to the constitution.
- Display a map of the United States and point out the eleven confederate states and the five border states that did not join the confederacy. All were slave states in 1860.
    - Confederate states – Alabama, Arkansas, Florida, Georgia, Louisiana, Mississippi, North Carolina, South Carolina, Tennessee, Texas and Virginia
    - Border states – Maryland, Delaware, West Virginia, Kentucky and Missouri
- Print the worksheet you plan to use with your class, based upon math concepts learned. Project the worksheet for demonstration purposes.
    - Slavery Data Worksheet A displays the information from the 1860 United States Census computed with the percentages of families who owned slaves and the percentages of slaves in the population.
    - Slavery Data Worksheet B contains the identical statistics; however, the computation of percentages is left for the students to complete.
- Using the projected worksheet, formulate math questions about the confederate and border states. Some suggestions include:
    - Which state had the greatest population?
    - What was the difference between the number of slaves in Virginia and the number in Alabama?
    - What was the difference between the state with the lowest number of slaves in the confederate states and the highest number of slaves in the border states?
- Demonstrate how the percentages of slaves in Alabama is computed by dividing 435,080 by 964,201. You may round off to make the division simpler, for example, by rounding to the nearest thousand, divide 435,000 by 964,000.
- Demonstrate how the percentage of families owning slaves in Alabama is computed by dividing 33,730 by 96,603 (or 34,000 by 97,000).

DO
- Divide students into small groups and distribute Slavery Data Worksheets.
- Students follow the directions on the worksheet and present their work to the class.

Slavery Data Worksheet A

Use the data to write five word problems that include the following math functions:
- Addition of three or more addends
- Multi-digit subtraction
- Percentages
- Fractions
- Place value and rounding

Confederate States 1860 Census Data

STATE	POPULATON	SLAVES	NO. OF FAMILIES	FREE POPULATION	SLAVE HOLDERS	% OF FAMILIES OWNING SLAVES	% OF SLAVES IN POPULATION
AL	964,201	435,080	96,603	529,121	33,730	35%	45%
AK	435,450	111,115	57,244	324,335	11,481	20%	26%
FL	140,424	61,745	15,090	78,679	5,152	34%	44%
GA	1,057,286	462,198	109,919	595,088	41,084	37%	44%
LA	708,002	331,726	74,725	376,276	22,033	29%	47%
MS	791,305	436,631	63,015	354,674	30,943	49%	55%
NC	992,622	331,059	125,090	661,563	34,658	28%	33%
SC	703,708	402,406	58,642	301,302	26,701	46%	57%
TN	1,109,801	275,719	149,335	834,082	36,844	25%	25%
TX	604,415	182,566	76,781	421,649	21,878	28%	30%
VA	1,596,318	490,865	201,523	1,105,453	52,128	26%	31%

Border States 1860 Census Data

STATE	POPULATON	SLAVES	NO. OF FAMILIES	FREE POPULATION	SLAVE HOLDERS	% OF FAMILIES OWNING SLAVES	% OF SLAVES IN POPULATION
DE	112,216	1,798	18,966	110,418	587	3%	2%
KY	1,155,684	225,483	166,321	930,201	38,645	23%	20%
MD	687,049	87,189	110,278	599,860	13,783	12%	13%
MO	1,182,012	114,931	192,073	1,067,081	52,128	26%	31%

Slavery Data Worksheet B

Complete the census data tables as follows:
- Compute the percentages of families owning slaves.
- Compute the percentages of slaves in the population.
- Write at least two word problems using the data below.
- Compare the percentages your group computed with those of another group and check any discrepancies for errors.
- Share your word problems with the class.

Confederate States 1860 Census Data

STATE	POPULATON	SLAVES	NO. OF FAMILIES	FREE POPULATION	SLAVE HOLDERS	% OF FAMILIES OWNING SLAVES	% OF SLAVES IN POPULATION
AL	964,201	435,080	96,603	529,121	33,730		
AK	435,450	111,115	57,244	324,335	11,481		
FL	140,424	61,745	15,090	78,679	5,152		
GA	1,057,286	462,198	109,919	595,088	41,084		
LA	708,002	331,726	74,725	376,276	22,033		
MS	791,305	436,631	63,015	354,674	30,943		
NC	992,622	331,059	125,090	661,563	34,658		
SC	703,708	402,406	58,642	301,302	26,701		
TN	1,109,801	275,719	149,335	834,082	36,844		
TX	604,415	182,566	76,781	421,649	21,878		
VA	1,596,318	490,865	201,523	1,105,453	52,128		

Border States 1860 Census Data

STATE	POPULATON	SLAVES	NO. OF FAMILIES	FREE POPULATION	SLAVE HOLDERS	% OF FAMILIES OWNING SLAVES	% OF SLAVES IN POPULATION
DE	112,216	1,798	18,966	110,418	587		
KY	1,155,684	225,483	166,321	930,201	38,645		
MD	687,049	87,189	110,278	599,860	13,783		
MO	1,182,012	114,931	192,073	1,067,081	52,128		

National Freedom Day
Poetry Lesson: Bury Me in a Free Land

Bury Me in a Free Land was written in 1864 one year before the signing of the Emancipation Proclamation. Frances Ellen Watkins Harper writes about the horrors of slavery in a hope for change. She would prefer to be buried "among earth's humblest graves," rather than in "a land where men are slaves." She could "not rest" and "could not sleep" in a grave in a land where slavery existed. Using this poem as a model, students explore their thoughts about intolerance and injustice.

MATERIALS
- Frances Ellen Watkins Harper Biography and her poem *Bury Me in a Free Land*
- Word processing or desktop publishing software or pencils and paper

PLAN
- Read and discuss Frances Ellen Watkins Harper biography and poem.
    - What does she mean when she writes she "could not rest" and "could not sleep"?
    - Find the images in the poem that keep her from resting.
    - Find the images in the poem that will allow her to sleep.

DO
Getting Ready to Write
Ask students the following questions to encourage discussion.
- What have you experienced that keeps you from sleeping or resting?
- Have you read about or experienced injustice such as bullying or teasing?
- What do you imagine seeing in a world where there is kindness for everyone?

Writing the Poem
- Students write poems with at least two stanzas, using Harper's as a model. Encourage line breaks so that the poem looks like a poem and not like a story.
    - Students write the first line of their poem with either *I could not rest* or *I could not sleep*.
    - Students continue their first stanza with an experience regarding injustices they have seen, read about or imagined that would make it difficult to sleep.
      For example: *if a boy sat and cried*
      the classmate laughed saying I'll never be your friend
      and walked away laughing
    - Students may add another stanza following the above instructions.
    - Students begin their last stanza with either *I would rest* or *I would sleep*.
    - Students continue this stanza describing a scene where justice and tolerance exists.
      For example: *at school, children holding hands*
      dancing in a circle
      inviting a new student to join the dance

Editing and Publishing
- Students read and edit poems with partners. Students send their poems to a publisher who accepts student writing. Here are three websites to consider: kid-lit.net; magicdragonmagazine.com; skippingstones.org.

Frances Ellen Watkins Harper
September 24, 1825 – February 25, 1911

Frances Ellen Watkins Harper was born in Baltimore, Maryland. Her parents were free African Americans. When she was three years old, her mother died. She was raised by her aunt and uncle. She began her education at the Academy for Negro Youth, a school run by her uncle. When Frances was thirteen, she left school but her education did not stop. She worked for a Quaker family who had a large library filled with works of literature. She read everything she could.

Frances loved writing poetry. At the age of twenty, she had her first book of poetry published. She continued to write and publish poetry through most of her life. In many of her poems, she described the horrible living conditions of slaves. She was the first African American to publish a short story.

Most important to Harper was the freeing of slaves. At twenty-five, she became active in the Underground Railroad, a name used to describe groups of people who helped slaves escape to freedom. At thirty-three, she joined the American Anti-Slavery Society and became a public speaker and political activist.

Harper worked for anti-slavery newspapers and became known as the mother of African American journalism. She was a social activist fighting to secure equal rights for women. She joined the Women's Christian Temperance Union and also founded The National Association of Colored Women. Eleven years after her death on August 18, 1920, the 19th Amendment to the United States Constitution was ratified granting women the right to vote.

Harper was a poet, teacher, suffragist, author, public speaker, journalist and abolitionist. In her poem *Bury Me in a Free Land*, she expresses the need for the end of slavery. She was among those people whose words helped make freedom possible.

Bury Me in a Free Land
by Frances Ellen Watkins Harper

Make me a grave where'er you will,
In a lowly plain, or a lofty hill;
Make it among earth's humblest graves,
But not in a land where men are slaves.

I could not rest if around my grave
I heard the steps of a trembling slave;
His shadow above my silent tomb
Would make it a place of fearful gloom.

I could not rest if I heard the tread
Of a coffle gang to the shambles led,
And the mother's shriek of wild despair
Rise like a curse on the trembling air.

I could not sleep if I saw the lash
Drinking her blood at each fearful gash,
And I saw her babes torn from her breast,
Like trembling doves from their parent nest.

I'd shudder and start if I heard the bay
Of bloodhounds seizing their human prey,
And I heard the captive plead in vain
As they bound afresh his galling chain.

If I saw young girls from their mother's arms
Bartered and sold for their youthful charms,
My eye would flash with a mournful flame,
My death-paled cheek grow red with shame.

I would sleep, dear friends, where bloated might
Can rob no man of his dearest right;
My rest shall be calm in any grave
Where none can call his brother a slave.

I ask no monument, proud and high,
To arrest the gaze of the passers-by;
All that my yearning spirit craves,
Is bury me not in a land of slaves.

Valentine's Day
Math Lesson: Memory Matching Game with Candy Kisses

In this delicious Valentine-themed lesson, students work in groups to create and play math memory matching games. They build the games by writing paired problems and solutions on the bottom of candy kisses.

MATERIALS
- Candy kisses (30 per group)
- Round 3/4 inch self-sticking labels (30 per group)
- Black fine-tipped markers (several per group)
- Chart paper or board

PLAN
- During a class discussion, have students suggest paired math problems and solutions for math concepts they are learning.
- Write their suggestions on a board or chart. For example:
  - 3 x 8 = 24 (multiplication)
  - ¼ + ¼ = ½ (addition of equivalent fractions)
  - 2 pints = 1 quart (measurement)
- After demonstrating how to create matched problems with the candy kisses and the self-sticking labels, divide the class into small groups to create memory matching games with candy kisses.
- Distribute candy kisses, self-sticking labels and felt tipped pens to each group.

DO
- Students work together to create and write fifteen math problems and their solutions on pairs of round labels.
- Place the labels on the bottom of the candy kisses.
- Lay out the mixed-up kisses on a table.
- Taking turns, turn over two kisses at a time.
- When they match a problem with its solution, they keep the kisses.
- The person who has the most kisses wins.
- If time permits, have students lay their kisses back on the table and change places with another group.
- Continue game play with the new math problems.
- After the last time the game is played, students divide and eat the kisses.

Noa – 4th grade

Valentine's Day
Poetry Lesson: A Red, Red Rose

There couldn't be a more perfect poem for Valentine's Day than *A Red, Red Rose* by Robert Burns. With the use of similes, Burns compares his "Luve" to the beauty of a rose, "O my Luve is like a red, red rose." He pledges to love her forever "Till a' the seas gang dry."

MATERIALS
- Robert Burns Biography and his poem *A Red, Red Rose*
- Word processing or desktop publishing software or pencil, pens and paper
- Red construction paper doilies, heart stickers, candy hearts, and more

PLAN
- Read and discuss Robert Burns biography and poem.
- Discuss the poem with the following questions:
  - Where in the poem does Burns write in a Scottish dialect?
  - Where does he use similes?
  - How do you know he will love his "luve" forever?

DO
Getting Ready to Write
- Students write a Valentine to an important person in their life.
  For example: *their mother, father, grandparent, aunt or uncle.*
- Ask the following questions and list a few responses on the board to stimulate ideas.
  - To what beautiful object would you compare this person?
  - What things in the universe will last forever?
  - What things will never happen?

Writing the Poem
- Students title their poems to their chosen person.
- Students follow the steps below to write their poems:
  1. Have them use at least two similes in the first stanza comparing that person to something beautiful, warm or comforting.
  2. In the second stanza, have students tell their person they will love them forever using at least two examples of things that will never end or never happen.

Editing and Publishing
- Print or handwrite completed poems on red paper.
- Decorate them using some of the materials listed above to give an original touch to their valentine poems.

Robert Burns Biography
January 25, 1759 - July 21, 1796

Robert Burns, poet, writer and songwriter was born on January 25, 1759 in an ancient village on the west coast of Scotland. Although his parents were poor farmers, it was important to them that their son received a good education, which he began at the age of six.

Because of his family's poor financial condition, Burns was forced to work as a farm laborer. His first love, Nelly Kirkpatrick, encouraged him to write poetry. He wrote regularly and passionately. By the time he was twenty-seven, his poems, most of which written in the Scottish dialect, had become famous throughout his country.

He died at the age of thirty-seven and was buried with full civil and military honors. Many of his songs and poems have become more famous after his death, gaining international popularity. He is known as the national poet of Scotland. He has influenced much of Scottish literature.

A Red, Red Rose
by Robert Burns

O my Luve is like a red, red rose
That's newly sprung in June;
O my Luve is like the melody
That's sweetly played in tune.

So fair art thou, my bonnie lass,
So deep in luve am I;
And I will luve thee still, my dear,
Till a' the seas gang dry.

Till a' the seas gang dry, my dear,
And the rocks melt wi' the sun;
I will luv thee still, my dear,
While the sands o' life shall run.

And fare thee weel, my only luve!
And fare thee weel awhile!
And I will come again, my luve,
Though it were ten thousand mile.

Presidents' Day
Math Lesson: Presidents' Day Data Crunch

Presidents' Day holiday is celebrated on the third Monday of February. The date was picked because it is the closest to George Washington's birthday, February 22nd. We honor all our past presidents on this day. Student mathematicians analyze and organize raw data about the Presidents and complete a bar graph showing birth months. Students also complete a map displaying the number of presidents born in various states along with a corresponding map key.

MATERIALS
- Presidents' Day Data Handout
- Presidents' Day Data Crunch Worksheet
- Paper, pencils, crayons, markers, colored pencils

PLAN
- Distribute and discuss the Presidents' Day Data Handout.
- Have students refer to the handout to answer the following questions:
  - How many presidents were born in the State of Virginia?
  - Who was the youngest president to take office?
  - Who was the oldest?
  - How many presidents were born in the 1700s? 1800s? 1900s?
  - Have student volunteers ask questions using the handout for reference.

DO
- Distribute and discuss the Presidents' Day Data Crunch Worksheet.
- Tell students they will be working in groups to create a bar graph displaying the birth months of our nation's presidents.
- Use the bar graph to complete a color-coded map and map key of presidential birth states.
- Divide the class into small groups.
- Groups complete the worksheet and exchange it with another group to check their work.
- To extend the lesson, students can do some or all of the following:
  - Create a circle graph or pie chart by hand or by using a spreadsheet program on the computer to show the presidents' ages when they took office.
  - Write several word problems that can be answered by crunching the data on the worksheet.
  - Create a timeline to show the years United States Presidents first served ranging from George Washington to the current president.

Presidents' Day Data Handout

PRESIDENT	BIRTHDAY	AGE HE TOOK OFFICE	BIRTH STATE
George Washington	02/22/1732	57	Virginia
John Adams	10/30/1735	61	Massachusetts
Thomas Jefferson	04/13/1743	57	Virginia
James Madison	03/16/1751	57	Virginia
James Monroe	04/28/1758	58	Virginia
John Quincy Adams	07/11/1767	57	Massachusetts
Andrew Jackson	03/15/1767	61	South Carolina
Martin Van Buren	12/05/1782	54	New York
William Henry Harrison	02/09/1773	68	Virginia
John Tyler	03/29/1790	51	Virginia
James K. Polk	11/02/1795	49	North Carolina
Zachary Taylor	11/24/1784	64	Virginia
Millard Fillmore	01/07/1800	50	New York
Franklin Pierce	11/23/1804	48	New Hampshire
James Buchanan	04/23/1971	65	Pennsylvania
Abraham Lincoln	02/12/1809	52	Kentucky
Andrew Johnson	11/29/1808	56	North Carolina
Ulysses S. Grant	04/27/1822	46	Ohio
Rutherford B. Hayes	10/04/1822	54	Ohio
James A. Garfield	11/19/1831	49	Ohio
Chester A. Arthur	10/05/1829	51	Vermont
Grover Cleveland	03/18/1837	55	New Jersey
Benjamin Harrison	08/20/1833	55	Ohio
William McKinley	01/29/1843	54	Ohio
Theodore Roosevelt	10/27/1858	42	New York
William Howard Taft	09/15/1857	51	Ohio
Woodrow Wilson	12/28/1856	56	Virginia
Warren G Harding	11/02/1865	55	Ohio
Calvin Coolidge	07/04/1872	51	Vermont
Herbert Hoover	08/10/1874	54	Iowa
Franklin D. Roosevelt	01/30/1882	51	New York
Harry S. Truman	05/08/1884	60	Missouri
Dwight D. Eisenhower	10/14/1890	62	Texas
John Kennedy	05/29/1917	43	Massachusetts
Lyndon B. Johnson	08/27/1908	55	Texas
Richard M. Nixon	01/09/1913	56	California
Gerald R. Ford	07/14/1913	61	Nebraska
Jimmy Carter	10/01/1924	52	Georgia
Ronald Reagan	02/06/1911	69	Illinois
George H. W. Bush	06/12/1924	64	Massachusetts
William J. Clinton	08/19/1946	46	Arkansas
George W. Bush	07/06/1946	54	Connecticut
Barack Hussein Obama	08/04/1961	47	Hawaii
Donald John Trump	6/14/1946	70	New York

Presidents' Day Data Crunch Worksheet

	Birth Months of Presidents											
12												
11												
10												
9												
8												
7												
6												
5												
4												
3												
2												
1												
	Jan	Feb	Mar	Apr	May	Jun	Jul	Aug	Sept	Oct	Nov	Dec

Number of Presidents (y-axis)

Months the Presidents Were Born

Complete the color-coded map key and color the map to represent the number of presidents born in a particular state.

Number of Presidents Born in Each State   Map Key

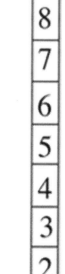

Presidents' Day
Poetry Lesson: Excerpt from The People, Yes

This excerpt is from a three-hundred-page book-length poem *The People, Yes*. Carl Sandburg writes about Lincoln and his understanding of the positive and negative aspects of a democracy. He valued these contradictions and said "Yes to the paradoxes of democracy."

MATERIALS
- Carl Sandburg Biography and excerpt from *The People, Yes*
- Word processing or desktop publishing software or pencils, pens and paper
- Board or chart and marker

PLAN
Read and discuss Carl Sandburg's biography and poem. Some sample guiding questions include:
- What are some of the paradoxes of democracy in our country?
- In the poem, President Lincoln says, "Yes to the hopes of government." To what else does he say "yes?"
- President Lincoln says, "No to the constitution when a hindrance." To what else does he say "no?"

DO
Getting Ready to Write
During a class discussion, have students do the following. Write responses on a board or chart.
- Identify presidents that the class knows something about.
- What issues would they like to discuss with the president they select?

Writing the Poem
- Students title their poem "To (the president of their choice)."
- Suggest their first line be the name of the president they have selected followed by a question mark.
- Continue their poem telling the issues they think their president would say "yes" and the issues they think their president would say "no."
- Students can make their poem more interesting mixing "yes" and "no" lines.

Editing and Publishing
- Students read and edit poems with partners.
- Students read their poems as if they are questioning the president of their choice.

Carl Sandburg Biography
January 6, 1878 – July 22, 1967

Carl Sandburg was born in Illinois. When he was thirteen, he left school and went to work. Initially, he did not have a formal education, but his many jobs gave him much life experience. Sandburg is known as the Poet of the Industrial Revolution. He worked in a theater, barbershop, in a brickyard, as a dishwasher in hotels and as a harvest hand in the wheat fields. These jobs and the people he met through them became the subject matter of his poetry.

In 1898 when war with Spain was declared, Sandburg enlisted into the United States Army. Afterwards, he went to college and became interested in literature. He left college without a degree and traveled the country riding the railroads. Eventually, he became a journalist.

While he worked as a newspaperman, he struggled to keep writing poetry. Sandburg was unknown in the literary world until he was thirty-six years old. A group of his poems finally appeared in a famous poetry journal. A year later, his first book of poems was published. Those in the literary world thought he should pay more attention to the craft of writing. But the reading public appreciated his subjects and his honest words. In his lifetime he won three Pulitzer prizes. Two of them were for his poetry and a third for a biography he wrote about Abraham Lincoln. In 1964 he received the Presidential Medal of Freedom from President Lyndon B. Johnson.

Excerpt from The People, Yes
by Carl Sandburg

The excerpt from the poem is available online at:

http://www.poetryfoundation.org/poem/182329

In one portion of his three-hundred-page poem, Carl Sandburg writes about Abraham Lincoln's views on both the positive and negative aspects of a democratic form of government. Lincoln says "Yes to the hopes of government," "Yes to the Constitution when a help," and "No to the Constitution when a hindrance."

Lincoln saw what was good for the country. He didn't try to have laws passed to harm the people of his land, but to make his land a place where freedom is the right of all people. In the poem, Sandburg quotes Lincoln:

> "I have not willingly planted a thorn
> in any man's bosom.
> I shall do nothing through malice: what
> I deal with is too vast for malice."

March Monthly Holidays

Adopt a Rescued Guinea Pig Month • American Red Cross Month Employee Spirit Month • Expanding Girls' Horizons in Science and Engineering Month • Humorists are Artists Month • International Ideas Month • Irish American Heritage Month • Mad for Plaid Month • Music in Our Schools Month • National Cheerleading Safety Month • National Craft Month • National Flour Month • National Frozen Food Month • National Hobby Month • National Multiple Sclerosis Education and Awareness Month • National Noodle Month • National Nutrition Month • National Peanut Month • National Umbrella Month National Women's History Month • Optimism Month • Play the Recorder Month • Poison Prevention Awareness Month • Social Work Month • Youth Art Month

March Weekly Holidays

First Week of March
Help Someone See Week • National Aardvark Week • National Cheerleading Week • National Ghostwriters Week National Write a Letter of Appreciation Week • National Consumer Protection Week • National Procrastination Week • National School Breakfast Week • National Women's History Week • National Words Matter Week • Newspaper in Education Week • Read an E-Book Week • Return the Borrowed Books Week • Save Your Vision Week • Universal Human Beings Week

Second Week of March
Bubble Gum Week • Children and Healthcare Week • Garden Book Week • Girl Scout Week • Music in Our Schools Week • National Professional Pet Sitter's Week • National Surveyor's Week • Newspaper in Education Week Teen Tech Week

Third Week of March
American Chocolate Week • Brotherhood Week • Camp Fire Boys and Girls Week • Children and Hospitals Week • Health Information Professionals Week • National Agriculture Week • National Free Paper Week • National Manufacturing Week • National Poison Prevention Week • National Yo-Yo and Skills Toys Days • Shakespeare Week • Termite Awareness Week World Folktales and Fables Week

Fourth Week of March
American Crossword Puzzle Days (27-29) • Brotherhood/Sisterhood Week National Agricultural Week • National Energy Education Week Pediatric Nurse Practitioner Week • Root Canal Awareness Week

March Moveable Holidays

Namesake Day	first Sunday
Daylight Saving Begins	second Sunday
Casimir Pulaski Day	first Monday
Fun Facts About Names Day	first Monday
Peace Corps Day	first Tuesday
Read Across America Day	school day nearest March 2nd
Middle Name Pride Day	first Friday
Employee Appreciation Day	first Friday
Sock Monkey Day	first Saturday
Girl Scout Sunday	Sunday closest to March 12
Fill Our Staplers Day	day after Daylight Saving begins
Popcorn Lover's Day	second Thursday
International Fanny Pack Day	second Saturday
National Urban Ballroom Dancing Day	second Saturday
Absolutely Incredible Kid Day	third Thursday
National Quilting Day	third Saturday
American Diabetes Association Alert Day	fourth Tuesday
Manatee Appreciation Day	last Wednesday

March Days for STEAM Makers and Poets

1. Peanut Butter Lover's Day
2. Dr. Seuss Day
3. If Pets Had Thumbs Day
4. National Grammar Day
5. Hula Hoop was Patented Day
6. Dentist Day
7. National Cereal Day
8. National Proofreading Day
9. National Meatball Day
10. Harriet Tubman Day
11. Paper was Invented in China Day
12. National Alfred Hitchcock Day
13. Pluto is Discovered Day
14. National Potato Chip Day
15. National Everything You Think is Wrong Day
16. National Panda Day
17. St. Patrick's Day
20. World Storytelling Day
21. National Fragrance Day
22. National Goof-Off Day
23. United Nations World Meteorological Day
24. Chocolate Covered Raisin Day
25. Tolkien Reading Day
26. Make Up Your Own Holiday
27. Quirky Country Music Song Titles Day
28. Something on a Stick Day
29. Smoke and Mirrors Day
30. National Pencil Day
31. Cesar Chavez Day

Integrating March Math Days

Science   Technology   Engineering   Arts   Math

Day		Make and Do
1	Peanut Butter Lover's Day	Do you like smooth or crunchy? Perhaps you like your peanut butter laced with jam or chocolate. There are hundreds of kinds of peanut butter available and Americans on average eat three pounds a year. Create three word problems using some fun peanut butter facts. For example, it takes 540 peanuts to make a 12-ounce jar of peanut butter. Did you know that an acre of peanuts makes 30,000 peanut butter sandwiches? What fun facts did you discover?
5	The Hula Hoop was Patented Day	The Hula Hoop was patented on this day in 1963. Arthur Melin and Richard Knerr, the founders of Wham-O, began making a plastic hoop similar to the wooden hoop that they saw Australian children use in gym class. The name Hula came from the Hawaiian dance. Twenty-five million Hula-Hoops were sold in the first four months of production in 1958. Hula-Hoop mania took off and Wham-O became a great success story. Find out why the company was called Wham-O and learn about its famous products including the Frisbee (first known as the Pluto Platter), the Water Wiggle, Silly String, Hacky Sack and Slip 'N' Slide. Create a sales brochure to advertise some of Wham-O's products. Include graphics and pictures in your brochure. Hold a Hula Hoop contest to find out who can Hula Hoop the longest with one hoop and with two hoops. Create a graph to display how your classmates did.

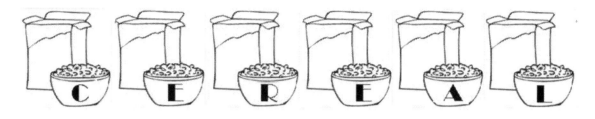

7	National Cereal Day	John Kellogg and his brother Will accidently let some wheat go stale and found that it flaked when forced through rollers. The patent for flaked cereals soon followed. Their cereal was considered a 19th-century wonder food. Rice Krispies were their next big hit in 1928. What is your favorite breakfast cereal? Learn to read the nutritional information on the box. What is the healthiest cereal you can find in the cereal aisle of your local supermarket?
9	National Meatball Day	Who doesn't like meatballs? Spaghetti and meatballs, porcupines, Swedish or sweet and sour – there is a meatball for every taste. What is your favorite meatball? Find a recipe and create a recipe card. Create a spreadsheet to determine the quantities of each ingredient and the cost to make enough meatballs so that everyone in your class could eat one. How much of each ingredient and what would be the cost to make a meatball for everyone in your school?
18	Sloppy Joe Day	Sloppy Joe Sandwiches were first served in Havana, Cuba in the early 1900s, although some historians attribute the original Sloppy Joe to a café in Sioux City, Iowa. A cook named Joe added tomato sauce to ground beef and served his "loose meat" between bread. Today, Sloppy Joes continue to be a favorite in Iowa and in other parts of the Midwest. In 1969, Hunt's introduced the Manwich, a Sloppy Joe in a can. Find a recipe for Sloppy Joes, create a shopping list and make dinner for your family. Keep track of the cost of each item and determine how much it costs per serving. Use a spreadsheet to determine how much of each ingredient you would need to serve ten people, twenty-five people and one hundred people.

19	National Quilting Day	National Quilting Day is a great day to study the mathematics of tessellating shapes and applying transformational geometry in quilt patterns. Slide (translate), turn (rotate), and flip (reflect) quilt pieces to create a tessellating quilt. Start with a Quilt Square Challenge. Each student needs nine squares. Use a two-inch paper square and draw a diagonal line. Make half of the square black, leave the other half white. Starting with four squares, create as many patterns as possible on a four square grid. When proficient, do the same with all nine squares on a nine square grid. Try making quilts with unified color schemes like red, white and blue for patriotic quilts and black and orange for Halloween. When you are pleased with your design, paste it onto a separate piece of paper. Combine class tessellations into a larger bulletin board display.
22	National Goof-Off Day	Today is a day to relax, unwind and do everything except what you are supposed to do. In other words, goof-off, assuming you won't get in trouble at school. If you can goof-off, what would you like to do? Would you play games, take a walk, read a book, or watch television? Perhaps you have other activities that would be fun. Create a survey to find out what people like to do when they goof-off. Does it change with age? Display your results in a pictorial graph.
24	Chocolate Covered Raisin Day	Today is Chocolate Covered Raisin Day. You can make your own by melting ¼ cup dark chocolate chips and ½ tablespoon of coconut oil in the microwave for one minute. Stir well and add one and half cups of raisins. Pour the mixture onto parchment paper in a thin layer and freeze to firm. Break apart. Alternatively, you can buy ready-made Raisinets. If you eat ten pieces, you have consumed 41 calories. How many minutes of walking will it take you to burn off 41 calories? How many minutes of running? How many minutes of jumping rope?

March Overview

Women's History Month
Math Lesson: Women's Barrier-Breaking Years
Poetry Lesson: Praised Be Diana's Fair and Harmless Light
by Sir Walter Raleigh
This is the month to praise women for who they are and what they have accomplished. In this Women's History Month math lesson, students solve and create word problems based on women's barrier breaking achievements. Students study a poem by Sir Walter Raleigh praising a powerful Roman goddess and write poems praising a woman in their own life.
NCTM STANDARD 5: Data Analysis and Probability, Gr 3 – 5A-2; Gr 4 – 5A-2, 5A-3; Gr 5 – 5A-2, 5A-3; Gr 6 – 5A-1, 5A-3, 5A-4

Music in Our Schools Month
Math Lesson: Fractionated Rhythms
Poetry Lesson: The Violin – A Little Bit Nervous by Vladimir Mayakovsky
Music in Our Schools Month is sponsored by the National Association for Music and promotes the benefit of music instruction. In this lesson students link their understanding of NCTM math concepts to the beat of musical notes. In the poetry lesson, Mayakovsky brings an orchestra to life and students write poems about an orchestra in his style.
NCTM STANDARD 1: Numbers and Operations, Gr 3 – 1A-5; Gr 5 – 1A-7, 1A-8; Gr 6 – 1A-2, 1A-3, 1B-6

St. Patrick's Day
Math Lesson: Charming Math
Poetry Lesson: Limericks by Edward Lear
Both St. Patrick's Day and limericks originated in Ireland. Across the globe on March 17th the Irish at heart celebrate the holiday with parades, shamrocks, leprechauns and the color green. In this magically delicious math lesson, students explore math concepts using boxes of Lucky Charms Cereal. What would this day be like without limericks? Poet Edward Lear, well known for his limericks, gets us started.
NCTM STANDARD 2: Algebra, Gr 4 – 2A-4, 2A-5; Gr 5 – 2A-2; Gr 6 – 2A-1

Suddenly It's Spring
Math Lesson: Fractional Spring Words
Poetry Lesson: The Caterpillar by Robert Graves
Spring begins on a day when the Earth's equator passes through the center of the sun. During the Spring Equinox between March 21st and 23rd daylight and nightime are nearly equal. Students sharpen fraction skills by solving, creating and illustrating Spring math puzzles. In his poem Robert Graves playfully describes the life of a caterpillar. Students write their own poems about a spring insect.
NCTM STANDARD 2: Algebra, Gr 3 – 1A-5; Gr 5 – 1A-8; Gr 6 – 1B-6, 1C-7

Women's History Month
Math Lesson: Women's Barrier-Breaking Years

In this Women's History Month math lesson, students solve and create word problems based on women's barrier-breaking achievements in (1) the United States Senate, (2) Space and (3) the Supreme Court. Working in pairs, small groups or on their own, students search the Internet and complete a worksheet as they learn about meritorious women. When the worksheets are completed, students share and check their answers. Students present the word problems they created to the class. Answer keys and suggested websites to find further information conclude the lesson.

MATERIALS
- Internet capable device
- Women's Barrier Breaking Years Worksheet
- Women's Barrier Breaking Years Answer Key
- Board or chart and marker

PLAN
- Tell students that the American Feminist Movement that took place in the 1960s and 1970s in the United States opened opportunities for women to break prior barriers and have greater participation on a political and a public level.
- Write the names Barbara Boxer, Diane Feinstein, Sally Ride, Eileen Collins, and Sandra Day O'Connor on a board or chart.
- Have students discuss what they know about each woman.

DO
- Divide the class into pairs or small groups.
- Distribute the Women's Barrier-Breaking Years Worksheet.
- Students use Internet capable devices to find answers to the worksheet questions.
- Students solve the math problems and write problems of their own in each section.

Women's Barrier-Breaking Years Worksheet

1. United States Senate
a. In what year did California elect the first two women to the United States Senate? _____
b. How many women from other states were elected with them? _____
c. What fractional number elected in that year did the two senators represent? _____
d. Write a math word problem of your own. _____
_____

Suggested website to visit:
http://www.senate.gov/artandhistory/history/minute/year_of_the_woman.htm

2. Space
a. Who was the first American woman to travel to space? _____
b. In what year did she achieve this milestone? _____
c. When did Eileen Collins become the first woman space shuttle pilot? _____
d. How many years passed between the two events? _____
e. Write a math word problem of your own. _____
_____

Suggested website to visit:
http://starchild.gsfc.nasa.gov/docs/StarChild/whos_who_level2/

3. Supreme Court
a. In what year did George Washington appoint John Jay as the first Supreme Court Justice? _____
b. Who was the first female Supreme Court justice? _____
c. When did the first female justice join the Supreme Court? _____
d. How many years was the Supreme Court all male? _____
e. Write a math word problem of your own. _____
_____

Suggested websites to visit:
https://www.constitutionfacts.com/us-supreme-court/first-chief-justice-john-jay/
http://www.supremecourt.gov/visiting/SandraDayOConnor.aspx

Women's Barrier-Breaking Years Answer Key

1. United States Senate
  a. In what year did California elect the first two women to the United States Senate? <u>1992, Diane Feinstein and Barbara Boxer</u>
  b. How many other women were elected with them? <u>two</u>
  c. What fractional number of women elected in that year did the two senators represent? <u>½</u>

  Suggested website to visit:
  http://www.senate.gov/artandhistory/history/minute/year_of_the_woman.htm

2. Space
  a. Who was the first American woman to travel in space? <u>Sally Ride</u>
  b. In what year did she achieve this milestone? <u>1983</u>
  c. When did Eileen Collins become the first woman space shuttle pilot? <u>1995</u>
  d. How many years passed between the two events? <u>12</u>

  Suggested website to visit:
  http://starchild.gsfc.nasa.gov/docs/StarChild/whos_who_level2/

3. Supreme Court
  a. In what year did George Washington appoint John Jay as the first Supreme Court Justice? <u>1798</u>
  b. Who was the first female Supreme Court justice? <u>Sandra Day O'Connor</u>
  c. When did the first female justice join the Supreme Court? <u>1981</u>
  d. How many years was the Supreme Court all male? <u>183</u>

  Suggested websites to visit:
  https://www.constitutionfacts.com/us-supreme-court/first-chief-justice-john-jay/
  http://www.supremecourt.gov/visiting/SandraDayOConnor.aspx

Women's History Month
Poetry Lesson:
Praised Be Diana's Fair and Harmless Light

This is the month to praise women for who they are and what they have accomplished. In his poem, Sir Walter Raleigh praises Diana, a powerful Roman goddess of the hunt, moon, birthing and fertility. He praises her power that moves "the floods." He praises the spirits and "her nymphs, with whom she decks the woods." He praises her beauty that will last eternally "Time wears her not—she doth his chariot guide." In the last two lines of the poem, Raleigh writes that Diana has pure knowledge. People who do not believe in her should dwell with Circes, a minor goddess, who is a magician and spreads lies with her magic.

MATERIALS
- Sir Walter Raleigh Biography and his poem *Praised Be Diana's Fair and Harmless Light*
- Word processing and/or desktop publishing software

PLAN
- Read and discuss Sir Walter Raleigh's biography and poem.
- Read and discuss the poem using the following questions and discussion points.
  - For what is Diana praised?
  - Why does Diana not grow older?
  - Discuss what the last two lines mean. "A knowledge pure it is her worth to know/With Circes let them dwell that think not so."

DO
Getting Ready to Write
- Conduct a brainstorming session by asking students to list women to praise. Tell students to praise a woman in their life, in their world or in mythology.
  - Who would they praise?
    For example: *mother, aunt, grandmother, a mythological woman, or an historical woman*
  - Continue with the following question. What would they praise about this woman?
    For example: *Praised be her spirit that lights my life; Praised be her beauty that outshines all the flowers in an English spring garden.*

Writing the Poem
- Students write their own poems following the directions below.
  - Students title their poem "Praise to" and the name of whom they are praising.
  - Begin the first line "Praised be" and add to whom they are praising.
  - Embellish the line with a praise about the woman.
  - Begin the second line and all lines that follow with "Praise be her".
  - Suggest that students write at least seven praises.

Editing and Publishing
- Have students read and edit poems with partners.
- Students handwrite their poems in fancy penmanship and draw a decorative border.
- Mount and display the finished poems.

Sir Walter Raleigh Biography
Circa 1552 – October 29, 1618

Walter Raleigh was born in England. The date of his birth is unknown but historians believe it was 1552. Although his father came from a wealthy family, his family's finances had dwindled by the time Raleigh was born. He attended Oxford University but did not graduate. At the age of twenty-six, he sailed to America with his half-brother, an explorer.

Raleigh served in the army of Queen Elizabeth 1 of England. He fought in Ireland and was honored by the Queen for his service. She rewarded him with knighthood, a large estate in Ireland and the right to establish colonies in America.

Raleigh sailed with a fleet of seven vessels. His 108 men reached Roanoke Island (today part of North Carolina) and established the colony of Virginia. Raleigh was the first person to bring back potatoes and Virginian tobacco to Europe. He was also responsible for making smoking tobacco popular in the European court.

There is a myth that Raleigh once threw his cloak over a mud puddle to protect the queen as she walked by. He repeated this myth in a famous novel. The myth ends with the queen blushing and nodding her head, as she 'hastily passed on, and embarked in her barge without saying a word."

He was loved by Queen Elizabeth for the poems he wrote praising her. When she found out that he was secretly married to one of her maids of honor, she went into a jealous rage. She had Raleigh and his wife imprisoned in the Tower of London.

After his release, he went on two expeditions to the New World searching for El Dorado, a city of gold, which he never found. After the first failure, James 1 put him in prison for plotting against the king. He spent twelve years there, occupying himself by writing books. He was released and after his second failure to find the city of gold, and defying the king's instructions not to attack the Spanish, Raleigh was put back into prison, given the death sentence and executed.

Praised Be Diana's Fair and Harmless Light
by Sir Walter Raleigh

Praised be Diana's fair and harmless light,
Praised be the dews wherewith she moists the ground;
Praised be her beams, the glory of the night;
Praised be her power, by which all powers abound.

Praised be her nymphs, with whom she decks the woods;
Praised be her knights, in whom true honor lives;
Praised be that force by which she moves the floods;
Let that Diana shine, which all these gives.

In heaven queen she is among the spheres;
In aye she mistress-like makes all things pure;
Eternity in her oft change she bears;
She beauty is; by her the fair endure.

Time wears her not—she doth his chariot guide;
Mortality below her orb is placed.
By her the virtue of the stars down slide,
In her is virtue's perfect image cast.

> A knowledge pure it is her worth to know;
> With Circes let them dwell that think not so.

Music in Our Schools Month
Math Lesson: Fractionated Rhythms

In this lesson students link their understanding of math concepts to the beat of musical notes. They study the fractional values of notes and use these values to review addition and subtraction of fractions. Students learn about equivalent fractions. They work in groups to create their own songs using four beats per measure. By clapping, stomping, humming and using plastic cups, students perform their compositions for the class.

MATERIALS
- Musical Beats Chart
- Projection device
- Pencil, paper
- One plastic cup per student

PLAN
- Project the Musical Beats Chart in the front of the room. The notes on the chart are whole notes, half notes, quarter notes, eighth notes, sixteenth notes, dotted half notes, dotted quarter notes, and dotted sixteenth notes.
- Introduce the notes displayed on the chart, one at a time, while pointing to them.
- Student volunteers are guided to tell whether the note is solid or open; whether it has a vertical line attached or not; whether it has one or more flags attached to the line; and whether it is followed by a dot.
- Have the class join you as you count, clap and say each note as follows:
    - Whole notes: hold for four beats
    - Half notes: hold for two beats
    - Quarter notes: hold for one beat
    - Eighth notes: hold for ½ beat
    - Sixteenth note: hold for ¼ beat
- Dots add half the value of the note to the original note. For example, a dotted half note has three beats.
    - Count, clap and tap the dotted whole, quarter and half notes on the chart.
- Practice counting and humming the beats in the first four measures of the song, "Twinkle, Twinkle Little Star."

DO
- Divide the class into small groups.
- Challenge each group to draw four groups of notes to create four-beat measures showing their equivalent fractional values. Each measure needs to be different than the other three measures. Here is an example of one measure:
- Once the four measures are created, the groups use their plastic cup to tap their four-measure creation.

1/2 + 1/4 + 1/8 + 1/8 = 1 MEASURE
4/8 + 2/8 + 1/8 + 1/8 = 8/8 = 1 WHOLE

Musical Beats Chart

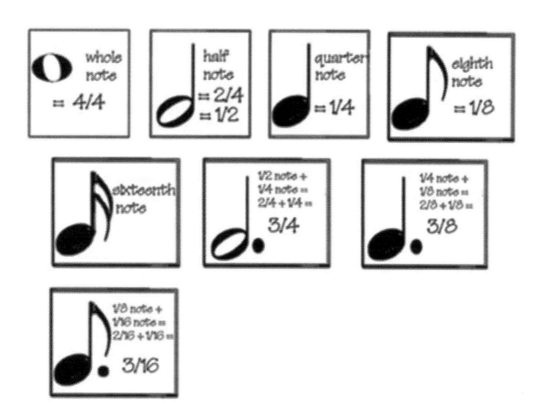

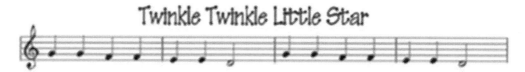

Music in Our Schools Month
Poetry Lesson: The Violin – A Little Bit Nervous

Vladimir Mayakovsky in a humorous, complex and story-like way presents a character study of the personalities of some of the instruments found in an orchestra. In this lesson, students think about which instrument in the orchestra reminds them most of themselves and write a poem in which they become that instrument. They will include how they feel about themselves and the other instruments.

Mayakovsky's poem is narrated by the orchestra's conductor. The violin with its "child-like" complaining voice and manner irritates the other members of the orchestra. The members include the instruments and the musicians. At first, the drum tries to soothe the violin: "All right, all right, all right!" But the drum can't take it any longer and slips out going to the "Kuznetsky" a famous street in Moscow. The cymbal with his clashing sound becomes irritated with the violin's noise and says, "What is it, what's all the racket about?" At the end of the poem, the conductor realizes that he loves the violin since it reminds him of himself "we're awfully alike;/I too/always yell." He decides to take the violin home saying, "Let's live together."

MATERIALS
- Vladmir Mayakovsky Biography and his poem *The Violin – A Little Bit Nervous*
- Word processing or desktop publishing software (optional)

PLAN
- Read and discuss Vladimir Mayakovsky's biography and poem.
- Read and discuss the poem using the following possible questions:
    - Why does Mayakovsksy choose the violin as the instrument that bursts into sobs?
    - Where is personification used in the poem?
    - Who is the poem's narrator?
    - Is the narrator's description of the instruments accurate? Why or why not?
    - How does the narrator feel about the violin in the beginning and at the end of the poem? Why?

DO
Getting Ready to Write
- Have students brainstorm and discuss the following points. As the class gives their responses list them on the board or on a chart.
    - Have students name the different instruments in an orchestra.
    - Continue the discussion, asking them what type of personalities do each one of these instruments have, depending upon how they sound.
    - Ask students what instrument reminds them most of themselves and why?
    - What would their instrument say?

Writing the Poem
- Students use the instrument that reminds them most of themselves as the main character in their own poem. Refer to the instrument as I.
- Title their poems with the name of their selected instrument.
- Continue writing their poems with what they are saying, thinking and doing as their selected instrument.
- In their poems, refer to all other instruments using the pronouns he or she.
- Suggest they continue with how the other instruments react in speech and action.

Editing and Publishing
- Students read and edit their poems with partners.
- Students write their poems either by hand or in a word processing program.
- Students practice reading their poems mimicking the voice of their instrument.
- Work in groups to record their polished performances.

The Recorder
I toot through my holes
My sounds strong and sweet
And I listen to them
And say to the bossy piano
Let's play together
I wish the drum would stop banging
But I forgive him
by Tate – 4th grade

Vladimir Mayakovsky Biography
July 19, 1893 – April 14, 1930

Vladimir Mayakovsky was born in a small town in Russia. His father was a Cossack, an important member of the Russian army. When Vladimir was thirteen, his father died and his mother and two sisters moved to Moscow, the capital and largest city in Russia. Vladimir went to school at the Moscow Gymnasium, a school that spanned grades one through eleven. He dropped out at the age of fifteen and joined the underground Social Democratic Labor Party. Because of his involvement with the Party, he was imprisoned three times. He disobeyed prison rules and spent six months in solitary confinement. While in isolation, he began writing poetry.

After Vladimir's release from prison, he attended the Moscow Art School and became an independent thinker and writer. He was politically involved, wanting change in Russia. He believed that through art there could be change. He joined and became a prominent member of the Futurist movement that rejected the art of the past. Believing in this movement, he created a new form of Russian poetry. Vladimir began writing, directing plays and publishing his poetry. He moved to St. Petersburg where he became a leading writer. He appeared in three silent films, one of which he wrote and two he directed.

In the 1920s, Vladimir began traveling through Europe and America. He moved back to Russia for financial reasons. Back in Russia, his public appearances and poetry made him famous and financially successful. He bought a new car and hired a driver. Soviet officials became more irritated about Vladimir's ideas that did not conform with those of the government. He was under constant surveillance. His driver was a secret spy for the Soviets.

Vladimir became more and more critical of the Soviet government. Because of his criticisms, he was not allowed to travel out of Russia. He became very depressed and was found dead with a bullet in his heart. It was said that he committed suicide. Ten days after his death, the criminal investigator on his case was also shot dead.

The Violin - A Little Bit Nervous
by Vladimir Mayakovsky
(translated from the Russian text by Dorian Rottenberg)

The violin got all worked up, imploring
then suddenly burst into sobs,
so child-like
that the drum couldn't stand it:
All right, all right, all right!"
But then he got tired, couldn't wait till the violin ended,
slipped out on the burning Kuznetsky
and took flight.
The orchestra looked on, chilly,
while the violin wept itself out
without reason
or rhyme,
and only somewhere,
a cymbal, silly,
kept clashing:
"What is it,
what's all the racket about?"
and when the helicon,
brass-faced, sweaty,
hollared:
"Crazy!
Crybaby!
Be still!"
I staggered,
on to my feet getting,
and lumbered
over the horror-stuck music stands,
yelling,
"Good God"
why, I myself couldn't tell;
then dashed, my arms round the wooden neck to fling:
"You know what, violin,
we're awfully alike;
I too
always yell,
but can't prove a thing!"
The musicians commented,
contemptuously smiling:
"Look at him-
come to his wooden-bride –
tee-hee!"
But I don't care –
I'm a good guy-
"You know, what, violin,
let's live together,
eh?"

St. Patrick's Day
Math Lesson: Charming Math

Lucky Charms Cereal debuted in 1963 and for over fifty years has been a favorite at the breakfast table. The cereal features frosted oats along with marshmallow charms known as "marbits." In this magically delicious math lesson, students explore math concepts using boxes of Lucky Charms Cereal. They hone skills with graphs, percentages, fractions as well as statistics and probability.

MATERIALS
- One box of Lucky Charms Cereal for every six students
- Lucky Charms Tally Sheets
- Lucky Charms Special Power Chart
- Sandwich-size plastic bags for each student
- One-inch graph paper

PLAN
- Discuss student's prior experiences eating Lucky Charms Cereal. Some sample questions to ask include:
    - Who has eaten Lucky Charms?
    - Do they eat it often?
    - Do they have a favorite marshmallow marbit?
    - How many marbits do they remember finding in each cup of cereal?
    - What percentage of marbits do they think are in each cup?
- The marshmallows in each box of Lucky Charms are there to represent Lucky the Leprechaun's magical charms. Each charm is said to have its own special power.
- Display a Lucky Charms Special Power Chart to share with the class:

Charm	Special Power
Hearts	Power to bring things to life
Shooting Starts	Power to fly
Horseshoes	Power to speed things up
Clovers	Luck
Blue Moons	Power of invisibility
Rainbows	Power to instantaneously travel from place to place
Balloons	Power to make things float
Hourglass	Power to control time

- Open one of the boxes of cereal you are using to see if new marbits have been added.
- Update the chart if necessary.

DO
- Divide the class into groups of six.
- Give each group member a sandwich-size plastic bag.
- Randomly divide the contents of the cereal into the six sandwich bags.
- Students do the following:
    - Create a tally sheet by writing the names of each marshmallow marbit in a vertical row on a sheet of paper.
    - Individually count and sort the marshmallows in his or her bag and record the results on a tally sheet.
    - Distribute 1" graph paper to each student.
- Students create a graph as follows.
    - Write the names of the marbits on the horizontal axis at the bottom of the graph paper.
    - On the vertical axis, add numbers.
    - Color each square in the correct column to correspond with the data on the tally sheet.
- Depending on the math level of the class, have students do the following computations with the data they created:
    - Write each result as a fraction of the total charms found.
    - Reduce the fractions to the lowest common denominator.
    - Change the fractions to percentages.
    - Combine the group totals and use the results to create statistical information.
- Create stories of the marbit's special powers, writing math word problems, and/or research the history of Lucky Charms.

St. Patrick's Day Poetry Lesson: Limericks

Both St. Patrick's Day and limericks originated in Ireland. This fun and humorous form of poetry began in the 14th century in the Irish town of Limerick. Edward Lear made this form of poetry popular. Two of the limericks in this lesson are named for Irish towns. Students read *There Was an Old Man of Kildare*, *There Was an Old Man of Kilkenny* and *There Was a Young Lady of Norway*. Then they write their own limericks.

MATERIALS
- Edward Lear Biography and three of his limericks
- Word processing and/or desktop publishing software

PLAN
- Read and discuss Edward Lear's biography and his limericks.
    - Discuss how limericks are structured.
        - Limericks are humorous.
        - The first line ends with a name or place.
        - Lines one, two and five rhyme with one another.
        - Lines three and four rhyme with each other.
        - The last line repeats the place named in the first line.
- Read and discuss the selection of limericks to show students how each one of Lear's limericks follows the appropriate limerick rules.

DO
Getting Ready to Write
- During a brainstorming session, ask students the following questions. List their responses on a board or on a chart.
    - What places would they like to use in the first and last lines of their own limerick?
    - Who or what would be at that place?
- Have students participate in writing a group limerick beginning with "There was a" and follow the suggested rules.

Writing the Poem
- Following the suggested rules, students write their own limericks.

Editing and Publishing
- Students read their limerick to themselves to check for rhyme structure.
- Next, students read and edit limericks with partners.
- Plan a limerick reading party where students read their poems, eat green cookies and drink green punch.
- Create a class anthology of limericks.

Edward Lear Biography
May 12, 1812 – January 29, 1888

Edward Lear was born in Holloway, a district in London. He was second to the youngest of twenty-one children. Most of his siblings died when they were infants. He lived with his parents until he was four years old. His father, a stockbroker, had financial difficulties. Young Edward moved in with an older sister. Beginning at the age of five, he had epileptic seizures. He felt ashamed of his condition and suffered from depression. Edward had trouble developing relationships. At sixteen, he was earning a living by drawing illustrations for the Zoological Society. Later, he was employed by a wealthy man who had a private menagerie. He drew beautiful paintings of his employer's animals.

He loved to travel and created beautiful colored drawings of his travels. Queen Victoria hired him to teach her how to draw. Lear loved the Italian Mediterranean coast and settled there. He never married but had many close friendships that lasted his entire life. His best friend was his cat, Foss, who died two years before Lear did.

Lear was known as an artist, writer, illustrator, and poet. He was well known for his limericks. They were funny, perhaps hiding his own sadness. His limericks made him famous and he in turn, made limericks famous. Besides his limericks, he also is remembered for the beloved children's classic *The Owl and the Pussycat*.

Limericks
by Edward Lear

There Was an Old Man of Kildare
There was an Old Man of Kildare,
Who climbed into a very old chair;
When he said,-- "Here I stays--
till the end of my days,"
That immovable Man of Kildare.

There Was an Old Man of Kilkenny
There was an Old Man of Kilkenny,
Who never had more than a penny;
He spent all that money,
In onions and honey,
That wayward Old Man of Kilkenny.

There Was a Young Lady of Norway
There was a Young Lady of Norway.
Who casually sat in a doorway;
When the door squeezed her flat,
She exclaimed, "What of that?"
The courageous Young Lady of Norway.

Suddenly It's Spring
Math Lesson: Fractional Spring Words

Spring brings thoughts of flowers, butterflies, and baby animals. It is a growing time and a time for nature's renewal. Students sharpen fraction skills by solving, creating and illustrating math puzzles based on the special words that thoughts of spring bring to mind.

MATERIALS
- Board or chart
- Marker
- Pencil and paper
- Art paper
- Crayons, colored markers, colored pencils

PLAN
- Have students brainstorm and create a class list of words that remind them of spring.
- Write the words on the board or on a chart. Below are some possibilities:

rainbow	caterpillar	butterfly	flowers	bunny	chicken
lamb	green	blossom	Easter	planting	insect
season	caterpillar	equinox	leprechaun	clover	green

- Tell students they are going to create spring word puzzles by writing fractional clues for spring-themed words.
- As an example, write the following fractional clues for students to solve. Note, each of these fractions represent the first part of the word.
  - 1/2 of card + 1/3 of terminate + 1/2 of pillow + 3/4 of lard
    Answer: caterpillar
  - 1/3 of length + 1/2 of pretty + 2/5 of child + 1/3 of author + 1/6 of notice
    Answer: leprechaun

DO
- Divide the class into small groups.
- Groups write as many spring words and their fractional clues as they can in a defined amount of time, for example 20 minutes.
- Each group member selects a favorite fractional word to write and illustrate on art paper.
- The groups share their work with the rest of the class by showing their puzzles and illustrations for the others to solve.
- Display the fractional word puzzles on a spring bulletin board.

Suddenly It's Spring
Poetry Lesson: The Caterpillar

Spring is the season when caterpillars transform from creepy and hairy insects to colorful flying butterflies. The caterpillar in the poem says he wants to remain a caterpillar whose only quest in life is to "eat, eat, eat." He knows that sometime in his future "when I'm old, tired, melancholy, I'll build a leaf-green mausoleum" where I will "dream the ages away." He's heard that "worms win resurrection" and become butterflies, but to him this is not winning. He would still like to remain a caterpillar. In this lesson, students will become an insect that reminds them of spring and express how they think and feel.

MATERIALS
- Robert Graves Biography and excerpt from his poem *The Caterpillar*
- Word processing and/or desktop publishing software

PLAN
- Read and discuss Robert Graves's biography and poem.
- Encourage responses to the following questions:
  - Where does the caterpillar live?
  - Who is "I" in the poem?
  - What does the caterpillar do all day long?
  - Why does he want to remain a caterpillar?
  - Why is he going to build a mausoleum and what happens in the mausoleum?

DO
Getting Ready to Write
- Discuss the following questions with students.
  - What spring insect would they like to become?
  - Where does it live?
  - What does it look like? Encourage detailed descriptions.
  - What does it do all day long?
  - What does it think about?
  - What does it think about its past, present and future?
  - What is it happy or sad about?

Writing the Poem
Tell students they are going to write a poem in which they become an insect.
Have students use page breaks so that their writing looks like a poem.
- Have students title their poem the name of their spring insect.
- Begin their poem describing where the insect lives and what it looks like Graves does. For example: *On a grassy leaf crawling a short legged ant*
- Continue the poem becoming the spring insect. As in the poem, start with "I" and follow with what you are doing.

Editing and Publishing
- Students read and edit poems with partners.
- Have students draw their animal or insect and mount on a poster board with their poem.

Robert Graves Biography
July 24, 1895 – December 7, 1985

Robert Graves was born in Wimbledon, England in 1895. His father was a school inspector and published poet. His mother descended from nobility. He attended several schools before entering at age nine a very prominent private boarding school. He was bullied because of his seriousness, his outspokenness and his German name. To defend himself, he began boxing and became a school champion. He began writing poetry to express his troubles. His first poem was published in the school magazine in 1911.

When Germany invaded Belgium in 1914, Graves was nineteen and he joined the British Army to fight in World War I. Two years after joining the army, he was badly wounded and was expected to die. He suffered from shell shock and is quoted as saying "I couldn't face the sound of heavy shelling now; the noise of a car back-firing would send me flat on my face, or running for cover." The army accidently told his parents that their son was killed. He read his own obituary in the London Times.

Still feeling the need to defend his country, Graves returned to the army after his wounds healed. He spent a brief time in France and the remainder of the war in England. During this time, he had two books of poems published and developed the reputation as a war poet.

In January 1918, at the age of twenty-two, he began teaching at Oxford and married Nancy Nicholson. They had four children together. In 1926 he moved to Egypt where he taught at Cairo University. The following year he traveled back to England. Upon returning, he and his wife divorced. Eventually he moved to the Spanish Island of Majorca and became a full-time writer. By then, Graves had published many books of poetry. But poetry could not support him so he began to write historical novels, the most successful of which was *I Claudius*. It became an internationally famous BBC television series.

In 1936 he had to leave Spain because of the onset of the Spanish Civil War. He moved to London where he met Beryl Hodge who would become his second wife and with whom he would have another four children. They moved to the quiet English village of Devon. In 1939, war with Germany was declared. By the end of the war, Graves was ready to move back to Majorca where he and Beryl would spend the rest of their lives together.

Graves received the Queen's Gold Medal for Poetry. He was also one of sixteen Great War poets commemorated on a stone in the Poets' Corner in Westminster Abbey. During his lifetime he published more than 140 books, which included 55 books of poetry, 15 novels, 10 translations, and 40 works of nonfiction, autobiographies, and literary essays. His greatest love was poetry.

The Caterpillar
by Robert Graves

In his poem *The Caterpillar*, Robert Graves gives a new perspective on a caterpillar's life through the use of personification and a great imagination. He begins his poem establishing where the caterpillar spends most of his time: "Under this loop of honeysuckle." Graves describes what the caterpillar looks like: "A creeping, coloured caterpillar." He continues the poem, becoming the caterpillar "I gnaw the fresh green hawthorn spray." Throughout the poem, he writes about the caterpillar's love of his life and his reason for living: "I eat and swallow and eat again."

The caterpillar begins to think that, although he does not want to change, he must become a butterfly. He makes plans to build himself a cocoon which he refers to as a mausoleum. He writes that some say worms "win resurrection" by dying and becoming butterflies. But to this caterpillar the word "win" does not have a positive connotation because he would like to remain "A hungry, hairy caterpillar," and "crawl on my high and swinging seat, / And eat, eat, eat – as one ought to eat."

The poem is available online. You can search for it or go to the following website to find the poem. Copy, print and share the poem with your class.

http://www.poets.org/viewmedia.php/prmMID/20235

April Monthly Holidays

Alcohol Awareness Month • Cancer Control Month • Child Abuse Prevention Month • Foot Health Month • International Guitar Month Keep America Beautiful Month • Math Awareness Month • Month of the Young Child • Multicultural Communication Month • National Cable Month • National Food Month • National Garden Month • National Humor Month • National Knuckles Down Month • National Occupational Therapy Month • National Pest Control Month • National Welding Month National Woodworking Month • Pets Are Wonderful Month • Prevention of Cruelty to Animals Month • Stress Awareness Month • Thai Heritage Month • Un-huh Month

April Weekly Holidays

First Week of April
Cherry Blossom Festival • Bat Appreciation Week • Medic Alert Week National Birthparents Week • National Reading a Road Map Week Publicity Stunt Week • Straw Hat Week

Second Week of April
National Building Safety Week • National Gardening Week • National Guitar Week • National Home Safety Week • National Library Week

Third Week of April
Bike Safety Week • Boys' and Girls' Club Week • Lefty Awareness Week Library Forgiveness Week • National Coin Week • National Pan American Week • National Volunteer Week • National Week of the Ocean

Fourth Week of April
Big Brother and Big Sister Appreciation Week • Canada-U.S. Goodwill Week • Egg Salad Week • Forest Week Intergenerational Week • Keep American Beautiful Week • National Administrative Professionals Week National Give-a-Sample Week • National YMCA Week • Reading is Fun Week • Teacher Appreciation Week (begins the last Monday) • Week of the Young Child

April Moveable Holidays

Tater Day (It's Sweet Potatoes)	first Monday
National Day of Hope	first Wednesday
National Walking Day	first Wednesday
Every Day is Tag Day	first Saturday
National Be Kind to Lawyers Day	second Tuesday
Audubon Day	second Friday
Slow Art Day	second Saturday
Astronomy Week	the week of the first quarter moon
Professional Secretaries Day	Wednesday of the last full week
Take Our Daughters and Sons to Work Day	fourth Thursday
National Hairball Awareness Day	last Friday
Arbor Day	last Friday
Eeyore's Birthday Day	last Saturday
Save the Frogs Day	last Saturday
Sense of Smell Day	last Saturday
Penguin Day	last Saturday

April Days for STEAM Makers and Poets

1. April Fool's Day
2. National Peanut Butter and Jelly Day
3. Find a Rainbow Day
4. Vitamin C Day
5. Read a Roadmap Day
6. National Student-Athlete Day
7. Metric System Day
8. Zoo Lovers Day
9. Name Yourself Day
10. Safety Pin Day
11. National Pet Day
12. International Human Space Flight Day
13. Scrabble Day
14. Look Up in the Sky Day
15. Rubber Eraser Day
16. Day of the Mushroom
17. National Haiku Poetry Day
18. Animal Crackers Birthday Day
19. National Garlic Day
20. Volunteer Recognition Day
21. Kindergarten Day
22. National Jelly Bean Day
23. Movie Theater Day
24. National Teach Your Children to Save Day
25. Telephone Day
26. Audubon Day
27. Morse Code Day
28. Great Poetry Reading Day
29. Zipper Day
30. Bugs Bunny Day

Integrating April Math Days

Science • Technology • Engineering • Arts • Math

Day		Make and Do
1	April Fool's Day	April Fool's Day dates back hundreds of years. Some interesting and fun pranks and hoaxes happened in recent times. For example, in 1957, Swiss farmers reported to be harvesting a record spaghetti crop. The newscast on the BBC showed footage of people pulling noodles from trees. In 1996, Taco Bell announced that it had purchased the Liberty Bell and were renaming it the Taco Liberty Bell. Visit the online Museum of Hoaxes at hoaxes.org and select the April Fool's Day menu. Read some of the top 100 hoaxes of all time. Which ones are your favorites? Write up a hoax for the museum. Be sure to feature a hoax with numbers or other surprising math facts.
4	Vitamin C Day	Vitamin C, also known as ascorbic acid, is a nutrient found in some foods. Celebrate Vitamin C by learning about the foods that have it and the amount needed for good health. The amount you need changes with age and gender. Research the amount of Vitamin C you need per day for your age group. Vitamin C is found in fruits (especially citrus) and many vegetables. Make a chart displaying the amount needed, an illustration of foods that provide you with Vitamin C and the amount found per serving for your good health.

5	Read a Roadmap Day	Roadmaps may have been drawn as early as 1160 BC in Ancient Egypt. Maps were sold as consumer goods as early as the sixteenth century. In the 1920s, oil companies distributed road maps as promotional tools. Today, web mapping tools are a new form of cartography. Web maps deliver up-to-date information in real time, can be personalized and don't need to be printed and distributed. Create an Internet roadmap from your school to the nearest science museum. What will you see along the way? Write your directions in a guidebook, illustrated with street directions and pictures from the Internet. Create your guidebook in word processing software and save as a pdf (portable document format) for easy electronic distribution.
7	Metric System Day	The Metric System of decimal measurement was developed in the 18th century in France and became part of French law on this day in 1795. The "metrification" of America has been tried unsuccessfully since the 1800s. The United States, Burma and Liberia are countries that today do not use the metric system. In our global society, American business encounters numerous problems as we try to do business with the rest of the world. The metric system uses multiples and sub-multiples of decimals (tens). Working in a group, define millimeter, centimeter, meter, and kilometer. Compare the following to their metric counterparts, an inch, a yard, and a mile. Create a worksheet that will show what you've learned. For example, which is longer, a mile or a kilometer?
13	Scrabble Day	One hundred million sets of Scrabble have been sold worldwide dating back to 1948. Over a million new sets are sold each year. If you're lucky enough to have the right letters, spelling the word oxyphenbutazone in a single play of Scrabble will give you the highest possible scoring word on a Scrabble board. Read about the history of Scrabble at http://www.scrabble-assoc.com/info/history.html. Have a Scrabble tournament today. How many long words were created? What was their point value?

Animal Crackers

18	Animal Crackers Birthday Day	An animal cracker is a small cookie baked in the shape of a zoo or circus animal. A box of animal crackers is usually filled with lions, tigers, bears and elephants. They are slightly sweet and light in color, but there are also frosted and chocolate flavor varieties as well. They started in England in the nineteenth century and made their way to America in 1902. There have been 37 different animals included over the years in Barnum's Animal Crackers with the koala added on the 100th birthday in 2002. Take apart a box of animal crackers. In a group, list, count and graph the animals contained. Decide as a group which animal should be the next to get its own cracker.
24	National Teach Your Children to Save Day	In your lifetime, you will make four important money choices: to save, to spend, to donate and to invest. Today we learn about saving and compounding interest. When you save money in a bank account with compounding interest, your savings earn money on both your saved amount (known as the principal) and on the interest. That is why saving consistently and starting early will lead to greater returns. This lesson starter is great for students in grade five and above. What will you have at the end of five years? For younger students, find a compounding interest calculator on the web and see if you can answer the same question. Using a spreadsheet, build your own compounding interest calculator as you show what happens by saving $10 a week for 52 weeks. Show what happens if you earn 5% interest, assume that the interest is paid once a year. What do you have in five years? Assume that your interest is paid every four weeks, what will you have at the end of one year? What will you have at the end of five years? Assume that the interest compounds daily, what will you have at the end of the year?

April Overview

Children and Nature Awareness Month
Math Lesson: Nature Mastermind
Poetry Lesson: The Gladness of Nature by William Cullen Bryant

Children and Nature Awareness Month celebrates the natural world and all the benefits nature offers to children. Students collect items from nature to use in a Nature Mastermind game. In the poetry lesson they delight in the poet's observations of nature.
NCTM Process Standard – Problem Solving: Apply and adapt a variety of appropriate strategies to solve problems.

National Poetry Month
Math Lesson: OuLiPo Snowball Poems
Poetry Lesson: Introduction to Songs of Innocence by William Blake

National Poetry Month was established to increase an awareness of poetry and its importance in our lives. Students connect the art of poetry with mathematics by writing OuLiPo snowball poems. Students experience the joy of poetry and model the poem of William Blake by creating a magical world.
NCTM Process Standard – Connections: Recognize and apply mathematics in contexts outside of mathematics.

Math Awareness Month
Math Lesson: Math in the Real World Scavenger Hunt
Poetry Lesson: Arithmetic by Carl Sandburg

Math Awareness Month was established to increase public understanding of and appreciation for mathematics. Student groups participate in a math scavenger hunt and learn how math exists in their daily lives. Carl Sandburg's poem Arithmetic uses humor to present the joys and frustrations with math and numbers.
NCTM Process Standard – Connections: Recognize and apply mathematics in contexts outside of mathematics.

Earth Day
Math Lesson: May The Forest Be With You
Poetry Lesson: The Cloud by Percy Bysshe Shelley

Earth Day, the largest secular observance celebrated worldwide, was established to educate the public about the importance of environmental planetary concerns for the health of humans, animals and all nature. Students reuse old math textbooks for an Earth Day math lesson to write and solve problems following a given set of directions. In Shelley's poem, he follows a cloud's journey as it moves across the Earth and the sky interacting with nature. Students become an element of nature and write poems in the first person.
NCTM STANDARD 1: Numbers and Operations, Gr 3 – 5C all; Gr 4 – 5C all; Gr 5 – 5C all; Gr 6 – 1A all.

Children and Nature Awareness Month
Math Lesson: Nature Mastermind

Children and Nature Awareness Month promotes the benefit of children interacting with the natural world. Students collect items from nature to use in a mastermind game.

MATERIALS
- Twigs, pebbles, leaves, seeds, blades of grass and other items from nature
- Plastic baggies
- Paper

PLAN
- A few days before the game is played, students collect items from nature.
- Identify the types of items collected, for example leaves, twigs, pebbles, etc.
- Sort the items into separate piles.
- Select at least six piles with enough items for all class members to have four of each item to place in a large baggie.

DO
- Divide the class into pairs.
- Select two student volunteers to demonstrate the game directions below while the class gives suggestions to help break the code.
    - Make a paper tent to place between the two players.
    - One player becomes the code maker and the other the code breaker.
    - The code maker chooses a pattern of four single items selected from their six baggies and places them shielded from view.
    - The goal is for the code breaker to duplicate the same items and the position as the code maker.
    - The code breaker tries to guess the pattern by placing four items from their six plastic bags.
    - The code maker provides feedback by telling how many objects are correctly matched in both item and position and which have matching items placed in the wrong position.
    - For example, "of your four items, you have two correctly matched and only one is in the correct position."
    - After the feedback is provided the code breaker attempts another guess.
    - Again the code maker provides feedback.
    - The code breaker uses the feedback to deduce the next move.
    - The game is over when the code is broken or ten attempts have elapsed.
- When the class understands the game, have pairs of students play. Once they are proficient, make the game even more challenging by having the code makers select duplicate as part of the four that make up the code.

Children and Nature Awareness Month
Poetry Lesson: The Gladness of Nature

In his poem *The Gladness of Nature*, William Cullen Bryant takes us on a nature trip and delights us with the gifts that nature gives. Combining personification and descriptive writing, he gives nature a personality and voice. Through his sensitive ears and descriptive writing, children will hear: "… notes of joy from the hang-bird and wren, / And the gossip of swallows through all the sky." In this lesson, students model their poems after Bryant's poem as they personify nature.

MATERIALS
- William Cullen Bryant Biography and his poem *The Gladness of Nature*
- Word processing or desktop publishing software or pencils, pens and paper

PLAN
- Read and discuss William Cullen Bryant's biography and poem.
- Discuss the poem with the following questions:
  - What does Bryant mean by "is this a time to be cloudy and sad"?
  - What does Bryant see in nature?
  - What interesting descriptive words does he use?
  - Where is personification used in the poem?

DO
Getting Ready to Write
- The poet begins his poem with the words "Is this a time to be cloudy and sad." Exchange the words *cloudy* and *sad* with other synonyms.
  For example: *Is this a time to be angry and mean or Is this a time to be frowning and crying*
- List objects in nature they can use in their poems.
  For example: *clouds, birds, fruits and flowers*
- How would they use personification to describe these object's reaction to nature?
  For example: *dancing clouds, singing birds, smiling fruits and flowers*

Writing the Poem
Using *The Gladness of Nature* as a model, students write poems of their own. Encourage line breaks so that the poem looks like a poem and not like a story.
- Begin with "Is this a time to be cloudy and sad" using your synonyms for cloudy and sad.
- Continue the poem with "When" and describe an object in nature and what it is doing on such a beautiful day. Encourage personification.
- Continue the poem with other objects in nature and describe what each one does.

Editing and Publishing
- Students read and edit poems with partners.
- Have students use watercolors to paint a scene illustrating their poem.
- When painting dries thoroughly, write a part of their poem or their entire poem on the watercolor.

William Cullen Bryant Biography
November 3, 1794 – June 12, 1878

William Cullen Bryant was born in a log cabin in Cummington, Massachusetts. His mother's family came to America on the Mayflower. His father's family came to the American colonies about twelve years later. His father was a physician as well as state legislator. His home in Massachusetts is now a museum.

William's father had a strong influence on him. William learned English poetry at a young age in his father's large personal library. Bryant's father encouraged William's writing, at times even sending William's poems to magazines for publication without his knowledge. At the age of ten, William had his first poem published and at thirteen had his first book of poetry published. He loved nature and celebrated it in his poems.

William studied law in Massachusetts and at twenty-one he passed the bar and became a lawyer. He would walk seven miles to work every day. On these walks, he was moved by the nature he observed. His love of nature would be celebrated in his poems. Although his first love was poetry, the life of a poet was not practical for him. But his literary dreams would be fulfilled in journalism. He moved his family to New York City and began his career as editor-in-chief of the New York Evening Post, one of the nation's most respected newspapers. He wrote articles, essays and poems that defended human rights, free trade, Abraham Lincoln, and the abolition of slavery. His influence helped the establishment of Central Park and the Metropolitan Museum of Art. He held the position of editor-in-chief until his death.

In his lifetime, he didn't publish many poems but he was very popular due to his writing as a journalist, and his many public speeches where he spoke about his views. Bryant was one of the founders of the Republican Party, and at one time he even thought about running for President of the United States. New York City's Bryant Park is named in his honor.

The Gladness of Nature
by William Cullen Bryant

Is this a time to be cloudy and sad,
When our mother Nature laughs around;
When even the deep blue heavens look glad,
And gladness breathes from the blossoming ground?

There are notes of joy from the hang-bird and wren,
And the gossip of swallows through all the sky;
The ground-squirrel gaily chirps by his den,
And the wilding bee hums merrily by.

The clouds are at play in the azure space,
And their shadows at play on the bright green vale,
And here they stretch to the frolic chase,
And there they roll on the easy gale.

There's a dance of leaves in that aspen bower,
There's a titter of winds in that beechen tree,
There's a smile on the fruit, and a smile on the flower,
And a laugh from the brook that runs to the sea.

And look at the broad-faced sun, how he smiles
On the dewy earth that smiles in his ray,
On the leaping waters and gay young isles;
Ay, look, and he'll smile thy gloom away.

National Poetry Month
Math Lesson: OuLiPo Snowball Poems

It's National Poetry Month! As part of the celebration students connect the art of poetry and mathematics by writing OuLiPo snowball poems. The philosophy OuLiPo (Ouvoir de Litterature Potentielle) is an acronym from French roughly translated as "the seeking of new structures and patterns which may be used by writers in any way they enjoy." Developed by French scientists and mathematicians, OuLiPo poetry is written within a system of structural constraints and is designed to produce endless outcomes. In this lesson, students build a progressive OuLiPo snowball poem that starts with a one-word sentence and builds up sequentially with each line containing one more word than the last.

MATERIALS
- Chart paper
- Marking pens
- Dictionaries and thesauruses

PLAN
- Discuss the meaning of the French acronym OuLiPo poetry that roughly translates to English as the seeking of new structures and patterns.
- Discuss the math and science connections to OuLiPo poetry.
- Inform the class that the most popular type of OuLiPo poems is the progressive snowball poem.
- Demonstrate how the construction of the poem works by creating one with the whole class.
- Place a one-word beginning on the board or chart. Class members build the poem by adding lines that progressively have one more word than the next. Here is an example.

Flowers
Many colors
Arrival of spring
Blowing in the wind
Surrounded by bees and butterflies
Children have patiently waited for you
Your breathtaking fragrance fills the crisp air

DO
- Divide the class into small groups.
- Distribute chart paper and markers to each group.
- Groups choose a one-word noun to begin.
- Groups write additional lines as in the example.
- Set a goal of writing as many lines as possible within a twenty-minute time frame.
- At the end of twenty minutes, groups present their poems.
- Display the poems on a poetry month bulletin board.

VARIATIONS

- You can build on this foundation by constructing additional poems. There are many varieties of OuLiPo poetry exercises from which to choose. For example, begin a snowball poem with one word on the first line. The second line is also one word, but with one additional letter. The lines grow progressively by making each line with a new word one letter longer than the previous word.

I
Am
Sun
Leaf
Plant
Flower
Vibrant
Dazzling
Sparkling
Blossoming
Enthralling
Silhouetting

- Another exercise is the S+7. In this exercise, writers replace each common noun in a poem with the common noun that follows it in a dictionary. For example, "To be, or not to be – that is the question . . ." becomes "To be, or not to be – that is the quetsal . . ." The word used to replace the noun varies with the dictionary used.

National Poetry Month
Poetry Lesson: Introduction to Songs of Innocence

If William Blake were alive today, he would be the first to acknowledge the power and magic of poetry. In his poem, William Blake creates a magical world where his Piper has the power to make the innocent child happy. First the Piper is: "Piping songs of pleasant glee." Next he sings "songs of happy cheer!" Finally, the Piper writes his happy songs: "In a book, that all may read." This makes the poet's words eternal and accessible so that all children can experience the joy the Piper's words bring. In this lesson, students become the Piper and pipe a song that makes the listener happy.

MATERIALS
- William Blake Biography and his poem *Introduction to Songs of Innocence*
- Word processing or desktop publishing software or pencils, pens and paper

PLAN
- Read and discuss William Blake's biography and poem.
- Discuss the poem with the following questions:
    - Where is the Piper in the beginning of the poem?
    - Why does the child want the Piper to pipe a song?
    - What does the poet mean when he writes "he wept to hear?"

DO
Getting Ready to Write
- Students answer the following questions as if they were the Piper.
    - What will they be doing and where will they be at the beginning of their poem?
      For **example:** *sitting in a cloud, sitting by the ocean, walking in the meadow, lying in the garden*
    - Who will ask them to pipe a song?
      For example: *my grandmother, my mother, my uncle or my brother*
    - What will they ask them to pipe about?
      For example: *the river, the mountains,* or *the sun*
    - How will they expand their responses?
      For example: *the river's water splashes calmly, the mountains touch the clouds* or *the sun warmly smiles on me*

Writing the Poem
- Students write poems of their own referring to the brainstormed list on the board. You may wish to begin by writing a class poem together.
    - Begin the poem with where they are and what they are doing.
    - Continue by telling who will ask them to pipe a song.
    - Suggest they continue writing their poems creating a peaceful and beautiful world by describing places in nature that make it that way.

Editing and Publishing
- Students read and edit poems with a partner.
- William Blake often framed his poetry with borders. Look at some of his border designs and give your poem a beautiful border.

William Blake Biography
November 28, 1757 – August 12, 1827

William Blake was born in Soho, England. His father was a haberdasher and hosier. They had seven children. His parents always supported his genius. When he was only four years old, he began to have visions. In one, he saw a tree filled with angels who sang and waved their wings in the branches. These visions were to become the subjects of his drawings and poetry throughout his life.

William's love of drawing and writing began at a very young age. Although he never attended school, his mother taught him to read. When he was ten, his father, recognizing his artistic talent, sent him to drawing school. There he learned to develop his skills by copying prints in drawing books. His teacher at the school sent him to Westminster Abbey, a famous church in London. At the Abbey, he spent his time sketching the statues. These statues were a major influence on his drawings. He was admitted to the Royal Academy Schools as an engraver where he began to exhibit his work.

As a teenager, he started writing poetry and combining his writing with his drawings and engravings. Much of his poetry was written about the conditions in British cities. These cities were unsanitary and overcrowded. As he walked along the streets of London, he saw children being mistreated and working very long hours in city factories. There was discontent among the working classes. In his visions, he saw a different world. He saw angels dancing around the sun that shined over London and children laughing on clouds. He wrote about the innocence of children. Much of his artistic energy was used to bring about a change in the way people behaved towards children. In this spirit, he wrote *Introduction to Songs of Innocence*.

Introduction to Songs of Innocence
by William Blake

Piping down the valleys wild,
Piping songs of pleasant glee,
On a cloud I saw a child,
And he laughing said to me:

"Pipe a song about a Lamb!"
So I piped with merry cheer.
"Piper, pipe that song again;"
So I piped: he wept to hear.

"Drop thy pipe, thy happy pipe;
Sing thy songs of happy cheer!"
So I sung the same again,
While he wept with joy to hear.

"Piper, sit thee down and write
In a book, that all may read."
So he vanish'd from my sight,
And I pluck'd a hollow reed.

And I made a rural pen,
And I stained the water clear,
And I wrote my happy songs
Every child may joy to hear.

April Math Awareness Month
Math Lesson: Math Real World Scavenger Hunt

In this lesson, students conduct a real-world math scavenger hunt by searching newspapers and magazines. Working from a handout, teams search for items that depict how math exists in their daily lives. As sample items are found they are placed on a project board.

MATERIALS
- Newspapers
- Magazines
- Math Real-World Scavenger Hunt Handout
- Poster paper or poster boards
- Scissors
- Glue, paste, tape

PLAN
- Students bring newspapers and magazines in advance.
- Discuss the sections of a daily newspaper and the format of some sample magazines.
- Distribute the Real-World Scavenger Hunt Handout.
- Discuss where some of the items would be found in the sections of a daily newspaper or in magazines.

DO
- Students work in pairs to find items from the list and place their found artifacts on poster paper or poster boards.
- In the specified time, students find as many of the twenty items as they can and number the items on the poster board to match the list on the handout.
- Early finishers, may add to the list and to their project boards.
- Finished boards will be presented to the class and displayed in the classroom.
- Alternatively, the Internet could be used for this activity; however, it requires a networked printer and a lot of paper.

Math Real-World Scavenger Hunt Handout

1. Select a sports statistic where the total score is greater than or equal to 34
2. Ad that includes a telephone number or Internet address
3. Item of clothing with a two-digit number
4. Product reduced 50% or more
5. A business logo with a geometric shape
6. Item that costs more than $1500
7. Ad that tells or shows how much money you can save
8. Sudoku or other number puzzles
9. Picture of clothing with parallel lines
10. Ad that illustrates identical items
11. Something that lists miles per gallon
12. Comic strip or cartoon that relates to math
13. Listing of the time and date of an event
14. Measurement of an item (weight, length, etc.)
15. Real estate listing for property over one million dollars
16. A bar, circle, or line graph
17. Television schedule showing time or date
18. Current mortgage or interest rates
19. A picture of a consumer using math
20. Ad that shows a monthly payment amount

Math Awareness Month: Poetry Lesson: Arithmetic

Arithmetic, the poem by Carl Sandburg, with its fresh and imaginative language, appeals to all children, young or old, with its fanciful and imaginary use of language. His descriptions call attention to arithmetic. This poem for Math Awareness Month makes the reader aware of arithmetic in a new light.

MATERIALS
- Carl Sandburg's Biography and a summary of his poem *Arithmetic*
- Word processing or desktop publishing software or pencils, pens and paper

PLAN
- Read and discuss Carl Sandburg's biography and poem.
- Discuss the poem with the following questions:
    - How does Sandburg feel about arithmetic?
    - What arithmetic problems give the author the most trouble? Explain your answer.
    - What makes this poem enjoyable?
    - Where does Sandburg use humor in his poem?

DO
Getting Ready to Write
Ask students what the world would be like without arithmetic. Write responses on the board or a chart.
Writing the Poem
- Students write a poem in which they write about things in their everyday life that would change if arithmetic did not exist.
  For example:
  I would not know how old I am
  I could not count how many toes I have
  I would not know how many planets there are in the sky
  I would not be able to say how many teeth I am missing
- Students title their poem "Without Arithmetic."
- Encourage line breaks so that the poem looks like a poem and not like a story.
- Continue their poem writing about all the things they would not know or could not do if arithmetic did not exist.

Editing and Publishing
- Students read and edit poems with partners.
- Students write their poem in a poetry book or enter them in a word processing program.
- Have students illustrate their final masterpiece.

Carl Sandburg Biography
January 6, 1878 – July 22, 1967

Carl Sandburg is known as the poet of the Industrial Revolution. Sandburg was born in Galesburg, Illinois. His parents, August and Clara Sandburg were immigrants from the north of Sweden. His parents were very poor and he had to leave school when he was thirteen to work. He took any job available. He worked in a theater, barbershop, in a brickyard, as a dishwasher in hotels and as a harvest hand in wheat fields. These jobs and the people he met through them became the subject matter of his poetry.

When Sandburg was eighteen he visited Chicago and fell in love with the city. Chicago and the Industrial Revolution were to become the subject of much of his poetry. Eventually he would win a Pulitzer Prize for his *Chicago Poems*, a collection of nine poems written about Chicago. Sandburg wrote about the beautiful skyscrapers and of the people who constructed and worked in them.

In 1897, when Carl was nineteen, he decided to see the country. Hopping on trains, he spent a year as a hobo. In 1898, when war with Spain was declared, Sandburg enlisted in the United States Army. After the war, he went to college and became interested in literature. Eventually, he became a journalist.

As a newspaperman, he struggled to keep writing poetry. Sandburg was unknown in the literary world until he was thirty-six years old. A group of his poems finally appeared in a famous poetry journal. A year later, his first book of poems was published. Those in the literary world thought he should pay more attention to the craft of writing. But the reading public appreciated his subjects and his honest words. In his lifetime, he won three Pulitzer prizes. Two of them were for his poetry and a third for a biography he wrote about Abraham Lincoln. In 1964, he received the Presidential Medal of Freedom from President Lyndon B. Johnson.

Arithmetic
by Carl Sandburg

In his poem *Arithmetic*, Carl Sandburg begins in a humorous way, letting the reader know his own difficulty with numbers as they "fly like pigeons in and out of your head." He can't get ahold of them. He also describes how sometimes you feel good "where the answer is right and everything is nice and you can look out of the window and see the blue sky." Other times you feel bad when "the answer is wrong and you have to start all over and try again and see how it comes out this time." This is a perfect poem for most children who have had wonderful moments with numbers and other times would have liked to forget that numbers exist. Students will enjoy reading the poem and enjoy Sandburg's humor as expressed in the last three lines of the poem:

> "If you ask your mother for one fried egg for breakfast and she gives you two fried eggs and you eat both of them, who is better in arithmetic, you or your mother?"

The complete poem is available online. You can search for the poem or you can go to the following website to print, copy and share with your class.

http://www.poemhunter.com/poem/arithmetic/

Also check out YouTube for videos of Sandburg's poem.

Earth Day
Math Lesson: Reusing Old Math Textbooks – May The Forest Be With You!

Every year on April 22nd nations across the world celebrate Earth Day by holding events to show support for the protection of the environment. One way to celebrate Earth Day is to reuse paper, a major contributor to waste landfills. Every year many old textbooks are thrown out. Your school probably has a stack of old math textbooks that will work well for this activity. Your students will feel a great sense of accomplishment as they work through these fun directions.

MATERIALS
- Old math textbooks, one for every two students
- Paper and pencils
- Chart paper and markers
- May the Forest Be With You Worksheet

PLAN
- Discuss the fact that paper pollution has a large negative effect on the environment. Its production uses chemicals that pollute the environment. Its overuse is responsible for a great number of trees to be cut down and is a major contributor to waste landfills.
- Ask students to suggest ways to stop paper pollution and write them on a board or chart.
- Tell students they will be reusing old mathematics textbooks for an Earth Day math lesson.

DO
- Divide the class into pairs.
- Distribute an older mathematics textbook, one for each pair of students.
- Distribute a May The Forest Be With You Worksheet to each pair.
- Have students write their names and the name and edition of their math book at the top of the worksheet.
- Modulate the amount of time to complete the worksheet depending upon the grade level of your students.
- Have pairs swap their book and worksheet with another pair to check answers.

EXTENSION
- Have your students create their own list of directions to further extend learning on the back of the worksheet.

May the Forest Be With You Worksheet

- Open textbook to a random page and write the page number.
- Open to a new page and write that number.
- Add both numbers together to find the sum.
- Subtract to find the difference.
- Multiply the numbers to find the quotient.
- Open your textbook to the last numbered page.
- Round the page number to nearest tenth.
- Round the page number to the nearest hundredth.
- Write and solve the last problem on the first three odd numbered pages.
- Write and solve the first problem on the last four even numbered page.
- Write a one-digit page number and a two-digit page number. Use them to create and solve a division problem.
- Open a new random page and write the page number.
- Open to another page and write that number.
- Use both numbers to create a fraction with the smallest number as the numerator and the largest number as the denominator.
- Reduce the fraction to its lowest terms.
- Turn to a page near the end of the book and write the number on that page as a decimal.
- What number is in the hundreds place?
- What number is in the tens place?
- What number is in the ones place?
- Write the title of your math book.
    - How many vowels are in the title?
    - How many consonants?
    - Write the difference.
- Use a ruler to measure your math book.
    - How many inches wide is it?
    - How many inches long is it?
    - What is the area of your math book?

Earth Day
Poetry Lesson: The Cloud

Percy Bysshe Shelley was a Romantic poet. The Romantics admired and respected the untouched beauty of all that existed naturally on the earth. It was in nature they wrote their powerful and majestic poetry. In Shelley's poem *The Cloud*, he follows a cloud's journey as it moves across the Earth and the sky interacting with nature. In this lesson, students become an element of nature and write poems in the first person describing how their element interacts with the Earth.

MATERIALS
- Percy Bysshe Shelley Biography and excerpt from his poem *The Cloud*
- Word processing or desktop publishing software or pencils, pens and paper

PLAN
- Read and discuss Percy Bysshe Shelley's biography and poem.
- Discuss the poem with the following questions:
    - Where does Shelley use personification?
    - Why does Shelley use the word "I" when the cloud speaks?
    - What interesting verbs does Shelley use?
    - How does the cloud interact with nature?
    - Where in the poem does the poet describe the water cycle?
    - Why does the cloud laugh "at my own cenotaph"?
    - In what way does the cloud "change but cannot die"?
    - How does the cloud morph like a magician?

DO
Getting Ready to Write
- Students discuss which of the following elements of nature they want to become and why: *rain, ocean, moon, sun, wind, cloud, fog, snow, ice*.
- Have students pick an element from the discussion list and describe how it affects aspects in nature.
- Encourage the use of personification.

Writing the Poem
- Begin the first line with *I*.
- Describe how their selected element interacts with nature.

Editing and Publishing
- Students read and edit poems with partners.
- Students illustrate their poems.
- Students dramatically perform their poems using an appropriate voice.
- View videos of *The Cloud* on YouTube and create their own.

Percy Bysshe Shelley Biography
August 4, 1792 – July 8, 1822

Shelley was born in England. His father was a member of Parliament. He grew up in the countryside. In the meadows near his home, he enjoyed hunting and fishing. He was the oldest of seven children. He had a happy and imaginative childhood playing games that involved witches, wizards and demons.

At ten, he was sent to boarding school. He remained there for two years and then enrolled at Eton College. Within the first year at Eton, Shelley had two novels and two volumes of poetry published. He had an extremely difficult time at Eton. He was abused both physically and mentally, everyone bullying and making fun of him because of his eccentric ways. They called him "Mad Shelley." He had imagination and energy far beyond his physical strength. He loved to learn about magic and witchcraft and he could watch all night for ghosts. His interests were not like most of the other students who loved popular games. He did, however, enjoy boating and shooting. In the classroom, he was a Latin scholar. He loved to read and was also interested in science. During vacations back home, he was always telling his sisters tales of supernatural wonders.

At eighteen, Shelley enrolled at Oxford which seemed a better environment for him. After a few months there, Shelley was expelled from Oxford after publishing and distributing an essay *The Necessity of Atheism*. He went home to his angry parents. At nineteen, he went to Scotland with Harriet Westbrook and married. They separated and he began a relationship with Mary Godwin, who later wrote the novel *Frankenstein*. Eventually Harriet committed suicide leaving them free to marry.

From his childhood on, Shelley did not conform to the ideas of his society. As an adult, he believed that the changes proposed by the French Revolution would help society. He used his poetry to provoke a sense of revolution in people. He challenged authority in the way he lived, and was ostracized because of it. Shelley became one of the most well-loved and popular poets of his time. During his tumultuous life, he spent much of it thinking and appreciating nature, his work being an example of Romantic poetry. Shelley's imagination was constantly excited by the never-ending cycle of life that to him mirrored the human spirit. No poet has ever come closer to capturing in words the fullness of human emotion. After his death from drowning, Mary Shelley published a collection of his poetry and essays.

The Cloud
by Percy Bysshe Shelley

I bring fresh showers for the thirsting flowers,
    From the seas and the streams;
I bear light shade for the leaves when laid
    In their noonday dreams.
From my wings are shaken the dews that waken
    The sweet buds every one,
When rocked to rest on their mother's breast,
    As she dances about the sun.
I wield the flail of the lashing hail,
    And whiten the green plains under,
And then again I dissolve it in rain,
    And laugh as I pass in thunder.

I sift the snow on the mountains below,
    And their great pines groan aghast;
And all the night 'tis my pillow white,
    While I sleep in the arms of the blast.
Sublime on the towers of my skiey bowers,
    Lightning my pilot sits;
In a cavern under is fettered the thunder,
    It struggles and howls at fits;
Over earth and ocean, with gentle motion,
    This pilot is guiding me,
Lured by the love of the genii that move
    In the depths of the purple sea;
Over the rills, and the crags, and the hills,
    Over the lakes and the plains,
Wherever he dream, under mountain or stream,
    The Spirit he loves remains;
And I all the while bask in Heaven's blue smile,
    Whilst he is dissolving in rains.

The sanguine Sunrise, with his meteor eyes,
    And his burning plumes outspread,
Leaps on the back of my sailing rack,
    When the morning star shines dead;
As on the jag of a mountain crag,
    Which an earthquake rocks and swings,
An eagle alit one moment may sit
    In the light of its golden wings.
And when Sunset may breathe, from the lit sea beneath,
    Its ardours of rest and of love,
And the crimson pall of eve may fall
    From the depth of Heaven above,

With wings folded I rest, on mine aëry nest,
    As still as a brooding dove.

That orbèd maiden with white fire laden,
    Whom mortals call the Moon,
Glides glimmering o'er my fleece-like floor,
    By the midnight breezes strewn;
And wherever the beat of her unseen feet,
    Which only the angels hear,
May have broken the woof of my tent's thin roof,
    The stars peep behind her and peer;
And I laugh to see them whirl and flee,
    Like a swarm of golden bees,
When I widen the rent in my wind-built tent,
    Till calm the rivers, lakes, and seas,
Like strips of the sky fallen through me on high,
    Are each paved with the moon and these.

I bind the Sun's throne with a burning zone,
    And the Moon's with a girdle of pearl;
The volcanoes are dim, and the stars reel and swim,
    When the whirlwinds my banner unfurl.
From cape to cape, with a bridge-like shape,
    Over a torrent sea,
Sunbeam-proof, I hang like a roof,
    The mountains its columns be.
The triumphal arch through which I march
    With hurricane, fire, and snow,
When the Powers of the air are chained to my chair,
    Is the million-coloured bow;
The sphere-fire above its soft colours wove,
    While the moist Earth was laughing below.

I am the daughter of Earth and Water,
    And the nursling of the Sky;
I pass through the pores of the ocean and shores;
    I change, but I cannot die.
For after the rain when with never a stain
    The pavilion of Heaven is bare,
And the winds and sunbeams with their convex gleams
    Build up the blue dome of air,
I silently laugh at my own cenotaph,
    And out of the caverns of rain,
Like a child from the womb, like a ghost from the tomb,
    I arise and unbuild it again.

May Monthly Holidays

American Bike Month • Asian/Pacific-American Heritage Month
Breathe Easy Month • Flower Month • National Asparagus Month
National Barbeque Month • National Bike Month • National Egg Month
National Hamburger Month • National Mental Health Month • National
Photo Month • National Physical Fitness and Sports Month • National
Radio Month • National Salad Month • National Strawberry Month
Older Americans Month • Personal History Awareness Month

May Weekly Holidays

First Week of May
Cartoon Art Appreciation Week • National Herb Week • National Music
Week • National Photo Week • National Postcard Week • National Raisin
Week • Pen-Friends Week International • Public Service Recognition

Second Week of May
Conserve Water/Detect-a-Leak Week • Goodwill Industries Week
National Nurses Week • National Pet Week National Postcard Week
National Tourism Week • National Transportation Week

Third Week of May
Art Week • Buckle Up America! Week • Girls Incorporated Week
National Bike Week • National Educational Bosses Week • National Police
Week • National Salvation Army Week • Public Relations Week
Public Transportation Week

Fourth Week of May
Anonymous Giving Week • International Pickle Week • National Backyard
Games Week • National Safe Boating Week

May Moveable Holidays

International Tuba Day	first Friday
Mother's Day	second Sunday
Hawaiian Song Day	second Sunday
National Teacher Day	second Tuesday
Armed Forces Day	third Saturday
International Jumping Frog Jubilee	third Saturday
Indianapolis 500 Auto Race	Sunday before Memorial Day
Memorial Day	last Monday

May Days for STEAM Makers and Poets

1 Mother Goose Day
2 Make-a-Book Day
3 Famous Funnies Day
4 Movie Day
5 Cinco de Mayo
6 National Teacher Day
7 National School Nurse's Day
8 World Red Cross Day
9 Lost Sock Memorial Day
10 Clean Up Your Room Day
11 Surrealistic Art Day
12 Limerick Day
13 National Apple Pie Day
14 Stars and Stripes Forever Day
15 United Nations International Day of Families
16 Biographer's Day
17 Pack Rat Day
18 International Museum Day
19 Malcolm X Day
20 Eliza Doolittle Day
21 National Waiter and Waitresses Day
22 Sherlock Holmes Day
23 National Taffy Day
24 National Escargot Day
25 National Tap Dance Day
26 Birth Anniversary of Sally Ride
27 San Francisco's Golden Gate Bridge Day
28 National Hamburger Day
29 Bing Crosby's White Christmas Recorded
30 Lincoln Memorial Dedication Day
31 American Poetry Day

Integrating May Math Days

Science Technology Engineering Arts Math

Day		Make and Do
2	Make-a-Book Day	Today is Make-a-Book Day. Make a Math Alphabet Book. Think of a math word for each letter of the alphabet. Write and illustrate your book. Each page of your book should have a math term, its definition and an example of how it is used. You may wish to lay your book out in a word processing program and add illustrations to each page.
5	Cinco de Mayo	This Mexican national holiday celebrates a victory over the French at the Battle of Puebla, on May 5, 1862. Everyone loves chips and guacamole. Use the following recipe to make your guacamole to serve 8. Use a spreadsheet to multiply the number of servings for your class. How much of each ingredient will you need? To serve eight use: 2 avocados 1 large garlic clove minced 1 tablespoon lemon juice 2 tablespoons olive oil ½ teaspoon salt Mash and serve with chips.
8	World Red Cross Day	Learn about Henri Dunant and Clara Barton, great humanitarians. What is a humanitarian? Kids can make a difference through education, volunteering, writing letters and fundraising. Plan a fundraiser for the Red Cross. Research what the Red Cross does and create a promotional campaign for your class. Set a goal for a classroom project. Determine the dollar amount of funds you wish to raise.

9	Lost Sock Memorial Day	Today is the day to recognize your drawer of unmatched socks. Let's face it; they probably aren't coming back so why not make sock puppets today? Memorialize your missing socks, reflect upon how warm and fuzzy they made you feel and move on. Your sock puppets can put on a show in your very own do-it-yourself puppet theater. Create a math puppet show all about things that come in pairs. Come up with a math sock challenge. Use this as a model. If a drawer contains 6 red socks and 8 blue socks, what is the probability that you pull a pair of socks on the second time? For more activities, try graphing the color of the socks worn in your class today.
13	National Apple Pie Day	What is more American than apple pie? Pie is part of America's history dating back to the earliest colonial settlers. Find out how apple pie became a national symbol. Also find a favorite recipe and learn how apple pie a la mode came to be. Does your family have a special apple pie recipe? Here are two math fractional pie problems to solve. Be sure to illustrate your solution to explain how you solved the problem. For example, if six pieces of pie are eaten and two are leftover, how much of the pie can be eaten tomorrow? After a Sunday celebration, your family has three apple pies left. How do you divide them into equal portions so that each of your eight cousins can take home the same amount of pie?
17	Pack Rat Day	Are you a pack rat? Make a list of all things that pack rats should do and not do today. For example, clean your room and gather together items that you are willing to sell. How will you price your items? Make a list of your prized possessions and go on ebay to determine the value your items might get at a typical garage sale. See if your list can add up to more than $25.

18	International Museum Day	Organized by the International Council of Museums, over 35,000 museums in 143 countries participated in 2013. Museums engage their community with the ability to tell a story and educate their visitors. Design your own museum. Create a scale model floor plan where one inch equals one foot.
20	Eliza Doolittle Day	Just you wait Henry Higgins! Eliza Doolitle is the Cockney Flower girl of George Bernard Shaw's *Pygmalion*, 1912, and Lerner and Lowe's *My Fair Lady*, 1956. After a chance meeting in Covent Garden, Eliza takes elocution lessons from Professor Higgins and most famously learns "The rain is Spain falls mainly in the plain." How many times in one minute can you correctly say this tongue twister? Have a contest to see who can say it the most times without making an error. Graph your class results.
31	American Poetry Day	Today celebrates the birthday of Walt Whitman in 1819 and honors all poets and poetry lovers. Walt Whitman was known for his free verse style of poetry. Hold a Numerical Poetry Day Pageant. Each student writes a five-line poem with fifteen words. Begin with one word on line one. Add a word on every line. For example: Number Poems Are Easy to write They make you count As you add new words

May Overview

Wildflower Month
Math Lesson: Wildflower Calculations
Poetry Lesson: I Wandered Lonely as a Cloud by Williams Wordsworth
National Wildflower Week celebrates nature's bounty of wildflowers. This unit integrates planting and growing wildflowers with the study of fractions. Students categorize the growth of the wildflowers by colors, sizes, and types and then express the results in fractional terms. Students write poems describing wildflowers they see on an imaginary journey.
NCTM STANDARD 3: Geometry, Gr 3 – 3C-2; Gr 5 – 3B-7, 5B-8; Gr 6 – 4B-3
NCTM STANDARD 4: Measurement, Gr 3 – 4B-2, 4B-4; Gr 4 – 4B-1; Gr 5 – 5B-1
Gr 6 – 4B-3

May Day
Math Lesson: Hawaiian Lei Day
Poetry Lesson: In May by William Henry Davies
May Day is celebrated on May 1st as a traditional spring holiday in many cultures. To celebrate May Day known as Lei Day in Hawaii, students create circles with a compass, hone measurement skills to determine straw lengths, practice fraction knowledge to fold flowers and design patterns to make unique leis. In the poetry lesson they write about a beautiful day in May.
NCTM STANDARD 1: Numbers and Operations, Gr. 5 – 1A-6, 1A-7; Gr 6 – 1A-2, --1A-3
NCTM STANDARD 3: Geometry, Gr. 6 – 3D-10; NCTM STANDARD 4: Measurement,
Gr 3 – 4B-2

Mother's Day
Math Lesson: Flower Power Bar Graph
Poetry Lesson: Child and Mother by Eugene Field
Mother's Day falls on the second Sunday in May. On this day we take time to honor our mothers and other mother figures in our lives. Students create a flower bar graph representing the heights of each family member to present as a Mother's Day gift. They write a poem inviting their mother to a place where everyday problems disappear.
NCTM STANDARD 5: Analysis and Probability, Gr 4 – 5A-4; Gr 5 – 5A-4, Gr 5 – A-5

Memorial Day
Math Lesson: Savings Bonds
Poetry Lesson: Decoration Day by Evaleen Stein
Memorial Day is a legal holiday for America to honor and remember those who have served our country. Students learn about the Series E defense bonds sold to contribute to the financing of World War II. They use spreadsheets and calculators to compute their earnings over time. They write about how they would honor fallen soldiers and what they would say to them.
NCTM STANDARD 1: Numbers and Operations, Gr 6 – 1C-7
NCTM Process Standard – Problem Solving: Apply and adapt a variety of appropriate strategies to solve problems.

Wildflower Month
Math Lesson: Wildflower Calculations

This lesson integrates planting and growing wildflowers with the study of fractions. Students categorize the growth of the wildflowers by colors, sizes, and types and then express the results in fractional terms. During this lesson, students should be able to apply their knowledge of fractions to the real world.

MATERIALS
- Large aluminum baking pans, one for each group
- Potting soil, wildflower seeds, water
- Paper cups, index cards, markers, rulers
- Two-page Counting Flowers Worksheet

PLAN
- Divide class into groups of five.
- Distribute aluminum baking pans, wildflower seeds in paper cups, potting soil, index cards, markers and rulers.

DO
- The groups do the following:
  - Write the names of the group members on an index card and affix to the pan.
  - Spread ¼ inch of soil on the bottom of the aluminum pan and sprinkle the seeds over the soil.
  - Cover the seeds with a thin layer of soil. One-quarter inch of soil works well.
  - Gently water the soil to keep moist without overwatering.
- Keep the aluminum pans in a warm, lighted place.
- When the plants are grown, groups complete the Counting Flowers Worksheet.

Counting Flowers Worksheet – Page 1

Names: _____

You will need rulers and colored pencils or crayons.
Draw a picture of your flowers in the box below.

[ ]

Count the colors of your wildflowers. Create a bar graph below to illustrate the results.

Colors

	1	2	3	4	5	6	7	8	9	10	11	12	13

Counting Flowers Worksheet – Page 2

Write fractions to represent your results. For example, there are 14 flowers altogether. If 2 flowers are red, 2/14 of the flowers are red. Reduce to the lowest common denominator, 1/7. Write the color of flowers along with the appropriate fraction in the box below.

Measure the tallest flower and the shortest flower.
Write the measurements in inches. _____ _____
Find the difference between them. _____

As a group, write three word problems relating to the flowers. Include both the problems and the solutions.

Wildflower Month
Poetry Lesson: I Wandered Lonely as a Cloud

William Wordsworth loved nature and all its delights. In his poem, *I Wandered Lonely as a Cloud*, Wordsworth captures the glory of the golden daffodils growing wild in the English countryside. In this lesson, students take an imaginary journey and write a poem describing wildflowers they come upon.

MATERIALS
- William Wordsworth Biography and his poem *I Wandered Lonely as a Cloud*
- Word processing or desktop publishing software or pencils, pens and paper

PLAN
- Read and discuss William Wordsworth's biography and poem.
- Ask the following questions:
    - Why does Wordsworth compare the way he is walking to the way a cloud moves?
    - How do the daffodils make him feel?
    - Where does he use personification?
    - How does Wordsworth feel when he is old and sees the daffodils again? Why?

DO
Getting Ready to Write
- Students close their eyes and imagine themselves in a beautiful place such as a garden, a tropical forest, or a park. They begin to look at the landscape until they arrive at some extraordinary wildflowers. Have students pay attention to their senses that this scene evokes in them.
- Students open their eyes and discuss what images they saw and heard. Write their responses on the board.
  For example: *wildflowers purple, red and blue, the golden sun, owls hooting, ocean roaring*
- How would they add personification to what they saw? Write responses on the board. For example: *purple, red and yellow wildflowers dancing; the sun waving goodbye to the clouds*

Writing the Poem
Using *I Wandered Lonely as a Cloud* as a model, students write poems of their own. Encourage line breaks so that the poem looks like a poem and not like a story.
- Begin poems by using the words *I wandered* or *I floated* or a similar phrase.
- Continue poems describing what the wildflowers look like and what they are doing.
- Continue describing other things they saw or heard along the way.
- Use personification to make descriptions interesting and vivid.

Editing and Publishing
- Students read and edit the poems with partners.
- Make crepe paper wildflowers and attach to a bulletin board along with student poems.
- For instructions on how to make crepe paper wildflowers go to this website: http://appetitepaper.com/paper-wildflowers-yellow-day-dreaming/

William Wordsworth Biography
April 7, 1770 – April 23, 1850

William Wordsworth was born in Cumberland in North West England, a rural paradise. This environment influenced Wordsworth's love of nature and became the subject of much of his poetry. His father was a wealthy landowner. As a child, he had two traumatic experiences. He lost his mother when he was eight and lost his father when he was thirteen. He had five siblings.

Wordsworth published his first poem when he was seventeen at the same time as he completed his studies at Cambridge. He then went to France where the French revolutionary ideas intrigued him. Because of tensions that were mounting between England and France, Wordsworth moved back to England. Eventually he married Mary Hutchinson and had five children with her.

He remained very close to his siblings especially Dorothy. William wrote the poem *I Wandered Lonely as a Cloud* after walking with her among the daffodils. This experience was also recorded by Dorothy in her journal.

Wordsworth was a major English Romantic poet and helped to launch the Romantic period in English literature. His poetry reflects the Romantic poets view of nature's healing properties. He was a poet concerned with the human relationship to nature. He became England's Poet Laureate in 1843 and remained so until his death.

Wordsworth believed that nature strengthens our character and allows us to see the mysteries of the universe. He also believed that nature once experienced remains in our memory forever. These memories can give people as much joy as when they were first experienced. He wrote that the world of things was "forever speaking." We have to listen and look to find a "tale in everything."

I Wandered Lonely as a Cloud
by William Wordsworth

I wandered lonely as a cloud
That floats on high o'er vales and hills
When all at once I saw a crowd,
A host, of golden daffodils;
Beside the lake, beneath the trees
Fluttering and dancing in the breeze.

Continuous as the stars that shine
And twinkle in the milky way,
They stretched in never-ending line
Along the margin of the bay:
Ten thousand saw I at a glance,
Tossing their heads in sprightly dance.

The waves beside them danced; but they
Out-did the sparkling waves in glee:
A poet could not but be gay,
In such a jocund company:
I gazed --- and gazed---but little thought
What wealth the show to me had brought:

For oft, when on my couch I lie
In vacant or in pensive mood,
They flash upon that inward eye
Which is the bliss of solitude;
And then my heart with pleasure fills,
And dances with the daffodils.

May Day
Math Lesson: Hawaiian Lei Day

While people around the world celebrate May Day on the first day of May, Hawaiians are celebrating Lei Day. This tradition began in 1927 when two newspaper columnists Don Blanding and Grace Tower Warren suggested the holiday. It was Grace that coined the term "May Day is Lei Day." Each Hawaiian Island produces a unique lei made of flowers generic to their island. Kauai's lei is made of purple berries. Maui's lei is made from the fragile pink Hawaiian rose. The Big Island of Hawaii's flower is red ohia and is the most traditional of all. Oahu's lei is made of the yellow ilima flower, often called the "Royal Lei" as it was worn by Hawaiian royalty. In this lesson students work in groups and use math skills to design and produce leis in celebration of Lei Day. To produce the leis, students use geometry tools to create circles, measurement skills to determine straw lengths, fraction knowledge to fold flowers and design patterns to make unique leis.

MATERIALS
- Assorted colors of tissue paper
- Math compass with a sharp pencil, one per student
- Four-inch squares of tag board or heavy card paper, one per student
- Embroidery needle, one per student
- Rulers, scissors and tape
- Three or four drinking straws per student
- Pony beads and embroidery floss thread

PLAN
Students first learn to use a math compass to draw a circle. Draw a circle on the board and define the terms circumference, diameter and radius. During a teacher-led demonstration, students use the compass to draw a three-inch circle on the cardboard. Here are the steps to follow:

- Tighten the hinge on the top of the compass to prevent slippage.
- Insert the pencil into the holder.
- Make the tip of the pencil even with the sharp point of the compass.
- Tighten the screw on the pencil holder to firmly secure the pencil point.
- Place the pencil point and the compass point to a spread of 1½ inches on the ruler to make a circle with a 3" radius.
- Find the center point of the square. Hold the compass firmly at the hinge and place the pointed end of the compass on the center point to draw a 3" circle.
- Slowly and carefully rotate the compass to draw the circle.

DO
- Divide the class into small groups.
- Have the groups select the tissue paper color they will use to make lei flowers.
- Have group members follow the directions on the Hawaiian Lei Day Handout to create leis.

Hawaiian Lei Day Handout

Work as a group to complete the project in the most efficient way.

1. Cut out the tag board circles to use as your pattern.
2. Put tissue paper into three sheet stacks, one on top of another.
3. Place the patterns on top of the tissue paper stacks and trace around them.
4. Cut out the tissue paper stacks. Each stack will make one flower. You will need as many flowers as it will take to complete the length of your lei (approximately 30 to 40 flowers).
5. Fold the circles in half and then in half again as many times as possible to create pleats before unfolding.
6. Measure and cut the straws into ¼ inch segments. The numbers of straw segments need to be equal to the number of tissue circles.
7. Measure the length of embroidery floss you will need for each lei by laying a segment in a circle around the tallest group member's neck. Add an additional three inches.
8. Cut the thread to the measured length for each group member.
9. Complete the flowers as follows:
    a. Separate three strands from the embroidery floss.
    b. Thread the strands into the embroidery needle.
    c. Place a piece of tape on the other end of the floss to prevent items you sew from falling off.
    d. Alternate stringing pony beads, straw segments and tissue flowers to create the lei.
    e. Carefully push the needle straight through the middle of the flower as you proceed.
    f. Knot the ends to finish the lei.
    g. Group members wear the finished leis.
    h. Play Hawaiian music and have the class dance in a Lei Day parade.

May Day
Poetry Lesson: In May

William Henry Davies suggests that May is the time to "spend the livelong day with nature." In his poem *In May*, William Henry Davies imagines himself sitting under a tree on a typical day and celebrating nature by sharing bread with birds, listening to their songs and watching cows in the meadow. Davies escapes the everyday crowded world to a cottage near an ocean and listens to birds that sing rather than to the voices of men. In this poetry lesson, students write a poem about a beautiful day in May.

MATERIALS
- William Henry Davies Biography and his poem *In May*
- Word processing or desktop publishing software (optional)

PLAN
- Read and discuss William Henry Davies' biography and poem.
- Ask the following questions:
    - How does William Henry Davies use imagery to draw a picture with words?
    - Which words convey that this is the month of May?
    - What phrases set the mood of the poem?

DO
Getting Ready to Write
- Students draw a detailed picture of a beautiful day in May placing themselves into the picture. Their picture will be used as the inspiration for their poem.

Writing the Poem
- Encourage students to make their poems as descriptive as their drawings by using interesting adjectives, active verbs and modifying adverbs.
- Students include where they are in their picture, what they do and see.

Editing and Publishing
- Students edit their writing by checking adjectives, verbs and adverbs to make sure they are as descriptive as possible.
- Students publish their poems and share them with the class.
- Create a month of May anthology to print or for use on a class web page.

William Henry Davies Biography
July 3, 1871 – September 26, 1940

William Henry Davies was born in Newport, Monmouthshire, Wales. He had an older brother and a younger sister. His father died when he was three years old and his mother remarried. William's mother felt that the care of three children was too difficult for her so William and his two siblings were reared by his grandparents. He was not an obedient child. When William was twelve years old, he along with five of his school friends were caught stealing a purse. He was arrested.

His grandmother wanted him to be a frame maker but this type of work bored him. He didn't want the dreary life that so many of the poor people he grew up with endured. He dreamed for something more. William longed to go to America and he worked hard to save enough money to go.

William travelled from England to America and eventually to Canada, much of the time as a hobo. He travelled back and forth across the Atlantic Ocean on cattle boats at least seven times. He probably would have never stopped traveling except an accident derailed his plans. He lost his foot jumping from a train in Canada. He sailed back to England and supported himself as a street singer.

Most of Davies' poetry is about his adventures as a hobo. He never married and spent most of his time alone. His writing included descriptions of nature. He also wrote about life's hardships and the characters that he met on his travels. He wrote directly and innocently, even in a childlike way. His work reflected his love of life.

William Henry Davies self-published his first book of poetry and his reputation as a great poet began. Davies was well liked in the literary world and made many friends. Although he never graduated from college, at the age of fifty-five he received an honorary degree from the University of Wales. Davies accomplished what he set out to do. He lived an extraordinary life.

In May
by William Henry Davies

Yes, I will spend the livelong day
With Nature in this month of May;
And sit beneath the trees, and share
My bread with birds whose homes are there;
While cows lie down to eat, and sheep
Stand to their necks in grass so deep;
While birds do sing with all their might,
As though they felt the earth in flight.
This is the hour I dreamed of, when
I sat surrounded by poor men;
And thought of how the Arab sat
Alone at evening, gazing at
The stars that bubbled in clear skies;

And of young dreamers, when their eyes
Enjoyed methought a precious boon
In the adventures of the Moon
Whose light, behind the Clouds' dark bars,
Searched for her stolen flocks of stars.
When I, hemmed in by wrecks of men,
Thought of some lonely cottage then
Full of sweet books; and miles of sea,
With passing ships, in front of me;
And having, on the other hand,
A flowery, green, bird-singing land.

Mother's Day
Math Lesson: Flower Power Bar Graph

This flower bar graph makes a wonderful Mother's Day gift.

MATERIALS
- One-inch graph paper
- Colored construction paper
- Tape measure or measuring stick
- Scissors, glue, markers, crayons
- Projection device (optional)

PLAN
- Tell students they are going to make a Flower Power bar graph for Mother's Day.
- Students prepare for the lesson by measuring the height of each family member at home and bringing the results to class.
- In the classroom, students measure each other and add their height measurements to the family results.

DO
If possible, project the following directions in a place visible for student reference.
- Begin your bar graph by leaving a two-inch border at the bottom of your graph paper.
- Construct your graph so that you begin numbering with 0 feet at the bottom and continue up the left in ½ inch increments up to 8 feet.
- Each ½ inch equals ½ foot and this can be placed in the bar graph key.
- Write the name of each family member under the graph, evenly spaced. Don't worry about staying within the grid lines.
- Draw a line to represent the height of each person on the graph. The lines become the stem of a sunflower.
- Draw sunflowers at the top of each stem.
- The middle of the flower is where you will place a drawing of each family member.
- Finish the graph by adding the graph key, leaves, petals and pictures for the background.
- Mount the graph on a 9" x 12" piece of construction paper.
- Wrap with tissue paper and give your gift on Mother's Day.

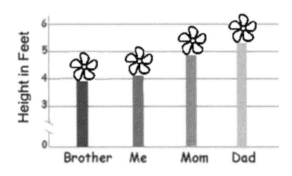

Mother's Day
Poetry Lesson: Child and Mother

On Mother's Day we take time to celebrate our mothers or a special mother figure. In this poem, the child describes a place where he would like to take his mother. He refers to it as a "Dreamland" where all her responsibilities dissolve and where all sorts of magical things occur to soothe her. Students write a poem inviting their mothers or a person they love to this place where everyday problems disappear. They present their finished poem as a Mother's Day gift.

MATERIALS
- Eugene Field Biography and poem *Child and Mother*
- Word processing or desktop publishing software (optional) and printer

PLAN
- Read and discuss Eugene Field's biography and poem.
- Discuss the poem using the following possible questions:
    - What makes this land a "Dreamland"?
    - What awaits his mother in this "Dreamland"?
    - The boy says that the "Dreamland" is "out yonder." Where is "out yonder"?
    - Why does the boy repeat "out yonder" at the end of the poem?

DO
Getting Ready to Write
Have students respond to the following sample questions:
- Where is your dreamland?
- What about your land makes it seem dreamlike?
- What chores that exist in your mother's real life would disappear in your dreamland?

Writing the Poem
- Using Eugene Field's poem as a model, suggest students begin their poems with the first line replacing the words "out yonder" with the location of their dreamland.
- Students continue their poems describing their dreamland.
- Suggest they include what they would do for their mothers in this land both practical and magical.

Editing and Publishing
- Have students read and edit poems with partners.
- Make a class Mother's Day Anthology with student poetry. Include each poet's name, the title of their poem and an illustration.
- As a class, students think of a name for their anthology.

Eugene Field Biography
September 2, 1850 - November 4, 1895

Eugene Field was born in St. Louis, Missouri. His father was an attorney who was famous for his defense of a slave who sued for his freedom. This case is sometimes referred to as "the lawsuit that started the Civil War." His mother died when Eugene was only two years old and his cousin in Massachusetts raised him and his brother. His father died when Field was nineteen. At that time, he was attending college but dropped out. He enrolled in and dropped out of two other colleges. He unsuccessfully tried his hand at acting. Eugene also studied law for a while but gave that up as well.

With an inheritance his father left him, he traveled to Europe and returned having used up all of the money. Shortly after his return, he worked as a journalist for the St. Joseph Gazette in Missouri. That same year he married Julia Comstock with whom he had eight children. He eventually became city editor of the Gazette and later worked for many newspapers. Field eventually moved to Chicago and wrote a humorous newspaper column for the Chicago Daily News. He became famous for his humorous language.

Field was also well known for his poetry written for children published in famous magazines. After his first poem *Christmas Treasures* was published, more than a dozen books of poetry followed. He became known as the poet laureate of children and the poet of childhood.

Eugene Field's name is memorialized in school names and parks. His poetry is represented in statues across the country. Many of his poems were set to music and became commercial successes. Some of his works were inspirations for paintings by Maxfield Parrish, a famous artist of the 20th century.

Child and Mother
by Eugene Field

The Dreamland that's waiting out yonder.
We'll walk in a sweet posie-garden out there,
Where moonlight and starlight are streaming,
And the flowers and the birds are filling the air
With the fragrance and music of dreaming.

There'll be no little tired-out boy to undress,
No questions or cares to perplex you,
There'll be no little bruises or bumps to caress,
Nor patching of stockings to vex you;
For I'll rock you away on a silver-dew stream
And sing you asleep when you're weary,
And no one shall know of our beautiful dream
But you and your own little dearie.

And when I am tired I'll nestle my head
In the bosom that's soothed me so often,
And the wide-awake stars shall sing, in my stead,
A song which our dreaming shall soften.
So, Mother-my-Love, let me take your dear hand,
And away through the starlight we'll wander, --
Away through the mist to the beautiful land,--
The Dreamland that's waiting out yonder.

Memorial Day
Math Lesson: Savings Bonds

President Franklin D. Roosevelt signed legislation in 1935 that created the first "baby bond" program. United States Savings Bonds continue to encourage participation by Americans in government financing and promote individual savings. The Series E of defense bonds were sold to contribute to the financing of World War II. On December 7th, 1942, the Japanese attacked Pearl Harbor. The bonds were renamed war bonds. American citizens were stimulated by advertisements and celebrity endorsements to purchase the bonds. School children saved quarters on a cardboard card with 75 slots ($18.75). When the card was full, they went to the post office and received a $25 war bond that matured in ten years, a 2.9% return on their investment. Billions of dollars' worth of war bonds were sold. Savings bonds are still a good method for a small investor to save without a lot of risk. Today, bonds are sold online at Treasury Direct:

http://www.treasurydirect.gov/indiv/products/prod_eebonds_glance.htm.

There you will find information about Series E savings bonds. In this lesson, students will create a savings plan using a spreadsheet or a calculator.

MATERIALS
- Digital device
- Spreadsheet software
- Calculator

PLAN
- Use the information above to discuss the selling of war bonds during WWII.
- Tell students that people filled special cards with quarters filling 75 slots. Each filled card was used to buy an $18.75 savings bond. After the cards were held for ten years they had a $25.00 value.

DO:
Have students do the following:
- Create a spreadsheet showing how much money saving 25 cents a day for one year would generate.
- Determine how many savings bonds could be purchased at the end of the one-year period. How much will these be worth in ten years?
- Show how many could be purchased if 50 cents, 75 cents and a dollar a day were saved for one year. How much will these be worth in ten years?
- If students made the same investment each year for three years, five years and ten years, what would the return on the investment be when the ten-year period was reached for each?

Memorial Day
Poetry Lesson: Decoration Day

We honor those who have died serving our country on Memorial Day, a federal holiday observed on the last Monday of May. Memorial Day originated as Decoration Day after the Civil War. Evaleen Stein's poem is about a Decoration Day parade. The poet invites children to follow soldiers and bring flowers to the fallen. In this lesson, students write about what they would do for the soldiers and what they would say to them.

MATERIALS
- Evaleen Stein Biography and her poem *Decoration Day*
- Word processing or desktop publishing software or pencils, pens, markers

PLAN
- Set the stage by researching and learning about Memorial Day.
- Read and discuss Evaleen Stein's Biography and poem.
- After reading the poem, ask the following questions:
  - Why are the flags tattered?
  - What is happening at the cemetery?
  - What does the narrator want the children to do?

DO
Getting Ready to Write
Have students respond to the following sample questions:
- How do you picture a military parade?
- What would you lay on the soldiers' graves?

Writing the Poem
- Title the poem Memorial Day or Decoration Day.
- Using *Decoration Day* as a model, students write poems of their own.
- The first stanza begins with the scene of a parade.
  For example:
  Soldiers marching in their crisp uniforms
  Up above airplanes flying with banners
- The second stanza includes what they would lay on the soldiers' graves.
  For example:
  I lay roses that grow in my garden
  A wreath with a circle of flowers, flags
- The third stanza includes what they would say to the soldiers.
  For example:
  Thank you for the peace I live with,
  I pray that you are at peace

Editing and Publishing
- Students read and edit poems with partners.
- Place poems on a Wall of Honor bulletin board in time for Memorial Day.

Evaleen Stein Biography
October 12, 1863 - December 11, 1923

Evaleen Stein was an artist, a writer and a poet. She was born and raised in Lafayette, Indiana. She lived with her parents and her brother, all of whom were writers. Her father was an attorney who also wrote for magazines and her mother wrote stories for young children.

After Evaleen graduated from high school, she studied at the Chicago Art Institute. She made a name for herself with her exquisite illuminations and original designs drawn on manuscripts. Her work drew attention and was exhibited in many cities in the United States. She would later write on parchment paper adorned with her border designs.

When Evaleen was in her early twenties, her father died. After his death, her mother became the city librarian at the Lafeyette Public Library, a position she held for thirty-two years. Evaleen spent many hours at the library working with her mother and reading. She also began writing books. At thirty-four her first book of poetry was published, *One Way to the Woods*. The poetry described the natural look and feel of Indiana including the rows of cornfields, marshes, forests and the large sycamore trees. The poems also included the names and description of birds commonly found in Indiana. Her second volume of poetry was titled, *Among the Trees Again*. Evaleen poetically describes the changing seasons as the days and months of the year went by.

She also became well known for children's stories. The main characters in these stories were often young people living in medieval times. She wrote twelve children's book and translated children's poems that were written in Japanese and Italian.

Her books began to draw attention by several Indiana authors. At forty-four, Evaleen was honored at Purdue University by Indiana-born writers. An interesting program and dinner party was arranged and featured the readings of prominent writer's works. She was presented a large monetary prize which she used to travel overseas with her mother. They visited many of the places she had dreamed about and used in her children's stories.

Evaleen was a private person. She spent much of her time alone in her beautiful garden surrounded by nature. She was a lover of birds and flowers. She died at age sixty. Stein is remembered for being the first Indiana poet to write about nature.

Decoration Day
by Evaleen Stein

See the soldiers, little ones!
Hark the drummers' beat!
See them with their flags and guns
Marching down the street!

Tattered flags from out the wars,
Let us follow these
To the little stripes and stars
Twinkling through the trees.

Watch them waving through the grass
Where the heroes sleep!
Thither gently let us pass
On this day we keep.

Let us bring our blossoms, too,
All our gardens grow;
Lilacs honey-sweet with dew,
And the lilies' snow.

Every posy of the May,
Every bloomy stem,
Every bud that breaks to-day
Gather now for them.

Lay the lilies o'er them thus,
Lovingly, for so
Down they laid their lives for us,
Long and long ago.

Heap above them bud and bough;
Softly, ere we cease,
God, we pray Thee, gently now
Fold them in Thy peace!

June Monthly Holidays

Adopt-a-Shelter-Cat Month • American Rivers Month • Black Music Month
Cancer in the Sun Month • Candy Month • Dairy Month • Fiction is Fun
Month • Fireworks Safety Month • Gay Pride Month • Great Outdoors
Month • National Accordion Awareness Month • National Drive Safe Month
National Fresh Fruit and Vegetable Month • National Frozen Yogurt Month
National Iced Tea Month • National Rose Month • Own Your Share of
America Month • Portable Computer Month • Supreme Court Month of
Tough Decisions • Tony Awards Month • Turkey Lovers Month
Zoo and Aquarium Month

June Weekly Holidays

First Week
National Fragrance Week • National Fishing Week • National Rip Current
Awareness Week • National Sun Safety Week • National Tire Safety Week
Pet Appreciation Week

Second Week
Duct Tape Days • National Email Week • National Flag Week
National Little League Baseball Week

Third Week
Fink Week • Grasslands Week • National Nursing Assistants Week

Fourth Week
Carpenter Ant Awareness Week • Fish Are Friends, Not Food Week
Lightning Safety Awareness Week • National Mosquito Control Awareness
Week • National Tennis Week • Watermelon Seed Spitting Week

June Moveable Holidays

Leave the Office Earlier Day	first workday
National Running Day	first Wednesday
Donut Day	first Friday
Hug Your Cat Day	first Friday
National Trails Day	first Saturday
Turtle Races Day	first Saturday
Horseradish Days	first weekend
Say Something Nice Sunday	first Sunday

National Children's Day	second Sunday
Race Unity Day	second Sunday
Missing Mutts Awareness Day	second Saturday
Flip Flop Day	third Friday
Father's Day	third Sunday
Take Your Dog to Work Day	first Friday after Father's Day
National Eat at a Food Truck Day	fourth Friday
America's Kids Day	fourth Sunday
Drive Your Corvette to Work Day	last Friday

June Days for STEAM Makers and Poets

1. Flip a Coin Day
2. American Indian Citizenship Day
3. Repeat Day (movies that repeat)
4. Hug Your Cat Day
5. Apple II Day
6. National Yo-Yo Day
7. Daniel Boone Day
8. Best Friends Day
9. Donald Duck Day
10. Ball Point Pen Day
11. Corn on the Cob Day
12. Red Rose Day
13. National Kitchen Klutzes of America Day
14. National Flag Day
15. Nature Photography Day
16. First Roller Coaster Opens on Coney Island in 1884
17. Eat Your Vegetables Day
18. International Picnic Day
19. Juneteenth
20. Ice Cream Soda Day
21. Finally Summer Day
22. Onion Rings Day
23. National Pink Day
24. Swim a Lap Day
25. First Color TV Broadcast (1951)
26. National Canoe Day
27. Sun Glasses Day
28. Paul Bunyan Day
29. Camera Day
30. Leap Second Time Adjustment Day

Integrating June Math Days

Science　　Technology　　Engineering　　Arts　　Math

Day		Make and Do
1	Flip a Coin Day	Quick, without looking, who is on the penny, the nickel, the dime and the quarter? Choose your favorite coin and call heads or tails. Work with a partner. How many heads do you get in twenty coin flips? What percentage of your flips were tails? What is the chance of getting a heads or tails? Try flipping a coin 100 times. What percentage of your flips were heads and how many were tails? Graph your results and see if you achieved a bell-shaped curve. Compare your results with other classmates. How did your results differ?
6	National Yo-Yo Day	Can you walk the dog, go around the world or rock the baby? If so, you might be the next Yo-Yo champ. Yo-Yo's date back to 500 BC and are depicted on Grecian vases. In modern day, Pedro Flores started manufacturing Yo-Yos in Santa Barbara, California in 1928. Along with factories in Los Angeles and Hollywood, he was producing 300,000 Yo-Yos a day. Donald F. Duncan saw great potential in the Yo-Yo fad and purchased the Flores Yo-Yo company in 1932. Yo-Yo's became very popular again in 1962 due to television ads. The Yo-Yo was inducted into the National Toy Hall of Fame in 1999. Today is Duncan's birthday. Hold a Yo-Yo contest. Time how long you and your classmates can keep a Yo-Yo going. Chart, graph and summarize your results.

7	Daniel Boone Day	Frontiersman Daniel Boone founded one of the first American settlements west of the Appalachians on this day in 1769. Today, Boonesborough is in the state of Kentucky. Boone, an American folk hero, blazed a trail through the Cumberland Gap. The Wilderness Road opened up the frontier to thousands of settlers from the East. Over 70,000 people crossed by foot or horseback starting in 1775 and by 1780 it was wide enough for pack animals. By 1796, it became a wagon trail. Many people migrated westward and Kentucky became known as the "Mother of Western States." Research the life of Daniel Boone and find up to ten significant events in his life. Determine how many years ago each event occurred.
14	National Flag Day	Flag Day has its roots with two school teachers who began to observe an annual day celebrating the flag. A teacher in Wisconsin in 1885 and a teacher in New York City in 1889 created programs with patriotic ceremonies at their respective schools. President Woodrow Wilson proclaimed Flag Day in 1916 and President Harry Truman signed an Act of Congress in 1949 designating June 14th National Flag Day. Find out some interesting facts about the U.S. Flag. For example, the length of the flag should be ¼ the height of the pole. So a 40-foot pole needs a flag that is 6' x 10'. How tall must the pole be for a 4' x 6' flag? How about a 3' x 5' flag? Government buildings fly flags that are 8' x 12'. How tall must the flag pole be?

16	First Roller Coaster Opens on Coney Island in 1884	On this day in 1884, the first roller coaster in America opened at Coney Island in Brooklyn, New York. LaMarcus Thomas developed the ride known as the "Gravity Switch-back Railway." It cost a nickel to ride and went 6 mph. Today, amusement parks all over the world feature thrilling roller coasters. Create a guide to the world's tallest and fastest roller coasters. Find out how fast they go, what they are made of, and how far they drop. You may wish to create your project in presentation software with pictures and maps highlighting where in the world they are found. Make sure to include graphs that compare the fastest and the tallest.
17	Eat Your Vegetables Day	Right in the middle of National Fresh Fruit and Vegetables Month comes this special day. American kids are advised to consume a variety of approximately seven servings of fruit and vegetables each day. One serving of fruit is approximately 150 grams (about equal to one medium-sized apple). One serving of vegetables is equal to about 75 grams (about ½ cup cooked vegetables). Plan a week's worth of fruit and vegetable servings. Using measuring cups and a food scale, portion out a day's worth of fruit and vegetables. Add lots of variety and take pictures of sample servings.
29	Camera Day	It's National Camera Day and time to snap some pictures. Here are two ideas to help you celebrate. Using simple digital cameras, go on a math scavenger hunt. Look for pictures to take that illustrate math concepts, perhaps a pattern or a set of numbers. Another great camera activity involves stop motion. Write a simple word problem for addition, subtraction, multiplication or division. Put your device (tablet, phone or camera) on a tripod. Bring your problem to life by taking a series of single frames. There are several free programs that work on mobile devices including iMotion and Stop Motion Studio.

June Overview

National Fresh Fruit and Vegetable Month
Math Lesson: Fruit Divide Game
Poetry Lesson: Ode to Tomatoes by Pablo Neruda

National Fresh Fruit and Vegetable Month's goal is to call attention to the importance of fruits and vegetables. Students hone their skills in addition, division, probability and graphing, as they learn to play a simple math game. Pablo Neruda gives the tomato a life of its own. Students write their own ode to either a fruit or vegetable in his style.
NCTM STANDARD 5: Analysis and Probability, Gr 3 – 5B all, Gr3 – 5D-1; Gr 4 – 4B all; Gr 5 – A5B-1, 5B2; Gr5 – 5D-5; Gr 6– 5B-1, 5B-2

National Zoo and Aquarium Month
Math Lesson: Go Fish for Equivalent Fractions
Poetry Lesson: An Aquarium by Amy Lowell

National Zoo and Aquarium Month pays tribute to zoos and aquariums that help prevent wildlife extinction and educate the visiting public about animal welfare. Students observe patterns to complete an equivalent fraction chart, create game cards and play. Amy Lowell wrote an Imagist poem about the colors of the fish and fauna that live within an aquarium. Students learn about Imagism and write a poem about either an aquarium or a zoo in the Imagist style.
NCTM STANDARD 1: Numbers and Operations, Gr 4 – 1B-7, 1B-8; Gr 5 – 1A-7, 1B-7, 1B-8; Gr6 – 1A-2, 1B-6

Father's Day
Math Lesson: Geometric Art
Poetry Lesson: A Boy and His Dad by Edgar Guest

Father's Day honors the important role that fathers or father figures play in the lives of their children. Students create Father's Day artwork by placing geometric patterns using tissue paper circles that they divide into semi-circles, quadrants and smaller segments. Poet Edgar Guest writes about a fishing trip that he recalls taken by a boy and his dad. Students write about an experience they had with an important male figure in their lives modeling their writing after the poem by Guest.
NCTM STANDARD 5: Analysis and Probability, Gr 4 – 5A-4; Gr 5 – 5A-4, A-5

Finally It's Summer
Math Lesson: Summer Solstice
Poetry Lesson: I'll Tell You How the Sun Rose by Emily Dickinson

Summer is the warmest season of the year in the northern hemisphere. Students compute the change in hours between the time the sun rises and the time the sun sets for the month of June in the city in which they live. Poet Emily Dickinson employs personification and symbolism as she describes the sun as it rises and sets. Students write poems describing their personified images of the sun as it moves through the day.
NCTM STANDARD 1: Numbers and Operations, Gr 6 – 1C-7; NCTM Process Standard – Problem Solving: Apply and adapt a variety of appropriate strategies to solve problems.

National Fresh Fruit and Vegetable Month
Math Lesson: Fruit Divide Game

June is National Fruit and Vegetable Month. During June, the growing season is in swing. Fresh produce is readily available and students are encouraged to increase their daily consumption of fruits and vegetables. In this lesson students hone their skills in addition, division, probability and graphing as they play a simple math game.

MATERIALS
- Dice, a pair for every two students
- Napkins, small paper bowls, small paper cups
- Grapes or other small fresh fruit
- Fruit Divide Game Worksheet
- Projection Device

PLAN
- Project the Fruit Divide Game Worksheet on the board.
- Fill a small paper bowl with grapes.
- Select two student volunteers to demonstrate the Fruit Divide Game by first washing their hands and then proceed as follows:
    1. Give a pair of dice, the fruit bowl, an empty bowl and two small paper cups to the volunteers.
    2. Place one cup in front of each player and the fruit bowl and empty bowl in between the players.
    3. The volunteers throw the dice, add the numbers and place a tally mark next to the sum thrown.
    4. Place the corresponding number of grapes into the empty bowl to match the result. For example, if you threw a 4 and a 3, you place a tally mark next to the number 7 in the sum column.
    5. Move 7 grapes from the fruit bowl to the empty bowl. Divide the 7 by placing 3 grapes in each cup and leave the remaining grape in the bowl.
    6. If a grape remains, place a check mark in the corresponding odd column. If there is no remainder, place a check mark in the corresponding even column.
    7. Students may eat the grapes in their cup.
    8. Play two more times by repeating steps 3 through 7.
    9. Complete the Frequency column on the Fruit Divide Worksheet by adding the tally marks to determine the number of times the same sum was reached.
    10. Count the grapes in the small bowl to check how many odd numbers were thrown.

DO
- Divide the class into pairs.
- All students wash their hands before playing.
- Distribute, a pair of dice, two paper cups, a small empty paper bowl and a bowl of grapes to each pair.
- Give each pair a Fruit Divide Worksheet and review directions for completing.

- Students roll the dice and place the corresponding numbers of grapes in the paper bowl placed between them.
- They divide the grapes, placing an equal number in each player's paper cup.
- They record the results on the worksheet, tally the times the same number is thrown and place a check mark in either the odd or even columns.
- They can enjoy eating the evenly divided grapes as they play the game.
- When the games are finished and the worksheets are complete do the following:
  - Project a blank Fruit Divide Worksheet.
  - Have each pair present their tally and odd/even results and record on the projected worksheet.
  - Complete the Frequency column by combining all results.
  - What happened?
    - Were more even numbers or odd numbers thrown?
    - What number was thrown most frequently?
    - What number was thrown the least?
    - Which sum had the most combinations?
- Project the chart below showing the 36 possible combinations when two dice are thrown.

Total on Dice	Ways to Get to the Total	Probability
2	1+1	1/36
3	1+2, 2+1	2/36
4	1+3, 2+2, 3+1	3/36
5	1+4, 2+3, 3+2, 4+1	4/36
6	1+5, 2+4, 3+3, 4+2, 5+1	5/36
7	1+6, 2+5, 3+4, 4+3, 5+2, 6+1	6/36
8	2+6, 3+5, 4+4, 5+3, 6+2	5/36
9	3+6, 4+5, 5+4, 6+3	4/36
10	4+6, 5+5, 6+4	3/26
11	5+6, 6+5	2/26
12	6+6	1/36

- Looking at the chart, have the class discuss the possible dice throws.
  - What numbers are more likely to be thrown and why?
  - What numbers are least likely to be thrown and why?
- Compare the class frequencies from the Fruit Divide Worksheet.
- Do the class frequencies follow the probability?
  - How are they the same?
  - How are they different?
- Predict the number of times you would need to throw the dice to get closer to the expected probability.

Fruit Divide Worksheet

Sum	Tally	Frequency	Odd Number	Even Number
2				
3				
4				
5				
6				
7				
8				
9				
10				
11				
12				
Totals				

National Fresh Fruit and Vegetable Month
Poetry Lesson: Ode to Tomatoes

Many of Pablo Neruda's poems are odes – "a lyric poem that expresses a noble feeling with dignity." In the poem *Ode to Tomatoes*, Pablo Neruda describes an ordinary tomato. Neruda is known for taking ordinary things and making them extraordinary. In this poem he gives the tomato a life of its own. Students write an ode to either a fruit or vegetable and give it a life of its own.

MATERIALS
- Pablo Neruda Biography and his poem *Ode to Tomatoes*
- Word processing or desktop publishing software or pencils, pens, markers

PLAN
- Read and discuss Pablo Neruda's biography and poem.
- In what season of the year do we get fresh tomatoes? (Summer) Why in the poem are tomatoes fresh in December? (Chile is in the southern hemisphere which is opposite ours, so December is their summer.)
- What is an ode?
- What is your opinion about how Neruda divides his lines?
- Where is personification used?
- Why does Neruda use the word "wed" to describe the union of the tomato and the onion?
- What makes the tomato an easy fruit?
- How do you know that the tomato is beautiful?

DO
Getting Ready to Write
- Make a class list of favorite fruits and vegetables.
- How would you personify your favorite fruit or vegetable?

Writing the Poem
- Title the poem "Ode to" followed by your selected fruit or vegetable.
- Using Neruda's line structuring write poems of your own.
- Begin the first line describing your fruit or vegetable using personification in the style of Pablo Neruda.
- Continue poem describing its life from that moment on.
- Finish with an interesting ending

Editing and Publishing
- Students read and edit poems with partners.
- Students either draw their fruit or take a photo of it. Place it on their poem.
- On a bulletin board, display all to honor National Fruit and Vegetable Month.

Pablo Neruda Biography
August 20, 1904 – August 5, 1973

Pablo Neruda was born in Chile. His mother died when he was one month old and he was raised by a father whom he both loved and feared. His father remarried a woman who was warm with a great sense of humor. When he was very young, Neruda moved to an area in Chile that was filled with rich nature. The forest, the rain, and the smell of freshly cut wood would be the subjects of many of his poems. He began to write poetry at a young age which he hid on scraps of paper from his father who did not approve of poetry writing.

By the time Neruda was fifteen years old, he won a prize for poetry in a national competition. At the same time he began wearing a cape and a brimmed hat, an outfit he continued to wear his entire life. Neruda continued to win prizes and have his poetry published. He won, for example, the National Prize of Literature from Cuba, the International Prize for Peace, Stalin Prize for Peace, and the Nobel Prize.

The turmoil during the Spanish Civil War formed what he would become, a man dedicated to political action. He became politically and socially involved with the problems of the Spanish people who were trying to flee Spain. Although he was widely accepted by much of Europe and the United States, he was forced to live in exile because of his political beliefs.

In his lifetime, Neruda traveled to and lived in many places. He returned to his country that he wrote about all his life. At the same time, he began writing about all manner of material objects giving them a life of their own. In his odes he wrote about bicycles, woolen socks and even tomatoes. Neruda wanted his work to appear in the news section of the paper rather than the literary section because he wanted to reach a wide variety of people. He believed that an important purpose of poetry was to communicate with all people.

Ode to Tomatoes
by Pablo Neruda

The poem is available online. Print copies for use in your classroom.

http://famouspoetsandpoems.com/poets/pablo_neruda/poems/15736

Neruda describes a meal where the main attraction is the tomato and the preparation for its "wedding." We are introduced to the tomatoes in December, the Chilean summer, when "its juice runs through the streets." The tomato "invades the kitchen" and is seen "on countertops" among several items where it sheds its own light. The tomato is properly prepared for its "wedding" as it is halved "the knife/sinks" into its "flesh." The tomato is then united with a "clear onion." To celebrate "the union of the onion and tomato" seasonings are poured onto the new couple. "The wedding of the day" begins as the "parsley hoists its flag" and "the aroma/of the roast/knocks/at the door." Guests arrive to celebrate a festive meal. At the table, the tomato is hailed for its beauty. It is a fruit that does not have any of the imperfections of others, "no pit/no husk/no leaves or thorns." It is heralded for "its gift/of fiery color/and cool completeness."

National Zoo and Aquarium Month
Math Lesson: Go Fish for Equivalent Fractions

Every June we celebrate National Zoo and Aquarium Month to honor the role zoos and aquariums play in conservation, research, education and recreation. In this lesson, students create and play the game Go Fish for Equivalent Fractions.

MATERIALS
- 8 ½" x 11" tagboard or cardstock
- Markers, scissors
- Go Fish for Equivalent Fractions Worksheet, copied onto tagboard

PLAN
- Ask students, have you ever played the classic card game Go Fish? Students share experiences playing the game.
- Divide students into groups of four.
- Distribute ten copies of the Go Fish for Equivalent Fractions Worksheet on tagboard or card stock to each group.
- Working together, have the group complete the Equivalent Fraction Chart at the top of the worksheet. Suggest students find patterns to quickly complete the chart.
- Review the two examples below. The fraction 1/1 is on the first fish and the next three fish contain three equivalent fractions to 1/1. The second set begins with 1/2 and is followed by three equivalent fractions to 1/2.

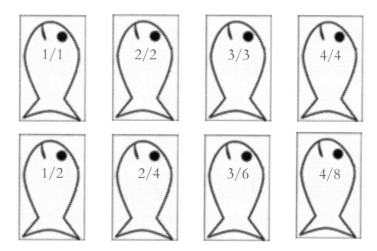

- Use the patterns on the worksheet to make equivalent fraction cards.
- Create ten sets of four cards. Each group makes forty cards.
- The first card of each set begins with a fraction from the first column of the chart. Select three equivalent fractions to go with 1/1. Do the same for each row.

DO
The group plays the game as follows:
- One group member is chosen as the dealer.
- Four cards are dealt to each player including the dealer.
- The dealer puts the remaining cards in a scattered pile to create a pond of cards in the middle of the group.
- Players check their cards and place any matching equivalent fractions in their personal pile.
- Players replace the number of cards laid down by taking new cards from the pond.
- The player to the left of the dealer goes first and asks the group member of his/her choice whether they have an equivalent fraction to a number in the player's hand. If that player does, all group members need to check for accuracy and the player takes the card and puts both cards in his/her personal pile and asks for another match.
- If there is no match, an opposing player says, "Go Fish."
- Again, if a match is found, all group members check for accuracy and the player takes the card and puts it in his/her personal pile.
- When no match occurs, the group member to the left of the first player takes a turn.
- If a group member runs out of cards he/she takes four more cards from the center pond.
- Continue play until the "pond" is depleted.
- The student with the most matches is the winner.
- Groups switch cards with another group to play with a new set of equivalent fractions.

Go Fish for Equivalent Fractions Worksheet

Equivalent Fraction Chart
Observe the pattern to complete the equivalent fractions chart.

1/1	2/2	3/3	4/4	5/5	6/6	7/7	8/8	9/9
1/2	2/4	3/6	4/8					
1/3	2/6	3/9						
1/4	2/8			5/40				
1/5						7/35		
1/6		3/18						
1/7				5/35				
1/8					6/48			
1/9							8/72	
1/10	2/20	3/30	4/40	5/50	6/60	7/70	8/80	10/90

Playing Cards Template for Go Fish

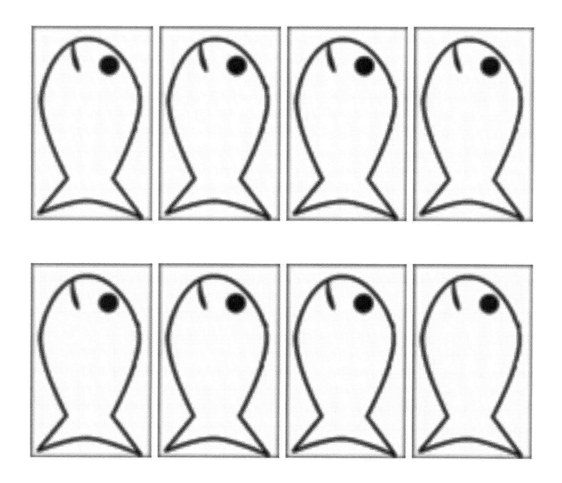

National Zoo and Aquarium Month
Poetry Lesson: An Aquarium

In the poem, *An Aquarium*, Amy Lowell writes about the colors of the fish and fauna that live within the aquarium. Lowell, one of the leaders of the imagist movement, observes the details of the inhabitants of the aquarium with vivid images. For example, "Blue shadows against silver-saffron water." In this lesson, students write a poem about either an aquarium or a zoo using Lowell's poem as a model.

MATERIALS
- Amy Lowell Biography and her poem *An Aquarium*
- Word processing or desktop publishing software or pencils, pens, markers

PLAN
- Read and discuss Amy Lowell's biography and poem.
- Ask the following questions:
    - What examples of imagism does Lowell employ in her poem?
    - If she didn't use the word fish or aquarium would you know what she is writing about and why?
    - Where is the aquarium?

DO
Getting Ready to Write
Ask students the following questions. As the class gives their responses, encourage discussion.
- What have you seen when gazing in an aquarium?
- What experiences have you had visiting a zoo?
- What images of fish can you find in Amy Lowell's poem?
- How would you write a description of a zoo animal using Imagism?
  For example:
  Large golden mane
  Slowly wandering from place to place
  Then lazily lying on its stomach

Writing the Poem
- Title the poem either An Aquarium or A Zoo.
- Using the poem as a model, students write poems of their own about a zoo or aquarium using images just as Lowell did in her poem. After each image, use a line break and continue to complete the image.

Editing and Publishing
- Students read and edit poems with partners.
- Students share their poems and the class determines what animal or fish they have described.

Amy Lowell Biography
February 9, 1874 – May 12, 1925

Amy Lowell was born into wealth. Her early education began at her home on a ten-acre estate. When Lowell was 8 years old, she began school. She was a social outcast because of her heavy weight, her "masculine" looks and "ugly" features. Her personality annoyed her classmates since she was outspoken about her opinions. But even at this young age she loved reading and had begun writing. Between the ages of thirteen and fifteen she wrote poetry. During these young years, Lowell travelled to Europe many times with her family.

Amy Lowell began writing poetry in free verse when she was a young girl. She never attended college because it was socially unacceptable for a woman to do so. She spent many of her days in her father's library that contained seven thousand books. She became obsessed with reading and collecting her own. At twenty-eight, after many years of not writing poetry, Lowell began to write again. She wrote in free verse.

At 39 she became involved with the Imagist movement. Ezra Pound, a famous poet, created the catchy name Imagism or the French term as it was first introduced *Imagiste*. He named the anthology *Imagiste* since he liked foreign language titles even though the poets included in the anthology were not French. Imagism presented a clear interpretation of images and concise speech to which Lowell was drawn. She was attracted to the status of French names. She also appreciated the importance of this new movement in the poetry world. When Lowell began to read imagist poetry, she felt that she had found her identity.

Des Imagistes, edited by Ezra Pound, was the first anthology of the Imagism movement and included Lowell's poetry. After its publication, Lowell felt that she had attained a name in the Imagist world. Because of wealth and connections in the literary world, Lowell took over leadership in the movement. She knew how to use her wealth to attract famous writers to appear in Imagist anthologies she edited and published.

Amy Lowell was very generous in her support of other Imagist poets and contributed to their success. Lowell spent much of her adult life writing and performing her poetry. About a year after her death, she was awarded the Pulitzer Prize for a collection of her poetry. Among her most famous poems is *An Aquarium*, a perfect example of Imagism. It presents an accurate interpretation of images.

An Aquarium
by Amy Lowell

Streaks of green and yellow iridescence,
Silver shiftings,
Rings veering out of rings,
Silver -- gold --
Grey-green opaqueness sliding down,
With sharp white bubbles
Shooting and dancing,
Flinging quickly outward.
Nosing the bubbles,
Swallowing them,
Fish.
Blue shadows against silver-saffron water,
The light rippling over them
In steel-bright tremors.
Outspread translucent fins
Flute, fold, and relapse;
The threaded light prints through them on the pebbles
In scarcely tarnished twinklings.
Curving of spotted spines,
Slow up-shifts,
Lazy convolutions:
Then a sudden swift straightening
And darting below:
Oblique grey shadows
Athwart a pale casement.
Roped and curled,
Green man-eating eels
Slumber in undulate rhythms,
With crests laid horizontal on their backs.
Barred fish,
Striped fish,
Uneven disks of fish,
Slip, slide, whirl, turn,
And never touch.
Metallic blue fish,
With fins wide and yellow and swaying
Like Oriental fans,
Hold the sun in their bellies
And glow with light:
Blue brilliance cut by black bars.
An oblong pane of straw-coloured shimmer,
Across it, in a tangent,
A smear of rose, black, silver.
Short twists and upstartings,
Rose-black, in a setting of bubbles:
Sunshine playing between red and black flowers
On a blue and gold lawn.
Shadows and polished surfaces,
Facets of mauve and purple,
A constant modulation of values.
Shaft-shaped,
With green bead eyes;
Thick-nosed,
Heliotrope-coloured;
Swift spots of chrysolite and coral;
In the midst of green, pearl, amethyst irradiations.
Outside,
A willow-tree flickers
With little white jerks,
And long blue waves
Rise steadily beyond the outer islands.

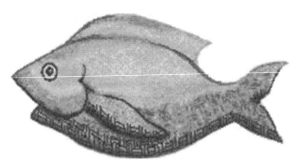

Father's Day
Math Lesson: Geometric Art

In this project students begin with tissue circles that they divide into semicircles, quadrants and smaller segments to create geometric Father's Day gifts. They arrange the shapes on a gridded flat surface. The art becomes more intricate as the lines of the circles intersect to create angles and other shapes. This project can be leveled for different math strategies. For example, if you are teaching symmetry, you can create a design where the quandrants are symmetrical. The finished product is presented as a Father's Day Gift.

MATERIALS
- 4 x 4 Graph Paper, 11" x 17"
- 4" tissue paper circles in several colors
- Glue sticks, rulers, scissors
- Fine or ultra-fine tipped markers
- Self-adhesive laminating sheets or a laminating sheet

PLAN
- Demonstrate the process with a piece of graph paper projected or taped to a board or chart.
- Distribute a small number of tissue paper circles to student volunteers.
- Have volunteers do the following:
    - Divide the paper into four quadrants.
    - Glue a tissue paper circle to the center of the page. Outline it with marker.
- Demonstrate pasting circle segments into the quadrants to create a design of patterns radiating from the circle. Outline each segment as you glue.

DO
- Distribute paper, tissue circles, glue sticks, black markers and scissors to students.
- Students do the following:
    - Measure and divide the graph paper into four quadrants.
    - Glue a whole circle into the center of the page and outline it with a thin black marker.
    - Fold the remaining circles into halves, fourths and smaller segments such as sixths and eighths.
    - Glue the segments to create patterns radiating from the center circle.
    - Outline each segment with black marker as it is placed.
    - Pay attention to shapes, portions of shapes, repeating shapes and spaces between the shapes.
    - Use the black marker to write a Father's Day message in the middle circle such as "World's Best Dad", "#1 Dad", "Love My Grandpa", etc.
    - Preserve the finished geometric artwork by covering with self-adhesive laminating sheets.
    - Wrap the artwork with tissue paper and give to dad.

Father's Day
Poetry Lesson: A Boy and His Dad

In the poem *A Boy and His Dad,* Edgar Guest writes about a father and son fishing trip. During this trip a bond develops between the two as they learn about each other. The father realizes "How close he has grown to his little son." In the last stanza, the reader becomes aware that the poet is the son fishing with his dad. In this lesson, students write a poem about an experience they had with an important male figure in their lives modeling their writing after the poem by Guest.

MATERIALS
- Edgar Guest Biography and his poem *A Boy and His Dad*
- Word processing or desktop publishing software or pencils, pens, markers
- Construction paper
- Decorations: sequins, stickers, etc.

PLAN
- Read and discuss Edgar Guest's biography and poem.
- Ask the following questions:
    - Who are the boy and his dad?
    - When do you find out who the boy and his dad are?
    - Why does the poet envy the boy and his dad?
    - What do they learn from each other on this trip?

DO
Getting Ready to Write
Ask students the following questions and encourage discussion.
- What memorable experience did you have with a male figure in your life?
- Describe the experience.
- What did you learn?

Writing the Poem
- Title the poem A Boy or A Girl along with the important male figure in your life.
  For example: *A Girl and Her Grandfather*
- Use page breaks so that their poem looks like a poem rather than like a story.
- Begin the first line with the title and what the experience was.
  For example: *A girl and her grandfather on a bike ride*
- Continue writing their poem as an observer (in the third person).
- In the last stanza, students write as the child (in the first person).
- Conclude the poem with what they discovered about their relationship.

Editing and Publishing
- Students read and edit poems with partners.
- Students create Father's Day cards.
    - Write their poem neatly in the inside of the card.
    - Write Happy Father's Day on the outside and decorate.

Edgar Guest Biography
August 20, 1881 – August 5, 1989

Edgar Allen Guest was born in Birmingham, England. He became a popular poet and was known as the People's Poet. His early life was difficult due to financial problems at home. When Edgar was ten years old, he and his family moved to Detroit, Michigan.

Because of the financial panic in the United States, his father needed Edgar to work after school. At fourteen, Edgar worked part time as an copy boy at the Detroit Free Press. His father died when he was in high school. He never finished school because he had to work full time to support his family. At sixteen, Edgar was promoted to the position of cub reporter. He worked the late shift and developed an aggressive reputation.

Edgar began writing poetry and submitted one of his poems to his editor. As an in-house reporter, it was unlikely that his poem would be printed, let alone a literary effort from a seventeen year old high school dropout. The editor decided to publish Edgar's poem. He continued to contribute his writing which included poetry, popular topics and clever observations. He had poem after poem published which led to a weekly column. His poetry became so popular that the weekly column turned into a daily column "Breakfast Table Chat." His writing described everyday life with sentimental expressions. Describing his poems he said, "I take simple everyday things that happen to me and I figure it happens to a lot of other people and I make simple rhymes out of them."

When Guest was twenty-five he married Nellie Crossman. They had three children. He began publishing books of his poetry with the help of his brother Harry, a typesetter. People were drawn to his writing. During his lifetime, over 20 volumes of his poetry were published.

Guest became well known as a broadcaster of a weekly radio program. He also became a popular TV personality with his own program called "A Guest in Your Home." He remained a faithful employee of the Detroit Free Press for almost sixty-five years until his death.

A Boy and His Dad
by Edgar Guest

A boy and his dad on a fishing trip –
There is a glorious fellowship!
Father and son and the open sky,
And the white clouds lazily drifting by,
And the laughing stream as it runs along
With the clicking reel like a martial song,
And the father teaching the youngster gay
How to land a fish in the sportsman's way.

I fancy I hear them talking there
In an open boat, and speech is fair;
And the boy is learning the ways of men
From the finest man in his youthful ken.
Kings, to youngster, cannot compare
With the gentle father who's with him there.
And the greatest mind of the human race
Not for one minute could take his place.

Which is happier, man or boy?
The soul of the father is steeped in joy,
For he's finding out, to his heart's delight,
That his son is fit for the future fight.
He is learning the glorious depths of him.
And the thoughts he thinks and his every whim,
And he shall discover, when night comes on,
How close he has grown to his little son.

Oh, I envy them, as I see them there
Under the sky in the open air,
For out of the old, old long-ago
Come the summer days that I used to know,
When I learned life's truth from my father's lips
As I shared the joy of his fishing trips-
A boy and his dad on a fishing trip –
Builders of life's companionship!

Finally It's Summer
Math Lesson: Summer Solstice

The beginning of summer occurs when the sun reaches its northernmost point on the equator. Depending on the shift of the calendar, the summer solstice occurs sometime between June 20th and June 22nd. The dates that summer will occur in the Northern Hemisphere in the years between 2017 and 2020 are: Wednesday, June 21, 2017; Thursday, June 21, 2018; Friday, June 21, 2019; and Saturday, June 20, 2020. In this lesson, students will compute the change of number of hours between the time the sunrises and the time the sun sets in June in the city in which they live.

MATERIALS
- Internet capable devices and/or newspapers
- Summer Daylight Hours Worksheet
- Pencils and paper

PLAN
- Discuss the following questions about the summer solstice with the class. Possible responses are in italics. Encourage students to expand on responses given.
    - Why is it that in summer the days seem longer even though a day is 24 hours long?
      Summer days feel longer because there are more daylight hours.
    - Why do we recognize the beginning of summer with the occurrence of the summer solstice?
      The summer solstice in the Northern Hemisphere occurs when the earth's orbit tilts the position of the North Pole farthest from the sun. This results in the sun reaching its highest point in the sky.
- A good website with video about the summer solstice that can heighten student interest and understanding is
  https://www.teachervision.com/winter/video/73032.html#prettyPhoto/1/
- The length of the day depends your geographical location. For example, in New York City on the first day of summer in 2017, the sun will rise at 5:25 AM and set at 8:31 PM. Have students calculate number of daylight numbers on that day.

DO
- Distribute the Summer Solstice Worksheet.
- Students work in pairs or small groups to search the Internet for sunrise and sunset times in their city to find the daylight hours for June.
- They enter their findings on the Summer Daylight Hours Worksheet.
- Using the data on the worksheet they answer math questions and create some of their own.
- Students present their math problems for their classmates to solve.

Summer Daylight Hours Worksheet

Complete the chart and use the data to answer the questions below.

Place_____ Year _____

Date	Sunrise	Sunset	Daylight Hours
June 1			
June 2			
June 3			
June 4			
June 5			
June 6			
June 7			
June 8			
June 9			
June 10			
June 11			
June 12			
June 13			
June 14			
June 15			
June 16			
June 17			
June 18			
June 19			
June 20			
June 21			
June 22			
June 23			
June 24			
June 25			
June 26			
June 27			
June 28			
June 29			
June 30			

1. What day has the greatest number of daylight hours? _____
2. What day has the shortest number of daylight hours? _____
3. What is the difference between the number of daylight hours on the 1st and 21st? _____
4. What is the difference between the number of daylight hours on 21st and 30th? _____
5. On June 21, 2016, the sun rose in Anchorage, Alaska at 4:21 AM and set at 11:43 PM. How many hours of sunlight will Anchorage experience? _____
6. What is the difference of sunlight hours in Anchorage and your city on June 21st? _____
7. Write two summer solstice math problems of your own.

Finally It's Summer:
Poetry Lesson: I'll Tell You How the Sun Rose

Throughout her poem, I'll Tell You How the Sun Rose, Emily Dickinson employs personification and symbolism as she describes the voyage of the sun from its rising to its setting. The narrator sees the beginning of the sun rising as "A ribbon at a time," then many ribbons follow until the sun appears. "The news" of the sun arriving as fast as squirrels. "The hills untied their bonnets" (women wore bonnets at night and untied them in the morning) and the song of the bobolink (birds) beginning, tell the narrator "That must have been the sun!" rising. The narrator describes its setting as the "dominie in gray," (a schoolmaster and gray being the color of dusk). He leads "little yellow boys and girls" (rays of sunlight) over the stile (steps to climb over a fence) as they disappear just as the sun does as it sets.

MATERIALS
- Emily Dickinson Biography and her poem *I'll Tell You How the Sun Rose*
- Word processing or desktop publishing software or pencils, pens, markers

PLAN
- Read and discuss Emily Dickinson's biography and poem.
- Ask the following questions:
    - What examples of personification does Dickinson employ in her poem?
    - How does the poet know the sun is rising?
    - How does the poet know the sun is setting?

DO
Getting Ready to Write
Ask students the following questions. As the class gives their responses, encourage discussion.
- What descriptive phrases would you use to describe the sun rising?
  For example: *the ocean began to laugh welcoming the children coming to its shore, flowers opening their mouths*
- What descriptive phrases would you use to describe the sun setting?
  For example: *the sky grew cold and covered itself with a grey blanket, leaves bowed their heads protecting themselves from the dark*

Writing the Poem
- Using *I'll Tell You How the Sun Rose* as a model, students write poems of their own about the sun using images and personification just as Dickinson did in her poem. After each idea, use a line break.
- Begin the poem with the words "I'll tell you _____". Also use this line as your poem's title.
- Continue writing describing what happens when the sun rises and sets.

Editing and Publishing
- Students read and edit poems with partners.
- Students use the images of their poem in a watercolor.

Emily Dickinson Biography
February 9, 1830 - 1886

Emily Dickinson was born in Amherst, Massachusetts over 150 years ago. Her father was a lawyer and businessman. Emily had an older brother and a younger sister. To her parents, education was very important and they sent their children to very fine schools.

Besides her school years away from home, she spent most of her time alone in her garden with her best friends: animals, plants, flowers, and her imagination.

Dickinson wrote to journalists and editors and they wrote back to her, but she did not allow any of them to visit. She loved to cook and she would give children in her neighborhood treats lowering them from her upstairs window in a basket attached to a rope. Her neighbors considered her to be a very eccentric woman and called her "the woman in white" because most of the time she wore white dresses.

Dickinson had an exceptional imagination probably strengthened because she was alone so much of the time. She had very few experiences outside of her own town or even outside of her own home. She died in the same house that she was born in and only left her town a few times. Withdrawn from the world, she undertook it as few ever have. Having a mind able to draw the most from what she saw combined with the isolation she lived with, gave her the ability to see the world with deep understanding. She saw and wrote about everyday life with the eyes of a child almost as if the everyday occurrences she wrote about were seen for the first time.

During her lifetime, almost no one knew she wrote poetry. Dickinson wrote only for herself. She wrote her poems on small pieces of paper and even the backs of envelopes. She wrote about her experiences with nature and animals and talked to them giving them feelings and thoughts. While she was alive, she had only seven poems published. When she died, her sister found hundreds of poems and arranged for publication.

I'll Tell You How the Sun Rose
by Emily Dickinson

I'll tell you how the sun rose,
A ribbon at a time.
The steeples swam in amethyst,
The news like squirrels ran.

The hills untied their bonnets,
The bobolinks begun.
Then I said softly to myself,
"That must have been the sun!"

But how he set, I know not.
There seemed a purple stile.
Which little yellow boys and girls
Were climbing all the while

Till when they reached the other side,
A dominie in gray
Put gently up the evening bars,
And led the flock away.

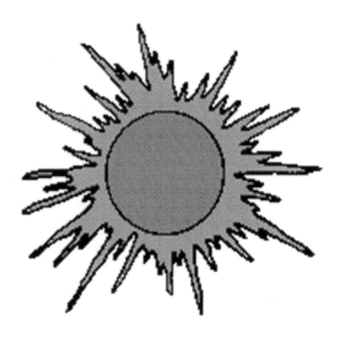

July Monthly Holidays

Anti-Boredom Month • Cell Phone Courtesy Month • Eggplant Month
Family Golf Month • Family Reunion Month • Fireworks Safety Month
Garlic Lovers Month • International Zine Month • Juvenile Arthritis
Awareness Month • Melon Month • National Baked Bean Month
National Blueberry Month • National Culinary Arts Month • National Hot
Dog Month • National Ice Cream Month • National Peach Month
National Picnic Month • National Recreation and Parks Month • National
Vacation Rental Month • Nectarine Month • Read An Almanac Month
Smart Irrigation Month • Sports and Recreation Books Month • Tour de
France Month • UV Safety Month • Wheat Month • Wild About Wildlife
Month

July Weekly Holidays

First Week of July

Beans and Bacon Days • Be Nice to New Jersey Week
National Tom Sawyer Days

Second Week of July

Creative Maladjustment Week • National Ventriloquism Week
Therapeutic Recreation Week

Third Week of July

Captive Nations Week • Everybody Deserves a Massage Week
National Independent Retailers Week • National Parenting of Gifted
Children Week • National Zoo Keeper Week • Soap Box Derby
(Akron, Ohio)

Fourth Week of July

Comic Con International • The Great Texas Mosquito Festival

July Moveable Holidays

Build a Scarecrow Day	first weekend
International Cherry Pit Spitting Day	first Saturday
International Town Criers Day	second Monday
Collector Car Appreciation Day	second Friday
Wayne Chicken Day	second Saturday
Get Out of the Doghouse Day	third Monday
Take Your Poet To Work Week	third Wednesday
National Hot Dog Day	third Saturday
Toss Away the "Could Haves" and "Should Haves"	third Saturday
Ice Cream Day aka Sundae Sunday	third Sunday
Lake Superior Day	third Sunday
Chili Dog Day	last Thursday
System Administrator Appreciation Day	last Friday
Lumberjack Day	last Friday of the last full weekend
Cowboy Day	fourth Saturday
Auntie's Day	fourth Sunday
Parents' Day	fourth Sunday

July Days for STEAM Makers and Poets

1   U.S. Postage Stamp Day
2   World UFO Day
3   Stay Out of the Sun Day
4   Fourth of July
5   Graham Cracker Day
6   National Fried Chicken Day
7   Macaroni Day
8   Math 2.0 Day
9   National Sugar Cookie Day
10   Don't Step on a Bee Day
11   World Population Day
12   Paper Bag Day
13   Embrace Your Geekness Day
14   Bastille Day
15   Shark Awareness Day
16   World Snake Day
17   Compass Day and Wrong Way Corrigan Day
18   John Glenn's Birthday
19   Stick Out Your Tongue Day
20   Moon Day
21   National Junk Food Day
22   Casual Pi Day
23   National Vanilla Ice Cream Day
24   Cousins Day
25   Merry Go-Round Day
26   Aunt and Uncle Day
27   Take Your Pants For A Walk Day
28   Buffalo Soldiers Day
29   NASA Created (by President Eisenhower in 1958)
30   Paperback Book Day
31   World Ranger Day

Integrating July Math Days

Science　　Technology　　Engineering　　Arts　　Math

Day		Make and Do
1	U.S. Postage Stamp Day	The first U.S. Postage stamp was issued on this day in 1847. The complete collection of all U.S. Postage stamps ever issued is available on Arago on-line at the Smithsonian National Postal Museum website at postalmuseum.si.edu/collections/arago.html. What famous mathematician would you recommend be featured on a stamp? Is your choice in the Arago database? Download a current U.S. Post Office price list. Find out how much it costs to mail a letter domestically. How much will it cost to send 110 invitations that weigh 3.5 ounces domestically? What happens if the invitation weights 4 ounces? What would the cost be then?
7	Macaroni Day	Today is the day to celebrate your favorite noodle. Macaroni is just one of hundreds of kinds of pasta. Pasta is made from just flour and water. Let's explore the mathematics of macaroni by creating macaroni necklaces that have patterns of color. First make various colors of macaroni. Measure one tablespoon of rubbing alcohol with three drops of food coloring in a jar large enough to hold one cup of dry macaroni. Screw on the lid and shake to color. Lay out on newspaper to dry overnight. Create patterns with the pasta and string.
8	Math 2.0 Day	The world runs on numbers. On Math 2.0 day we celebrate the intersection of mathematics and technology. Let's plan a fun-filled math day. Solve some fun mathematical problems. Tell some math jokes. Imagine what the world would be like without math and write a story.

10	Don't Step On A Bee Day	Bees work very hard. It takes eight bees all of their life to make one single teaspoon of honey. Bees are also great mathematicians and excel in geometry. Bees build honeycombs out of hexagons. Their hexagonal wax cells contain their larvae and store honey and pollen. Regular hexagons have six equal sides with equal interior angles. Similar to triangles and squares, hexagons tessellate themselves. Create a beautiful pattern of hexagons. Try dividing some of your hexagons into equilateral triangles. Quilts are often sewn together from hexagon pieces of cloth. Search the web for some beautiful examples of hexagonal quilts.
21	National Junk Food Day	The United States Food and Drug Administration (FDA) standardizes nutrition in America. The nutritional label provides guidance for consumers including serving size, calories and nutrient information based on either a 2,000 or 2,500 calorie diet (you will find this information in the label footnote). What do you consider a junk food? Select three favorite junk foods. Determine the calories per serving (the FDA considers 40 calories low, 100 calories medium, and 400 or more calories high). Determine which vitamins are in your food choice and what the fat content is. Create a chart or graph that compares your favorite junk food to an apple, a serving of carrot sticks, a serving of peanut butter or other favorite foods.
22	Casual Pi Day	Pi is the relationship of a circle's circumference to its diameter. That relationship is the fraction 22/7 that equals 3.14159265 and continues infinitely. We celebrate Pi Day on March 14 and Casual Pi Day on July 22 (22 divided by 7). This gives us an estimation of Pi. Visit the teachpi.org website for many activities for this special day. As we measure from the center of the circle to an edge, it is always the same distance at any point on the circumference of the circle. Measure some 10", 12" and 16" circles. If these were pizzas, which one would be the best value? Find some pizza prices from your local pizzeria and determine which pie is the better deal. (Hint, pi times the radius squared will give you the area of a circle).

July Overview

National Picnic Month
Math Lesson: Planning a Picnic
Poetry Lesson: Excerpt from Audley Court by Alfred Lord Tennyson

During National Picnic month friends and family celebrate outdoors and bring their favorite food to share. In this lesson, students create a budget for a friends and family picnic. In Tennyson's poem, he describes a picnic day with a friend and students write their own poems about their picnic.
NCTM STANDARD 1: Numbers and Operations, Gr 3 – 1C-13; Gr 4 – 1C-13; Gr 5 – 1C-5, 1C-13; Gr 6 – 1C-7; NCTM STANDARD 4: Measurement, Gr 4 – 4B2; Gr 5 – 4B6

Fourth of July
Math Lesson: Hot Dog Eating Contest
Poetry Lesson: Fearless Flying Hot Dogs by Jack Prelutsky

Every year close to 40,000 spectators celebrate Independence Day by attending Nathan's Famous Hot Dog Eating Contest. Students review contest winners to determine the mean, median and mode of participant scores. Jack Prelutsky invites us to read about a performance where hot dogs show off their aerobatic feats and Prelutsky shows off his hot dog puns. Students write a poem in which their hot dogs have unique personalities flavored by puns.
NCTM STANDARD 5: Data Analysis. Gr 3 – 5B1, 5B2, 5B3, 5B4 ; Gr4 – 5B1, 5B2; Gr5 – 5B1, 5B2; Gr6 – 5B1, 5B2, 5B3

Math 2.0 Day
Math Lesson: Website Round-Up
Poetry Lesson: Excerpt – The Hunting of the Snark by Lewis Carroll

Math 2.0 Day is an unofficial holiday observed each July 8 to celebrate the intersection of math and technology. In this lesson, students engage in on-line math games and critically review for content and fun. In this lesson, students learn about nonsense poems and write their own "complicated" math equations using the structure of Lewis Carroll's poem as a model.
NCTM Process Standard – Problem Solving: Apply and adapt a variety of appropriate strategies to solve problems.

Moon Day
Math Lesson: Moon Day Crossword
Poetry Lesson: The Eagle Has Landed by J. Patrick Lewis

National Moon Day is observed every July 20th to commemorate the first time man walked on the moon. Students read about the landing and create math questions to use in a lunar landing crossword puzzle. J. Patrick Lewis lends a poetic description to this historical event. Students imagine themselves as the first person to land on the moon and write poems describing their experiences.
NCTM Process Standard – Problem Solving: Apply and adapt a variety of appropriate strategies to solve problems.

National Picnic Month
Math Lesson: Planning a Picnic

It's easy to get family and friends out to celebrate the warm summer days and the joys of nature while eating some tasty food during National Picnic Month. In this lesson students plan a friends and family picnic with their classmates.

MATERIALS
- Internet capable device
- Picnic Planning Worksheet
- Pencil and paper
- Board or chart

PLAN
- Students work in groups to plan a picnic for friends and family.
- List the following categories on a board or chart:
  - Sandwiches
  - Type of bread
  - Condiments
  - Sides
  - Desserts
  - Paper goods
  - Outdoor picnic locations in the neighborhood
  - Groups of people to invite
- Brainstorm items for each category and write responses on the board or chart.
  - For example, responses under sandwiches might include: peanut butter and jelly, turkey and avocado, ham and cheese
  - Responses under groups of people to invite might include: family, friends, teachers.

DO
- Divide students into groups and distribute the Picnic Planning Worksheet.
- The group will divide the total cost of the picnic among the members so the group must decide how much each member is willing to spend.
- Groups select a location for the picnic and write it on their worksheet.
- Groups decide how many people will be invited.
- Groups determine the picnic menu and write what is needed on the worksheet in the item column.
- Search the Internet to complete the Picnic Planning Worksheet as follows:
  - Find the lowest cost of each item and record under cost per unit.
  - Determine the quantity of each item so that each guest gets at least one portion.
  - Compute the total cost per item and determine the total picnic cost.
  - Compute the expense for each group member.

Picnic Planning Worksheet

Picnic Location_____Number of Guests_____

Item	Cost Per Unit	Number Needed	Total Cost
Total Picnic Cost			
Price Per Group Member			

National Picnic Month
Poetry Lesson: Excerpt from Audley Court

In the poem, *Audley Court*, Alfred Lord Tennyson describes a picnic day enjoyed by two friends. Along with descriptions of the luscious food, the narrator describes the beautiful scenery, their gossip and songs. One friend arrives in a boat to Audley Court, a seaside area about a mile from London. His friend, the narrator of the poem is waiting for him. Upon arriving, the narrator's friend Francis, proceeds to set the elaborate feast. They sit, eat and talk about events in their lives. They are "glad at heart" after a satisfying picnic day.

MATERIALS
- Alfred Lord Tennyson Biography and excerpt from his poem *Audley Court*
- Word processing or desktop publishing software or pencils

PLAN
- Read and discuss Alfred Lord Tennyson's biography and poem. Students can look up unknown words in a dictionary as they read the poem.
- Ask the following questions:
  - Who prepares the picnic?
  - What did the two friends talk about?
  - Where does Francis live?

DO
Getting Ready to Write
Discuss the following points with your class.
- Describe the place where you have picnicked or where you want to picnic.
- Who would you like to be with on your picnic?
- Who brings the food and how is it presented?
  For example: *Mia laid the food she brought on a green tablecloth*
- Describe in detail foods that are presented at your picnic.
  For example: *turkey, cheese, and avocado topped with mayonnaise laid between whole wheat bread*
- What would you talk about?
  For example: *We spoke of our swimming in the warmth of the summer*
- Besides eating, what other activities would you do?
  For example: *We jumped rope until we couldn't breath, played rounders with a Frisbee*
- How did you feel about your picnic day?
  For example: *Talking about the past, loving my company will stay with me forever*

Writing the Poem
Students write about their own picnic. Use line breaks just as Tennyson did.
- Students begin their poem with "Let us picnic here."
- Continue the poem using some of the discussion points.

Editing and Publishing
- Students read and edit poems with partners.
- Create an anthology with each student's poem and a picnic recipe.

Alfred Lord Tennyson Biography
August 6, 1809 – October 6, 1892

Alfred Lord Tennyson is considered the greatest of the Victorian poets and was the most popular English poet of his time. Although Tennyson's father was a reverend, he didn't grow up in a peaceful environment. He had eleven brothers and sisters. His father was an alcoholic. One sibling was emotionally disturbed and another was addicted to drugs. There was a lot of arguing in his home between his father and one of his brothers.

Tennyson began to write poetry before he was ten years old. His father helped Tennyson by tutoring him in classical and modern languages to prepare him for college. By the time he was eighteen, he had published his first volume. When he began his studies at Cambridge University, his success as a poet made him very popular with a group of gifted students who encouraged Tennyson to devote his life to poetry. The friendships he formed at Cambridge gave him confidence to continue his work as a poet.

Although Tennyson did not have a happy childhood, he enjoyed his adult life. He got married and had a family. His earnings from poetry enabled him to buy a house in the country and to enjoy the kind of solitude he liked. Tennyson was a true character with his cloak and big hat. His powerful voice captured his listeners. In addition to being a poet, Tennyson was a wise man whose ideas on politics and world affairs represented the voice of his nation. Queen Victoria recognized him with the title of Poet Laureate.

The poem *Audley Court* is an example of Tennyson's power of creating scenery and states of feeling. He examined many religious issues that bewildered both his generation and future generations.

Excerpt from Audley Court
by Alfred Lord Tennyson

....
Let us picnic there
At Audley Court."
I spoke, while Audley feast
Humm'd like a hive all round the narrow quay,
To Francis, with a basket on his arm,
To Francis just alighted from the boat,
And breathing of the sea.
…………..
Then we shoulder'd thro' the swarm,
And rounded by the stillness of the beach
To where the bay runs up its latest horn.
We left the dying ebb that faintly lipp'd
The flat red granite; so by many a sweep
Of meadow smooth from aftermath we reach'd
………
There, on a slope of orchard, Francis laid
A damask napkin wrought with horse and hound,
Brought out a dusky loaf that smelt of home,
And, half-cut-down, a pasty costly-made,
Where quail and pigeon, lark and leveret lay,
Like fossils of the rock, with golden yolks
Imbedded and injellied; last, with these,
A flask of cider from his father's vats,
…………..
And talk'd old matters over;
…………..
discuss'd the farm,
The four-field system, and the price of grain;
…………..
He sang his song, and I replied with mine:
…………..
"Sleep, Ellen Aubrey, sleep, and dream of me:
…………..
So sang we each to either, Francis Hale,
The farmer's son, who lived across the bay,
My friend; and I,
…………..
but ere the night we rose
And saunter'd home beneath a moon, that, just
In crescent, dimly rain'd about the leaf
Twilights of airy silver, till we reach'd
The limit of the hills; and as we sank
From rock to rock upon the glooming quay,
The town was hush'd beneath us: lower down
The bay was oily calm; the harbour-buoy,
Sole star of phosphorescence in the calm,
With one green sparkle ever and anon
Dipt by itself, and we were glad at heart.

Fourth of July
Math Lesson: Hot Dog Eating Contest

A favorite annual Fourth of July event is the Nathan's Hot Dog Eating Contest. The contest takes place at the corner of Surf and Stillwell Avenues on Coney Island in Brooklyn, New York. The current men's champion is Joey Chestnut. He ate 70 hot dogs in ten minutes in the contest's 100th anniversary in 2016. Miki Sudo, the women's champion ate 38.5. In this lesson students learn about Nathan's Famous Hot Dog Eating Contest. They find the mean, median and mode as they analyze data from the competition.

MATERIALS
- Pencil and paper
- Board or chart
- Nathan's Hot Dog Eating Contest Handout

PLAN
- Distribute the Nathan's Hot Dog Eating Contest Handout to the class.
- Discuss the information about the contest and use the number of hot dogs in buns that Sonya Thomas ate.

Sonya Thomas Scores
In the 11 years between 2003 and 2013, women's champion Sonya Thomas ate the following number of hot dogs in buns.
25, 32, 37, 37, 39, 34, 41, 36, 40, 45, 36.75

Finding the Mean
To determine the mean, add up the number of hot dogs eaten and divide by the number of years she participated in the contest:
25 + 32 + 37 + 37 + 39 + 34 + 41 + 36 + 40 + 45 + 36.75 = 402.75 divided by 11 = 36.61

Finding the Median
To determine the median, arrange Sonya's scores in either ascending or descending order. The number in the middle is the median. Since there are 11 scores, the number 37 is the score between the first five and final five numbers and is the median. If there is an even number of scores, the average of the two middle scores is the median.
25 + 32 + 34 + 36 + 36.75 + 37 + 37 + 39 + 40 + 41 + 45

Finding the Mode
To determine the mode, arrange the data in order from least to greatest. The mode is the value that occurs most often. The number 37 occurs the most frequently and it is the mode.
25 + 32 + 34 + 36 + 36.75 + 37 + 37 + 39 + 40 + 41 + 45

DO
- Analyze the data on the handout.
- Answer the questions at the bottom of the handout.

Nathan's Hot Dog Eating Contest Handout

Background Information

Every year close to 40,000 spectators celebrate Independence Day on the Fourth of July by attending Nathan's Famous Hot Dog Eating Contest. In addition, over one million people watch the event on television. The competition takes place on Coney Island in Brooklyn, New York. About twenty prequalified contestants stand on a raised platform behind a long table. Nathan's hot dogs in buns are placed in front of the contestants along with drinks. Most contestants choose water. The contestant who consumes the greatest number is declared the winner. The length of the contest was set at ten minutes in 2008. Previously the contestants usually had 12 minutes of hot dog eating time. Until 2011, women had competed against the men in the same contest. In 2011, Nathan's Hot Dog Eating Contest for Women separated the two sexes.

Nathan's Hot Dog Eating Contest Results Chart

Year	Top Man	Hot Dogs in Buns	Top Woman	Hot Dogs in Buns
2016	Joey Chestnut	70	Miki Sudo	38.5
2015	Matthew Stonie	62	Miki Sudo	38
2014	Joey Chestnut	61	Miki Sudo	34
2013	Joey Chestnut	69	Sonya Thomas	36.75
2012	Joey Chestnut	68	Sonya Thomas	45
2011*	Joey Chestnut	62	Sonya Thomas	40
2010	Joey Chestnut	54	Sonya Thomas	36
2009	Joey Chestnut	68	Sonya Thomas	41
2008	Joey Chestnut	59	Sonya Thomas	34
2007	Joey Chestnut	66	Sonya Thomas	39
2006	Takeru Kobayashi	53.75	Sonya Thomas	37
2005	Takeru Kobayashi	49	Sonya Thomas	37
2004	Takeru Kobayashi	53.5	Sonya Thomas	32
2003	Takeru Kobayashi	44.5	Sonya Thomas	25
2002	Takeru Kobasyashi	50		
2001	Takeru Kobayashi	50		
2000	Kazutoyo Arai	25.125		

2011 was the first year of Nathan's Hot Dog Eating Contest for Women (previously women had competed with the men). In that contest, Thomas earned the inaugural Pepto-Bismol-sponsored pink belt and won $10,000.

Analyze the Data

Use the data above to do the following:
1. Find the mean, median and mode of Joey Chestnuts results.
2. Find the mean, median and mode of all the men's results.
3. Find the mean, median and mode of all the women's results.

Fourth of July
Poetry Lesson: Fearless Flying Hot Dogs

In the poem, *We're Fearless Flying Hot Dogs*, by Jack Prelutsky, the hot dog takes on an emotional and complex life of its own. This poem is filled with puns that add flavor to the hot dogs. Students write a poem using puns to add flavor to their hot dogs.

MATERIALS
- Jack Prelutsky Biography and his poem *We're Fearless Flying Hot Dogs*
- Word processing or desktop publishing software or pencils, pens, markers
- You Tube Recording of Fearless Flying Hot Dogs (optional)

PLAN
- Read and discuss Jack Prelutsky's biography and poem.
- Ask the following questions:
  - How does the alliteration in the title and first line add to the humor of the poem?
  - What words in the poem have puns (double meanings)?
  - What makes the hot dogs aerobatic?
  - How does the narrator show that the hot dogs are fearless? give hot dogs a personality?
  - What makes the hot dog performance entertaining?

DO
Getting Ready to Write
- How would your hot dogs introduce themselves using alliteration?
  For example: *We're smart studious hot dogs*
- Introduce the list of puns and discuss how each one has a double meaning and how they are related to hot dogs from a speech given by New York's Mayor Bloomberg on July 4, 2013: *let's be frank; people relish; not for the thin-skinned; can catch-up; cut the mustard; getting grilled; steam the competition; roast rivals; kick buns; top dog; blue ribbon wiener; landing in hot water*
- Which puns would you choose and how would you use them?
- Are there any other puns you can think of related to hot dogs?

Writing the Poem
- Title and the poem using an alliteration.
- Repeat the title in the first line of your poem.
- Continue poem using puns.
  - For example: *We're smart studious hot dogs*
    We relish every word we learn

Editing and Publishing
- Students read and edit poems with partners.
- Student sit in a circle and read their poems in a Pun Read-Along.
- Students listen to you tube recording of poem and perform their own.
  https://soundcloud.com/pbsnewshour/were-fearless-flying-hotdogs

Jack Prelutsky Biography
September 8, 1940 –

Jack Prelutsky was born in Brooklyn, New York. His father was an electrician and his mother a homemaker. He grew up in the Bronx with his parents and younger brother. His family was poor. He wasn't popular in school and was bullied. He was skinny and had a big mouth that irritated some children. He was beat up quite often. He was bored and didn't like school. He had a teacher who did not like poetry but who was forced to read a poem each week to her students. Jack was influenced by her dislike of poetry.

His high school teachers recognized his musical talent and he followed their suggestions by entering The High School of Music & Art. He thrived there honing his beautiful voice and participating in school musicals. At eighteen he entered Hunter College in New York where he failed English. After failing three times, he left school.

Jack had many jobs and worked as a bus boy, furniture mover, cab driver, salesman and others. He also sang in coffee houses. It was there that Bob Dylan heard Jack sing and was impressed by his voice. He and Bob Dylan became friends.

Jack loved to draw and spent hours creating imaginary animals. Before sending some of his drawings to a publisher, he quickly wrote poems to go along with them. The poetry he sent impressed a publisher and soon, at the age of twenty-four, he had a book of poems published.

Jack married a librarian named Carolyn who he met on a book tour in New Mexico. From the moment he saw her, he was in love. Today they live in Seattle. He surrounds himself with wind-up toys, frog miniatures, children's poetry books and art.

Prelutsky strives to make poetry enjoyable for children. He writes about subjects that are important to them and in humorous and unique ways that delight them. He is the author of more than fifty children's poetry books. He has also collected children's poetry from various authors and published them in anthologies. He became the first poet laureate of children's books. Besides writing, he is an accomplished singer and guitar player. He has several audio recordings of his poetry where he plays the guitar and sings his words.

We're Fearless Flying Hotdogs
by Jack Prelutsky

The poem is currently available online at:

        http://paulaoneil.tripod.com/id29.html

The poem appears in Jack Prelutsky's book *Something Big Has Been Here*. The book is more than likely available in your local library or school library. Also visit his website at jackprelutsky.com.

In his poem, We're Fearless Flying Hotdogs, Jack Prelutsky writes about the antics of five "famous" hotdogs. These hotdogs love "to climb, to dip, to dive." They "race with flair and style." They "swoop and spiral." And "then slide into a roll." His play on words using puns is something that children of all ages enjoy as he writes about the hotdogs with audiences that are "never a sour crowd" and where there's never "a chilly reception."

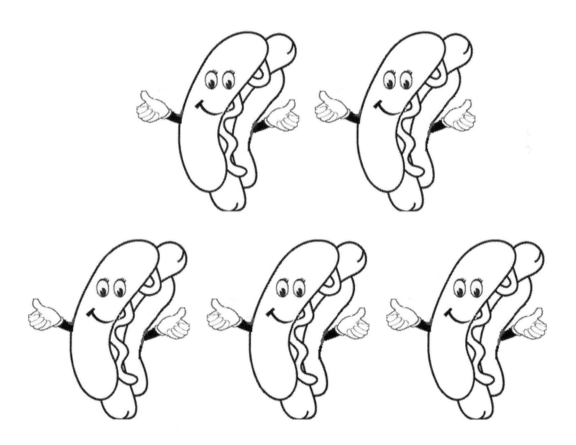

Math 2.0
Math Lesson: Website Round-Up

Math 2.0 Day is an unofficial holiday observed each July 8th. It is thought to have its beginning in 1979 to celebrate the intersection of math and technology. There are many industries and products that are based on a combination of the two. One of the most successful is the multi-billion dollar computer game industry. In this lesson students engage in online math-based games. They will explore and evaluate a variety of online math-related websites. Some evaluation criteria include: ease of use, closeness to math skills being learned, level of difficulty and amount of fun.

MATERIALS
- Internet capable device
- Pencil and paper
- Math Website Round-Up Game Evaluation Worksheet

PLAN
- Math 2 0 Day is an unofficial holiday that celebrates the intersection of math and technology.
- Discuss how students have used the computer to improve math understanding. Some examples are: math practice, math reviews, productivity tools and games.

DO
- Have the class name some of the math games they have played and instructional sites they have used.
- List responses on the board.
- Below are five popular sites to visit and check-out.
    - www.funbrain.com
    - www.mathplayground.com
    - www.coolmath-games.com
    - www.khanacademy.org
    - www.mathsisfun.com
- Divide the class into pairs and do the following:
    - Use computers, tablets and cellphones to play games and/or try lessons at some of the websites listed above.
    - Evaluate the math sites listed.
    - Complete the worksheet.
    - Share their evaluations with their classmates.

Math Website Round-Up
Game Evaluation Worksheet

Website _____

Internet Device Used_____

Math Games Evaluated _____

_____

Evaluators _____

_____

Check List

	Yes	No
Educational		
Grade level content		
Clear directions		
Easy to use		
Fun to use		
Promotes greater understanding		
Maintains interest		
Has a variety of skill levels		
Will use this math site again		
Recommend to classmates		

Description
Write a description and comments in the space below.

Math 2.0 Week
Poetry Lesson: Excerpt – The Hunting of the Snark

The Hunting of the Snark by Lewis Carroll is a nonsense poem. This form of poetry is filled with whims, humor and made-up words. This poem recounts the adventures, the relationships and the interactions between the crew members on a boat as they look for a mysterious creature, a Snark. In the fifth section called FIT THE FIFTH, *The Beaver's Lesson* stanzas 12, 16 and 17, a character named the Butcher teaches another character the Beaver a mathematics lesson. In this lesson, students learn how the Butcher complicates an easy mathematical addition equation, 2 + 1 = 3, using the four basic operations of elementary arithmetic: addition, subtraction, multiplication and division. Students write their own poems using all four operations.

MATERIALS
- Lewis Carroll Biography and three stanzas from his poem *The Hunting of the Snark*
- Word processing or desktop publishing software or pencils

PLAN
- Read and discuss Lewis Carroll's biography and the three stanzas from *The Hunting of the Snark* nonsense poem FIT THE FIFTH, *The Beaver's Lesson* stanzas 12, 16 and 17.
- Before discussion, tell students what constitutes a nonsense poem. Ask the following questions.
    - What makes these three stanzas fit the description of a nonsense poem?
    - What was nonsensical about the Butcher's calculation?

DO
Getting Ready to Write
During a class discussion, ask the following:
- What steps were taken to arrive at the answer of 3? Write the Butcher's calculation on the board: [(3 + 7 + 10) x (1000 - 8)] / 992 -17 = 3
- Do the math to see if the Butcher's calculation is correct.
- Have students complicate 3 + 2 = 5 and write a class nonsense poem using the four basic operations of arithmetic.

Writing the Poem
- Students use FIT THE FIFTH, *The Beaver's Lesson* stanzas 12, 16 and 17 as a model.
- Begin with stanza 12 and replace the numbers with numbers of your own choosing.
- The answer to your stanza 12 becomes the subject for your next stanza.
- Add, subtract, multiply and divide in a complicated nonsensical way in subsequent lines.
- Follow the poem and change the non-number words with words with similar meanings.
- End the poem with "…the answer must be / Exactly and perfectly true."
- For students who wish to replace the rhyming words with rhyming words of their own they may have to recalculate their original computations to arrive at rhyming words that work.

Editing and Publishing
- Students read and edit poems with partners.

Lewis Carroll Biography
January 27, 1832 - January 4, 1898

Charles Lutwidge Dodgson was born in England. His pen name was Lewis Carroll. His family was wealthy. He was the oldest boy in a family of eleven children. As a youngster, he wanted to be an artist and drew illustrations for his brothers and sisters. He was always creating either by writing poetry for his homemade newspapers or performing magic tricks. From the time he was a young boy, Carroll loved mathematics. At the age of twenty-three, he became a member of the faculty of mathematics at Oxford University and taught and lectured there.

Carroll was considered shy possibly because he had a stammer. With young children he seemed to be more relaxed and spent a great deal of time with them. He seemed to be two different people. When he was at Oxford, he wore black clergyman clothes with a black hat but when he went sailing he would wear white pants made of flannel and a straw hat.

Lewis Carroll is the author of *The Adventures of Alice in Wonderland*. The story revolves around a young girl named Alice who was modeled after Alice Pleasance Liddell, a friend of the author.

He also published mathematics papers and literature. Some of his poems employ formulas such as acrostic poetry and Nonsense poems. Nonsense poems are filled with whimsical ideas and made up words. In one of his Nonsense poems, *The Hunting of the Snark*, one can see the fun Carroll, the mathematician, had playing with numbers. Nonsense poems are enjoyed by many mathematicians probably because of the amusing mathematical discoveries they find when reading them.

Carroll took up photography as a hobby. His photographs were mainly of children and although he was an amateur at it, they were considered to be exceptional. Besides his hobby of photography, Carroll made up card games and all sorts of small inventions. The game Scrabble comes from one of his games.

Lewis Carroll was a man with many creative abilities; magician, photographer, mathematician, inventor but what he is most remembered for is his skill as a writer of novels and poetry. His words are quoted almost as frequently as Shakespeare and the Bible.

Excerpt – The Hunting of the Snark
by Lewis Carroll

Stanzas 12, 16 and 17 from
   FIT THE FIFTH
   The Beaver's Lesson

"Two added to one---if that could but be done,"
   It said, "with one's fingers and thumbs!"
Recollecting with tears how, in earlier years,
   It had taken no pains with its sums.

"Taking Three as the subject to reason about—
   A convenient number to state—
We add Seven, and Ten, and then multiply out
   By One Thousand diminished by Eight.

"The result we proceed to divide, as you see,
   By Nine Hundred and Ninety and Two:
Then subtract Seventeen, and the answer must be
   Exactly and perfectly true.

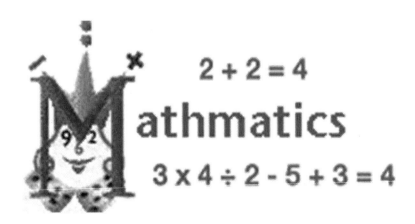

Moon Day
Math Lesson: Moon Day Crossword

MATERIALS
- Computer or tablet with printing capabilities
- Online crossword maker software
- Lunar Landing Handout
- Paper and pencils

PLAN
- Distribute the Lunar Landing Handout.
- Divide students into pairs to read along together or take turns reading aloud to each other.
- As a class discuss the reading and examine the text to find math questions to use in a Lunar Landing crossword puzzle. The answer to each question is written out in words for use in the puzzle without any spaces between words. Below are some examples:
  - What were the total round trip miles flown to the moon and back to earth?
    240,000 x 2 = 480,000; fourhundredeightythousand
  - How many days of flying did it take for the astronauts to arrive on the moon and return to earth?
    4 x 2 = 8; eight
  - How many miles did the spaceship fly each day?
    480,000/8 = 60,000; sixtythousand

DO
- Students work in pairs to create between ten and twenty questions and answers for a Lunar Landing crossword puzzle.
- Use the crossword puzzle maker found at http://www.puzzle-maker.com or a crossword puzzle generator of your choice.
- Follow the directions to input your questions and answers.
- Students print several copies of their finished crossword puzzle.
- Pairs exchange and solve each other's crosswords.

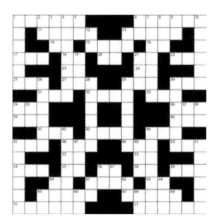

Lunar Landing Handout

National Moon Day is observed every July 20th to commemorate the first time man walked on the moon. The Apollo 11 spacecraft was launched from Cape Kennedy on July 16, 1969. The astronauts aboard the flight were: mission commander Neil Armstrong, age 38; command module pilot Lt. Col. Michael Collins, age 38; and lunar module pilot Eugene "Buzz" Aldrin, age 39.

Four days, 240,000 miles, about 109 hours and 42 minutes after the launch on July 20, 1969 at 10:56 PM, EDT, astronaut Neil Armstrong became the first human to walk on the moon. As he stepped off the ladder of the lunar module, nicknamed the Eagle, and placed a foot on the moon's surface, he said: "That's one small step for [a] man, one giant leap for mankind." Over 530 million people were estimated to have watched the televised event.

Armstrong's fellow astronaut Buzz Aldrin followed him onto the moon's surface about 20 minutes later. Armstrong, who had the responsibility of documenting the landing, recorded his descent. The two of them spent two-and-a-half hours on the moon's surface taking photographs, running some scientific tests, collecting samples and speaking with President Richard Nixon. They also left a plaque on the moon's surface that read "Here men from the planet Earth first set foot on the moon – July 1969 A.D. – We came in peace for all mankind." They returned to the lunar module and spent the night before returning to and successfully docking with the command module Columbia where Michael Collins had remained.

Apollo 11 began its journey home in the early morning of July 22nd. On July 24th, 1969, the spaceship safely splashed down in the Pacific Ocean at 12:51 PM, PDT.

Moon Day
Poetry Lesson: First Men on the Moon

July 20th is Moon Day. This observance commemorates man's first steps on the moon. J. Patrick Lewis lends a poetic description to this historical event. Using the poem along with images from the Internet and facts researched, students imagine themselves as the first person to land on the moon and write poems describing their experiences.

MATERIALS
- J. Patrick Lewis Biography and his poem *First Men on the Moon*
- Word processing or desktop publishing software or pencil
- Recording and movie software

PLAN
- Read and discuss J. Patrick Lewis's biography and poem.
- Ask the following questions:
    - Why does the narrator call the astronauts "pilgrims"?
    - Why does he describe the spaceship as "spidery"?
    - What does the poet mean by:
      They hopped like kangaroos because
      Of gravity. Or wanderlust?
    - What makes this accounting of landing on the moon poetic rather than a factual essay?

DO
Getting Ready to Write
- Before writing the poem, students learn about the moon and the first landing by reading accounts from astronauts, facts about the moon, photos from the internet and/or magazines illustrating the landing on the moon.
- Learn more facts about the moon on YouTube at
  https://www.youtube.com/watch?v=2iSZMv64wuU

Writing the Poem
- Students imagine themselves as astronauts and write a poem about their experience.
- Students start with the words "I stand here."
- Students describe what they see on the moon, how the earth looks from their vantage point, how they feel standing there and what they hear.
  For example:
  I stand here
  The ground with its craters
  Scars from so many attacks
  I dig my everlasting footprint into the ground

Editing and Publishing
- Record students as they read and combine their recordings into a movie.

Poet for National Moon Day
J. Patrick Lewis
May 5, 1942 -

J. Patrick Lewis, a writer of children's books, children's poetry and adult poetry, was born in Gary, Indiana, twenty minutes after his brother. Both of his parents loved words and loved reading to their sons. For as long as he can remember he loved writing and gives credit to his parents for this love. He attended Saint Joseph's College where he received a BA. He continued his education at Indiana University where he earned his MA degree. He received his PhD at Ohio State University in economics. He became a professor and taught in the Business, Accounting and Economics Department at Otterbein College. While teaching, he fell in love with poetry. At this point in his life he had already written and published ten children's books as well as poetry for adults in poetry journals.

At fifty-six, after thirty years as an educator, Lewis left teaching. He was happy to do so since he felt that he had spent enough time writing papers on economics. He wanted to write for children about many subjects and make these subjects entertaining for them. He is quoted as saying "I was certain I had discovered the best job in the world."

From thought-provoking to giggle-inducing, his poetry and books are about many subjects including mathematics, history, the animal kingdom and Russian legends. He says of his writing that "it runs higgledy-piggledy over the entire curriculum" casting an original light on all the subjects it embraces. He has authored over seventy-five children's books. His writing has been published in children's magazines such as Highlights for Children and Cricket. His writing has gained recognition and many awards. At the age of sixty-nine, Lewis became America's third Children's Poet Laureate. He has visited over 500 elementary schools and taught educators how to introduce poetry into the classroom. Lewis has also been recognized in the adult world where he received an Ohio Arts Council grant. The subjects of his adult poetry are family and history. According to Lewis, poetry "should transport him or her beyond the page." Lewis has definitely accomplished this by his thought provoking writing.

First Men on the Moon
by J. Patrick Lewis

The poem is available online at:

https://www.poetryfoundation.org/poems-and-poets/poems/detail/54725

First Men on the Moon by J. Patrick Lewis gives us a poetic description about the first manned moon landing on July 20, 1969. The astronauts are called "pilgrims" in the poem as they are travelling to a new place. He describes the spindly legs of the spaceship as "spidery." The words spoken by Neil Armstrong "One small step" as he climbed down the ladder will be remembered by many and memorialized in this poem.

August Monthly Holidays

Children's Vision and Learning Month • Get Ready for Kindergarten Month • International Air Travel Month • National Back to School Month National Catfish Month • National Eye Exam Month • National Golf Month National Inventor's Month • National Parks Month • National Water Quality Month

August Weekly Holidays

First Week of August
International Clown Week • National Smile Week • Simplify Your Life Week • Turtles International Awareness Week

Second Week of August
Diving Week • Don't Wait – Celebrate Week • Elvis Week • International Festival Week • National Apple Week • National Recreational Scuba Week

Third Week of August
Air Conditioning Appreciation Week • American Dance Week • National Aviation Week • Weird Contest Week

Fourth Week of August
Be Kind to Humankind Week • Carpenter Ant Awareness Week

August Moveable Holidays

Sister's Day	first Sunday
Nut Monday	first Monday
National Night Out	first Tuesday
Family Day	second Sunday
Hopi Snake Dance	third Saturday

August Days for STEAM Makers and Poets

1   The first U.S. Census in 1790
2   Friendship Day
3   National Watermelon Day
4   United States Coast Guard Day
5   American Bandstand Goes National
6   Lucille Ball Day
7   National Lighthouse Day
8   Happiness Happens Day
9   Moment of Silence for Nagasaki, Japan
10   The Smithsonian Institution is Established in 1846
11   Play in the Sand Day
12   National Vinyl Record Day
13   International Lefthanders Day
14   National Creamsicle Day
15   National Relaxation Day
16   Elvis Has Left the Building Day
17   First American Steamboat Trip in 1807
18   Hawaii Statehood Day
19   Ogden Nash Birthday
20   National Chocolate Pecan Pie Day
21   National Spumoni Day
22   Be an Angel Day
23   Permanent Press Day
24   National Peach Pie Day
25   National Don't Utter a Word Day
26   Women's Equality Day Begins in 1974
27   Guinness Book of World Records First Published in 1955
28   Anniversary of the 1963 March on Washington
29   Chop Suey is invented in New York City in 1896
30   National Marshmallow Toasting Day
31   National Trail Mix Day

Integrating August Math Days

 Science   Technology   Engineering   Arts   Math

Day		Make and Do
1	The first U.S. Census in 1790	*There are lies, damned lies and statistics.* — *Mark Twain* When the first census was taken in 1790, 3,939,326 citizens were counted in 16 states and the Ohio Territory. Compare that number to today's population. Have your students work in groups to discover five key facts about your hometown or your state. Get ready to integrate math lessons with graphs, statistics and maps.
3	National Watermelon Day	Watermelons are refreshing because they are 92% water. Europeans introduced them to America. Research, gather and make a watermelon cookbook. How will you enjoy them, sliced, diced or grilled? Be sure to include history of the watermelon. If your school has a community garden, try your hand at planting a county fair winning melon. How much does it weigh? What are its measurements? Hold a watermelon seed guessing day – how many seeds are in your class watermelon?
5	American Bandstand Goes National	American Bandstand (AB) broadcast on national television on this day in 1957. Hosted by Dick Clark, it brought rock 'n' roll music, dance steps, and fashion to millions of teenagers. Watch some AB clips and create your own "Rate-A-Record" segment. Make a list of ten popular tunes and administer a class survey. What percentage of your class voted for each song?

10	The Smithsonian Institution is Established in 1846	The Smithsonian Institution is a group of nineteen museums, nine research centers and a zoo in Washington, D.C. Design your own classroom museum. Make museum exhibits displaying math topics that you are studying. For example, some exhibit items could include a mobius strip, origami, patterns in nature, mazes, shapes, weights and measures and more. Here's a technology challenge. Use a digital camera to add pictures. Explore on-line museums. Take pictures of all of your classmate's exhibits and create an on-line class museum.
13	International Lefthanders Day	Celebrate your right to be left-handed. Make a list of the advantages and disadvantages of being left-handed. Did you know that ten percent of the world's population, on average is left-handed. What percentage of your class is left-handed? Your school's faculty? How many people might be left-handed in your city, county and state?
16	Elvis Has Left the Building Day	Elvis Aaron Presley was born in a two-room house in Tupelo, Mississippi on January 8, 1935 and died on August 16, 1977. He starred in thirty-three movies. Create a list of Elvis facts that include numbers. Write word problems incorporating the numbers in his life. Make a timeline of Elvis movies, records or highlights of his life.
20	National Chocolate Pecan Pie Day	Chocolate Pecan Pie recipes began in the mid-1920s. Celebrate this food holiday by learning about Karo syrup and trying out their recipe. What ingredients will you need? How much of each ingredient will you need to make enough pie to feed your class? Compare your recipe with one that uses corn syrup or other Karo syrup replacements.

27	Guinness Book of World Records	First published on August 27, 1955, learn all about it at http://www.guinnessworldrecords.com/explore-records/. Create a class record book of students' amazing feats such as who can jump the highest; who can add a long row of addition problems the quickest; and who has the longest hair. What other categories can you think of? Consider completing your world records with another class. Present your award winners in a class made book.
30	National Marshmallow Toasting Day	Marshmallows are great toasting over a campfire, but mini-marshmallows and toothpicks make great geometric figures. Experiment and make several multi-sided geometric figures. Begin by making two-dimensional shapes such as a square, rectangle, and triangle. Next build cubes, rectangular prisms and square pyramids. How many toothpicks and how many marshmallows did each require?
31	National Trail Mix Day	Trail mix is a tasty high-energy treat often made of nuts, dried fruits, seeds and more. Mix up equal parts for a delicious treat. Create and name your own mix and design the packaging. Try a second mix using a different proportion of each ingredient. Perhaps your favorite ingredient is a higher percentage. What will you call your new mix?

August Overview

National Back-to-School Month
Math Lesson: Figure Me Out
Poetry Lesson: The Village Schoolmaster by Oliver Goldsmith

Now that summer vacation will soon be a memory, thoughts of school days and how we begin the school year are in our minds. Figure Me Out introduces each student to their classmates, numerically. Students use math concepts related to their lives to create problems with solutions that unlocks their identity. Students read about the village schoolmaster and write a poem about an influential teacher.
NCTM STANDARD 5: Date Analysis and Probability, Gr 3 – 5A-1, 5A-5; Gr 4 – 5A-1, 5A-8; Gr 5 – 5A-1, 5A-8; NCTM STANDARD 2: Algebra, Gr 6 – 2B-3, 2B-4

National Sandwich Month
Math Lesson: Sandwich Shop
Poetry Lesson: Recipe for a Hippo Sandwich by Shel Silverstein

The name and popularity of the sandwich began in a town known as Sandwich in the County of Kent, England. Students become both diners and restaurateurs and practice math as they develop a sandwich shop menu and place orders. Shel Silverstein's delightful poem will inspire students to create their own unusual sandwich.
NCTM STANDARD 4: Measurement, Gr 3 – 4B-6; Gr 4 – 4B-2; Gr 5 – 4B-6

National Friendship Week
Math Lesson: Card Sharks
Poetry Lesson: Inviting a Friend to Supper by Ben Jonson

National Friendship Week is celebrated August 18th through August 24th. This is a time to appreciate your great friends. To help establish friendships in the classroom and to review and reinforce math skills, student work with partners and play a variety of math card games to see who is the greatest card shark. In Ben Jonson's poem, he invites a friend to supper. After studying his poem, students write their own poetic invitation inviting a friend to dine.
NCTM STANDARD 1: Numbers and Operations, Gr 3 – 1C-7, 1C-8; Gr 4 – 1C-3, 1C-4; Gr 5 – 1C-3; Gr 6 – 1B-9

National Ride the Wind Day
Math Lesson: Diamond Kites
Poetry Lesson: The Wind by Amy Lowell

Wind surfing, kite flying, sailboat racing and just feeling the warmth of the breeze running through your hair are a few of August's delights. National Ride the Wind Day is celebrated on August 23rd. Summer may be coming to an end and to enjoy the warm summer wind students use problem solving, measuring and basic geometry skills to build and fly a symmetrical diamond kite. Students write wind personification poems in the style of Amy Lowell.
NCTM STANDARD 3 Geometry: Gr 3 – 3D-1, Gr 4 – 3D4; Gr 5 – 3D-3

National Back-to-School Month
Math Lesson: Figure Me Out

This activity is a math version of the popular All About Me activity for Back to School. Students use math concepts related to their lives (number of letters in name, birthdates, number of boys/girls in family, house number etc.) to create a "Figure Me Out" activity. The finished product makes a perfect display for Back to School Night.

MATERIALS
- Lined writing paper
- Scissors
- Pencils, crayons, colored pencils
- Thin color markers in a variety of colors
- Chart paper

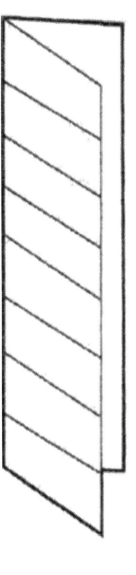

PLAN
- Tell students they are going to tell about themselves using the numbers in their lives.
- Ask students to create math problems to represent their age using math concepts they know. For example, 11 year olds can create some of the following:
    - I am $10 \times 2 - 9$ years old
    - I am $10 + 1/2 + 4/8$ years old
    - I am $10 \times 12 - 109$ years
    - I am $35 + 45 + 100 / 2 - 88 \times 5 + 1$
- Write the problems on a board or chart.
- Students create a list of other numbers in their lives. Examples:
    - Birthdays
    - Number of sisters/brothers
    - Number of pets
    - Street address
    - Birthday
    - Letters in first name/last name
    - Shoe size
    - Years until I can drive/vote
    - States I have visited
    - Rooms in my house

DO
- Fold a sheet of 8 1/2" by 11" lined paper in half lengthwise
- Cut every third line on front side of the folded paper from the outside to the fold to create flaps.
- Write the title Figure Me Out (Your Name) on the top flap.
- Write a math problem related to numbers in your life on the remaining flaps.
- Write the answers underneath each flap.

National Back-to-School Month
Poetry Lesson: The Village School Master

Oliver Goldsmith introduces us to an important "village schoolmaster" in his life in the poem *The Village Schoolmaster*. This detailed and honest dedication tells of his teacher's "severe" countenance that "every truant knew" and of his kindness and "love he bore to learning." His schoolmaster may have been forgotten if not for this poem.

MATERIALS
- Oliver Goldsmith Biography and poem *The Village Schoolmaster*
- Word processing or desktop publishing software or pencils, pens, and paper

PLAN
- Read and discuss biography and poem. Some sample guiding questions include:
- How does the setting draw us into the poem?
- Why did the schoolmaster frighten some students?
- Why did the students laugh at all their teacher's jokes?
- What were the schoolmaster's virtues?
- Why was the child happy to be taught by a stern teacher?

DO
Getting Ready to Write
- Have students think about and visualize an influential teacher.
- Students close their eyes and visualize the images that come to mind.
- The class discusses their thoughts.
- Encourage students to describe both physical and character details.
- Record descriptions as they are discussed, listing each one on a separate line.
- For example:
  A smile was on her face.
  She stood by the board.
  She smelled like chalk.

Writing the Poem
- Using The Village Schoolmaster as a model, students write their own influential teacher poem.
- Begin the first line of the poem by describing the image they see in their mind's eye.
- Students continue writing by including more details.
- For example: appearance, personality, traits, habits and gestures
- Each detail becomes a separate line of their poem.

Editing and Publishing
- Students trade papers with a partner. Each draws the teacher their partner described in his/her poem.
- Students write their poems in a poetry book or enter them in a word processing program.

Oliver Goldsmith Biography
November 10, 1730 - April 4, 1774

Oliver Goldsmith was born in a small village in Ireland. His father was a farmer and the head of a local church. After being educated at home he began school where he was bullied because of his small size and because his face was scarred from smallpox. He was not considered very bright and was mistreated by his teachers. But even at a young age, he showed a talent in writing and also loved reading great literature.

In college he was considered a character because he dressed in bright colors, not common in those days. He was not a good student and was always getting into trouble. After graduation he traveled through France and Germany and wrote about these travels. He probably earned money for his food and lodging by performing with his flute. He loved music and gambling and was always in debt. With his talent in writing and his need for money, he began working for a publisher where he produced some impressive literary work. He wrote plays and poetry. One play was called "The History of Little Goody Two-Shoes" from where the saying "goody two-shoes" probably comes.

Goldsmith wrote the truth that he saw in a sweet and gentle way and most of his writing describes happy memories. In his lifetime, he became friends with many famous artistic people not only for his writing but also his kind nature. After his death, his friends placed a monument to honor him in Westminster Abbey at the Poet's Corner featuring a bust of his profile. A monument was also erected in his honor in Ireland. Poetry historians believe it is possible that the village schoolmaster was Goldsmith's teacher when he was six years old.

The Village Schoolmaster
by Oliver Goldsmith

Illustrations by members of "The Etching Club" published in Bolton Corney, ed., The Poetical Works of Oliver Goldsmith, Lee and Shepard, Boston, 1872

Beside yon straggling fence that skirts the way
With blossom'd furze unprofitably gay,
There, in his noisy mansion, skill'd to rule,
The village master taught his little school;
A man severe he was, and stern to view,
I knew him well, and every truant knew;
Well had the boding tremblers learn'd to trace
The days disasters in his morning face;
Full well they laugh'd with counterfeited glee,
At all his jokes, for many a joke had he:
Full well the busy whisper, circling round,
Convey'd the dismal tidings when he frown'd:
Yet he was kind; or if severe in aught,
The love he bore to learning was in fault.
The village all declar'd how much he knew;
'Twas certain he could write, and cipher too:
Lands he could measure, terms and tides presage,
And e'en the story ran that he could gauge.
In arguing too, the parson own'd his skill,
For e'en though vanquish'd he could argue still;
While words of learned length and thund'ring sound
Amazed the gazing rustics rang'd around;
And still they gaz'd and still the wonder grew,
That one small head could carry all he knew.
But past is all his fame. The very spot
Where many a time he triumph'd is forgot.

National Sandwich Month
Math Lesson: Sandwich Shop

In this group project, students become both diners and restaurateurs as they create a special Sandwich Shop Menu for National Sandwich Month. Once all menus have been created, groups will exchange menus and become diners. They need to order at least five items from the menu. Depending on their math level they can do all or some of the following: add the bill, compute the tax and tip, and divide the bill between the group members to see how much each should pay.

MATERIALS
- Smart board or chart
- Internet access and word processing software (optional)
- Card stock paper, plain paper
- Art supplies, crayons, paints, pencils, colored pencils, markers, etc.

PLAN
- Students brainstorm to create a list of favorite restaurant sandwiches.
- Ask students to give brief descriptions of their favorite sandwich. Jot a few notes next to the various selections.
- Students work in groups to create a special Sandwich Shop menu. Students name their Sandwich Shop, create a menu and open for business.
- The menu should have five sections (appetizers, main course, sides, beverages and desserts). All items in the main course section are special sandwiches with illustrative descriptions. The prices should range from $1.00 to $15.00 per item.

DO
- Divide class into four or five groups.
- Group members plan their menus by creating, describing and pricing items for the five sections of their menu. Encourage students to include their own restaurant favorites.
- They write the menu selections, descriptions and prices on a "professionally designed" menu with the sandwich shop's name at the top. The final product is created using card stock paper and art supplies or if available they can create their menu on a word processor and add graphics from the Internet.
- Groups exchange menus and become diners using each other's menus.
- Each diner orders a meal of at least three items from the menu and totals up his/her bill.
- Depending on the math ability of the group, students add tax and tip to their meal. The group can total all the diner's meals and divide to split the bill equally between all diners at the table.
- Display the Sandwich Shop on a bulletin board celebrating National Sandwich Month.

National Sandwich Month Poetry Lesson: Recipe for a Hippopotamus Sandwich

In this delightful poem, Shel Silverstein, in his imaginative and original way, writes a recipe for a hippo sandwich. This is a perfect poem for National Sandwich Month where children imagine and write a poem about their own unusual sandwich and discover the challenges in devouring their creation.

MATERIALS
- Shel Silverstein's Biography and summary of his poem
- Word processing or desktop publishing software or pencils, pencils, pens and paper

PLAN
Read and discuss the biography and poem. Some suggested questions include:
- What ingredients in the recipe are found in the home or market?
- What ingredients work together in most sandwiches?
- What are the ingredients besides the hippopotamus that are not usually in a sandwich?
- What is the most unusual and silly ingredient?
- What might be the challenge in eating this sandwich?

DO
Getting Ready to Write
Have students brainstorm the following questions:
- What kind of sandwich will you write about?
- What usual and unusual ingredients will be in your sandwich?
- What would it be like to eat your sandwich?

Writing the Poem
- Students write a poem in which they make an unusual sandwich.
- Suggest they begin their poem with "A (name of sandwich) is easy to make"
- Have them continue their poem interspersing usual and unusual ingredients they will use.
- Have them write the most unusual and silliest ingredient last.
- End the poem by revealing something challenging about taking the first bite.

Editing and Publishing
- Have students check for errors with a partner.
- Students may wish to share their poems in a poetry book.
- Students illustrate their poem with Shel Silverstein style cartoons of their sandwich.

Shel Silverstein Biography
September 25, 1930 - May 10, 1999

Shel Silverstein was born in Chicago, Illinois. He was a talented and diversified artist. Silverstein was a popular poet and prose writer for young readers. He was also a well-known cartoonist, recording artist and songwriter. As a songwriter, he won a Grammy and was nominated for an Oscar.

He lived his early years with his parents, Nathan and Helen Silverstein. As a child, he was not popular since "When I was a kid – twelve to fourteen, around there – I would much rather have been a good baseball player or a hit with the girls, but I couldn't play ball. I couldn't dance. Luckily, the girls didn't want me. Not much I could do about that. So I started to draw and to write."

Silverstein attended Roosevelt High School in Chicago. After his graduation he began studying art at the Chicago Academy of Fine Arts now known as Art Institute of Chicago. He loved music and studied for a short time in a college for the performing arts.

He dropped out of college, joined the Army and had his cartoons published in the *Pacific Stars and Stripes* magazine. The editions were delivered to the troops on the front line so they could get the latest news. The soldiers enjoyed his drawings.

Silverstein was best known for his poetry. He also created the illustrations in his books. Two of his most popular books are *Where the Sidewalk Ends* and *A Light in the Attic*. In his poetry, readers are carried away by his unique imagination and his way of playing with words. Both the young and old throughout the world have been captured by his silly and serious poems.

Recipe for a Hippopotamus Sandwich
from Where the Sidewalk Ends by Shel Silverstein

In his poem, Shel Silverstein tells the reader know how easy it is to make a hippopotamus sandwich. He begins his recipe with ingredients that are found in most kitchens although not usually combined in one sandwich such as bread, some cake and an onion ring. The poem ends as he discovers a problem with the sandwich when he adds the final ingredient, a hippo.

The poem is available online. You can search for it or go to the following website and find the poem. It is ready to print, copy, and share with your class.

http://allpoetry.com/poem/8538979-Recipe-For-A-Hippopotamus-wbr--Sandwich-by-Shel-Silverstein

You can also find a movie on YouTube at:
https://www.youtube.com/watch?v=hdi-FPWwk60

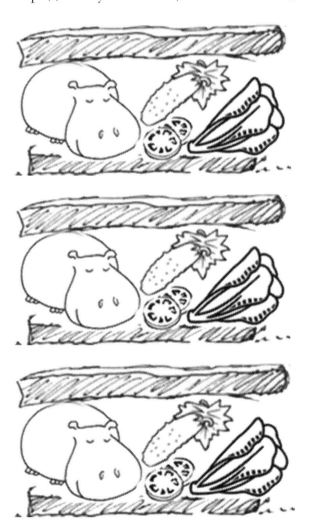

National Friendship Week
Math Lesson: Card Sharks

The three math card games introduced in this lesson help students begin the new school year rekindling old friendships and making new ones. In addition to promoting friendship, the following card games also serve as a back to school review of math concepts.

1. Multi-Digit Whole Number Multiplication War

MATERIALS
- Pencils and paper
- Deck of cards for every two players

PLAN
- Distribute pencils and paper to each player.
- Remove the tens and face cards from the deck.
- Divide the class into pairs of students.

DO
- Distribute a deck of cards to each set of partners.
- Aces have a value of one.
- Deal the deck evenly to each player.
- Players flip over the top three cards simultaneously.
- Players move the cards of their choice so that two of the cards represent a 2-digit number that is multiplied by the third.
- They compute the results.
- The player with the highest product wins all six cards.
- The above is repeated until all cards are played.
- The player with the most cards is the winner.
- For extra difficulty, four cards can be turned over simultaneously and the game can be played multiplying a three digit by one-digit number or a two-digit by two-digit number.

2. Make 24

MATERIALS
- Pencils and paper
- Deck of cards for every four players

PLAN
- Distribute pencils and paper to each player.
- Remove the tens and face cards from the deck.
- Divide the class into groups of four students.

DO
- Distribute a deck of cards to each group of four students.
- Partners remove all face cards and tens from the deck.
- Aces have a value of one.
- One person deals four cards face down to everyone in the group.
- When all the cards have been dealt, players turn their cards face up and try to arrange the cards in any order to get a total of 24 using three of the four math operations.
- The person who reaches the total of 24 first wins and gets a point.
- If no player can make 24 in that round no one gets a point and the game continues.
- The play continues until a predetermined number of rounds is completed.
- The winner is the player with the most points.

3. Fraction Number War

MATERIALS
- Pencils and paper
- Deck of cards for every two players

PLAN
- Distribute a deck of cards to each set of partners.
- Divide the class into pairs.

DO
- Give cards the following values: Aces = 11, Jacks = 12, Queens= 13 and Kings = 14.
- Deal the deck evenly to each player.
- Players flip over the top two cards simultaneously.
- Players make a fraction with their cards by making the card with the lowest number the numerator and the card with the highest number the denominator.
- The player with the largest fraction wins all four cards.
- If the fractions are equivalent, the four cards are placed in the middle and two more cards are turned over by each player. The player with the highest fraction takes all the cards.

National Friendship Week
Poetry Lesson: Inviting a Friend to Supper

In his poem, Ben Jonson invites a friend to supper, enticing him to attend by describing a sumptuous meal. Not only does he bribe his friend with food, he also writes that his friend will be entertained by a reading of Virgil along with several other Roman poets while they dine. In this lesson, students invite a friend to breakfast, lunch or dinner.

MATERIALS
- Ben Jonson Biography and poem *Inviting a Friend to Supper*
- Word processing or desktop publishing software or pencils, pens and paper, fancy stationery or art materials to create stationery.

PLAN
Read and discuss biography and poem. Some sample guiding questions include:
- What does he promise his friend to convince him to come to supper?
- What does he promise will be part of the entertainment?
- What does he promise will not be part of the entertainment?
- What does he say to convince his friend that he will be happy he accepted the invitation?

DO
Getting Ready to Write
Students discuss the follow questions:
- If you were to invite your friend to a meal, which meal would it be?
- What qualities does your friend have that makes you want to invite him or her?
- What would you promise your friend to insure that he or she will come?
- How would you exaggerate the occasion to make it so great that there is no way he or she would turn it down?
- What would you say to make your friend know how much you want him or her there?
- How would you let your friend know that coming would make him or her happy tomorrow?

Writing the Poem
Suggest students write a poem in which they invite a friend to a meal.
- Begin poems with "Please come to my home [whenever]"
- Continue the poem with the words "my friend" and describe something about their friend that makes him or her the person they want to invite.
- Describe what they will be served in an exaggerated and extraordinary way.
- End with how they will feel after such a great event.

Editing and Publishing
- Students embellish their poem with a fancy border and print.
- Students exchange printed invitations to find out if the person reading their invitation would be enticed to join them.

Ben Jonson Biography
June 11, 1572 – August 8, 1637

Ben Jonson was born June 11, 1572. Shortly after his father's death, when he was one month old, his mother remarried. His stepfather was a bricklayer and for a while Jonson worked in this trade as well. He escaped from his work by joining the army. When he returned to London he met the woman who was to be his wife, Anne Lewis.

Jonson loved the theatre, not only did he write dramas but also acted in them. He was imprisoned for writing and acting in a play that poked fun at the queen and government officials. Not long after that he killed a fellow actor in a duel. He was once again imprisoned. He narrowly escaped the gallows and when released from prison he was left penniless. Jonson continued to write plays that incited the law and was imprisoned repeatedly. He was impatient and known for having a temper. He thought of himself superior to most people because of his talent.

Jonson wrote plays called "masques" for the entertainment of the court. In his plays he demonstrated his great wit and wrote some of his best poetry.
He was appointed Court Poet. He then wrote a series of comedies that were considered his best work, and was named Poet Laureate.

When he grew old he was supported by the king and kept comfortable by his friends. Jonson was honored by being buried in the Poet's Corner of Westminster Abbey. Many people think that next to William Shakespeare, he was the greatest dramatic genius of his time.

Inviting a Friend to Supper
by Ben Jonson

Tonight, grave sir, both my poor house, and I
Do equally desire your company;
Not that we think us worthy such a guest,
But that your worth will dignify our feast
With those that come, whose grace may make that seem
Something, which else could hope for no esteem.
It is the fair acceptance, sir, creates
The entertainment perfect, not the cates.
Yet shall you have, to rectify your palate,
An olive, capers, or some better salad
Ushering the mutton; with a short-legged hen,
If we can get her, full of eggs, and then
Lemons, and wine for sauce; to these a cony
Is not to be despaired of, for our money;
And, though fowl now be scarce, yet there are clerks,
The sky not falling, think we may have larks.
I'll tell you of more, and lie, so you will come:
Of partridge, pheasant, woodcock, of which some
May yet be there, and godwit, if we can;
Knat, rail, and ruff too. Howsoe'er, my man
Shall read a piece of Virgil, Tacitus,
Livy, or of some better book to us,
Of which we'll speak our minds, amidst our meat;
And I'll profess no verses to repeat.
To this, if ought appear which I not know of,
That will the pastry, not my paper, show of.
Digestive cheese and fruit there sure will be;
But that which most doth take my Muse and me,
Is a pure cup of rich Canary wine,
Which is the Mermaid's now, but shall be mine;
Of which had Horace, or Anacreon tasted,
Their lives, as so their lines, till now had lasted.
Tobacco, nectar, or the Thespian spring,
Are all but Luther's beer to this I sing.
Of this we will sup free, but moderately,
And we will have no Pooley, or Parrot by,
Nor shall our cups make any guilty men;
But, at our parting we will be as when
We innocently met. No simple word
That shall be uttered at our mirthful board,
Shall make us sad next morning or affright
The liberty that we'll enjoy tonight.

National Ride the Wind Day – August 23rd
Math Lesson: Diamond Kites

In this lesson, students create a symmetrical diamond kite. They use problem solving, measuring and geometry skills to build and fly the kites to ride the fall wind.

MATERIALS (for each group)
- Kite picture
- Large sheet of paper about 2 feet square, chart paper
- Two wooden dowels or rods 18" long
- Large plastic garbage bag
- Strapping tape, kite string
- Rulers, protractors, pencils, markers

PLAN
- Project the kite picture.
- Ask geometry questions about the graphic. Some examples are:
- What makes the kite a quadrilateral? *It has four sides.*
- How many pairs of sides does it have? *It has two.*
- What makes the pairs congruent to one another? *The pairs are equal in size and shape and have the same endpoint.*
- What makes the intersecting lines perpendicular? *They intersect at 90 degree angles.*
- Have students come up with a joint definition for the shape of the kite based on the answers to the geometry questions.
  Example: The shape of a kite is a quadrilateral with two pair of congruent sides that have the same endpoint and are adjacent to each other.
- Select student volunteers to demonstrate how to draw a diamond kite using a large ruler or yardstick as follows:
  - Draw a vertical line that is 18 inches long.
  - Bisect the line by drawing an 18-inch horizontal line 4 inches from the top of the vertical line.
  - Join the endpoints of the lines to make a diamond kite pattern.
- Use the protractor to measure right angles of the kite where the lines intersect if grade appropriate.
- What are the measurements of the acute and obtuse angles?

DO
- Divide the class into small groups and distribute materials to each group.
- Group members draw a diamond kite with bisectors following the demonstrated steps.
- Trace the drawing onto a plastic garbage bag.
- Cut out the drawing. Place the wooden dowels on the bisector lines with strapping tape.
- Fold the kite in half lengthwise. Punch a hole just above the intersection of the bisectors.
- Turn over the kite and the kite string to the vertical dowel through the punched holes.
- Fly the kites.

Diamond Kite

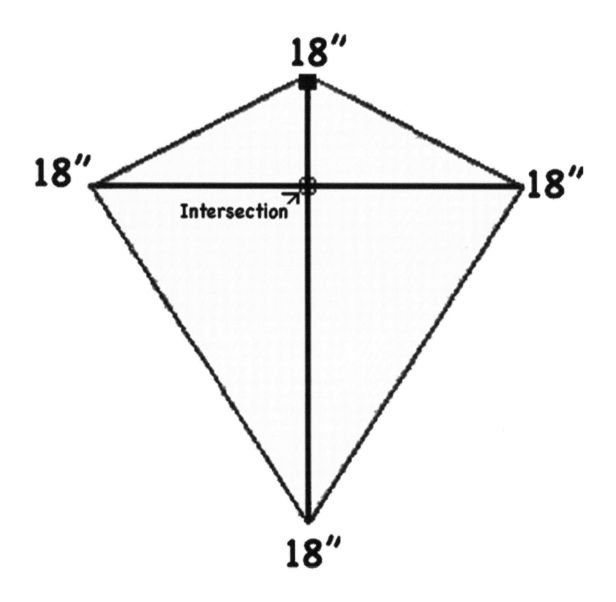

National Ride the Wind Day
Poetry Lesson: The Wind

In her poem *The Wind,* Amy Lowell uses personification as she describes the wind as a friendly and mischievous character who "steals the down from the honeybee." He is a contrary character: "Laughing, dancing, sunny wind, /Whistling, howling, rainy wind." The wind is not a force to fear, but loveable with four faces north, south, east and west, all of which the poet likes "the best."

MATERIALS
- Amy Lowell Biography and poem *The Wind*
- Word processing or desktop publishing software or pencils, pens and paper

PLAN
- Read and discuss Amy Lowell's biography and poem.
- Sample guiding questions include:
  - Who is "He?"
  - How does Lowell make you feel about the wind?
  - Where does she use personification?
  - How do the objects touched by the wind feel about him?
  - What does he do to make them feel that way?
  - How many personalities does the wind possess?
  - What interesting verbs and adjectives does Lowell use?

DO
Getting Ready to Write
- Using imagination and experience, students brainstorm a list of things the wind effects.
- Enhance the list using personification as they answer the following questions:
  - What verbs would you use to express the way the wind speaks?
    For example: shouts, laughs, wails
  - What adjectives would you use to describe the wind's personality?
    For example: invigorating, energetic, powerful
  - How do the objects you're writing about interact with the wind?
    For example: trees wait to be tickled, the ocean waves its fingers

Writing the Poem
- Students write a poem about the wind referring to it by using the pronoun he or she.
- Suggest they begin their poem describing how the wind speaks or acts to an object and how the object interacts with the wind.
- Have them continue their poem repeating the previous direction with new objects.

Editing and Publishing
- Have students read and edit poems with partners.
- Students compose or publish their poems in a word processing program.
- Students illustrate their final masterpieces.
- Create a class book or publish to a web site.

Amy Lowell Biography
February 9, 1874 – May 12, 1925

Amy Lowell was born in Brookline, Massachusetts. She was the youngest of five children. Lowell was from one of the most prominent families in New England. An English governess began teaching her to read and write when she was five or six. She was sent to school at age eight. By then she had developed a strong love of reading and had even begun some writing.

Lowell was very heavy from the time she was eight years old. As an adult, at only five feet tall she weighed 240 pounds. Her obesity made her self-conscious; so self-conscious that she didn't like being in school. Lowell loved the theater and may have become an actress if it weren't for her weight. Between the ages of thirteen and fifteen, she wrote poetry. After that time, she stopped writing until she was twenty-eight and continued writing until her death.

She became the founder of Imagism, a form of poetry which aimed particularly at "image" or clear pictures of what the poet had in mind. Lowell's reading tours helped to make the new poetry a matter of national interest. At the height of her fame, people had to be turned away from the auditoriums and halls she used. Even people who did not admire her poetry acknowledged her power over a live audience. In her final years she achieved her greatest success as a public reader. From the time she began writing poetry, she felt that poetry had chosen her. After her death, a book containing some of Lowell's best and most mature poems was awarded the Pulitzer Prize.

The Wind
by Amy Lowell

He shouts in the sails of the ships at sea,
He steals the down from the honeybee,
He makes the forest trees rustle and sing,
He twirls my kite till it breaks its string.
Laughing, dancing, sunny wind,
Whistling, howling, rainy wind,
North, South, East and West,
Each is the wind I like the best.
He calls up the fog and hides the hills,
He whirls the wings of the great windmills,
The weathercocks love him and turn to discover
His whereabouts -- but he's gone, the rover!
Laughing, dancing, sunny wind,
Whistling, howling, rainy wind,
North, South, East and West,
Each is the wind I like the best.

The pine trees toss him their cones with glee,
The flowers bend low in courtesy,
Each wave flings up a shower of pearls,
The flag in front of the school unfurls.
Laughing, dancing, sunny wind,
Whistling, howling, rainy wind,
North, South, East and West,
Each is the wind I like the best.

September Monthly Holidays

All American Breakfast Month • American Newspaper Month
Baby Safety Month • Chicken Month • Classical Music Month
Fall Hat Month • Hunger Action Month • Library Card Sign-Up Month
Little League Month • National Blueberry Popsicle Month
National Piano Month • National Breakfast Month • National Courtesy Month • National Hispanic Heritage Month (September 15 to October 15)
National Honey Month • Self-Improvement Month

September Weekly Holidays

First Week of September
National Childhood Injury Prevention Week • National Waffle Week
Cherokee National Holiday

Second Week of September
International Priorities Week • National Line Dance Week
Navajo Nation Fair • National Suicide Prevention Week

Third Week of September
Constitution Week • National Adult Services Week
National Flower Week

Fourth Week of September
Banned Books Week • International Week of the Deaf • National Ballroom Dancing Week • National Keep Kids Creative Week

September Moveable Holidays

Labor Day	first Monday
National Grandparents' Day	first Sunday after Labor Day
International Day of Peace	third Tuesday
Native American Day	last Friday
Rosh Hashanah, Jewish New Year	varies

September Days for STEAM Makers and Poets

1. Emma M. Nutt Day
2. V-J Day
3. Search for Tomorrow Day
4. Birthday of Los Angeles
5. Be Late for Something Day
6. Pilgrims Set Sail on the Mayflower in 1620
7. Neither Rain nor Snow Day
8. National Grandparents Day
9. Teddy Bear Day
10. Coast-to-Coast Day
11. 911 Memorial Day
12. Space Race Begins
13. Fortune Cookie Day
14. Star Spangled Banner Day
15. Agatha Christie Day
16. Mexican Independence Day
17. Constitution Day
18. National Cheeseburger Day
19. International Talk Like a Pirate Day
20. Magellan Sails Around the World
21. First Woman Supreme Court Justice Confirmed in 1981
22. Elephant Appreciation Day
23. McGuffey's Eclectic Readers Birthday
24. Miss Piggy Day
25. National Ask a Question Day
26. Johnny Appleseed Day
27. Ancestor Appreciation Day
28. National Good Neighbor Day
29. ESP Day
30. Chewing Gum Day

Integrating September Math Days

Science Technology Engineering Arts Math

Day		Make and Do
4	Birthday of Los Angeles	Happy birthday to Los Angeles, founded on this day in 1781 by 44 settlers from Mexico. Los Angeles is now the largest city in California and the second largest city in the U.S. When was the city you live in founded? How many years ago was that? To celebrate create a "tour book" (travel guide) to your hometown. Check out travel guides for ideas to develop the format you would like to use. What will you include? What great experiences will you suggest? Create a mileage map to show distances between places you will visit. How many miles will you need to drive to go from place to place?
5	Be Late for Something Day	Everyone is late for something sometimes and today is the day we celebrate lateness. Even the White Rabbit was late for a very important date in Lewis Carroll's *Alice in Wonderland*. Create your perfect daily schedule and then repeat the same schedule as if you were ten minutes early and ten minutes late.
7	Neither Rain nor Snow Day	The New York Post Office opened on this day in 1914. The following inscription was inscribed on the building: "Neither snow nor rain not heat nor gloom of night, stays these couriers from the swift completion of their appointed rounds." Mail delivery has changed over the years. Use a food scale or a postage scale for this activity. Go online and get the current rates for mailing a letter. Find five items that you would like to send to a friend and determine the weight and the cost.

10	Coast-to-Coast Day	The first paved coast-to-coast road in the U.S. opened on this day in 1913. The Lincoln Highway is also known as Interstate 80 and U.S. Highway 30. Using Google Maps, plan a coast-to-coast trip. For a two-week trip, how many miles would you drive in a day? Where would you stop and what sites would you see? Assuming you are covering sixty miles per hour, how many hours will it take you to get to each stop?
12	Space Race Begins	The first spacecraft to land on the moon, the Soviet Union's *Luna 2*, is launched on this day in 1959. This jump-started the space race. Schools across the country responded with stronger science lessons and activities. Today we are reaching towards other galaxies as astronomers learn more about the universe. Create a timeline that highlight at least ten historic space explorations. Make a chart that shows the date, the duration of the flight and a few interesting facts.
13	Fortune Cookie Day	Today is Fortune Cookie Day. Learn about the mysterious origins of the fortune cookie and trace its roots to California in the early 1900s. Note that many fortunes today include randomly generated numbers. Have each student create a fortune on a slip of paper. Place the numbers 1 to 69 on pieces of paper in a bowl and have each student pull six numbers to go on their original fortune. As a class, draw numbers and determine the percentages of students that matched no numbers, one number, two numbers, etc. Expand your discussion to include why the numbers are stacked against you in a lottery.
17	Constitution Day	Constitution Day (also known as Citizenship Day) commemorates the day the U.S. Constitution was signed in 1787. A great way to celebrate is to practice the right to vote. Make a voting booth and a ballot box. Tech-savvy kids can create a ballot in Google Docs and your class can electronically vote for class officers or mimic local or national elections. Graph the results.

21	First Woman Supreme Court Justice	In 1981, Sandra Day O'Connor was confirmed by the Senate and became the first woman Supreme Court justice. Come up with a list of women who were the first to become accomplished in their field. For example, who was the first woman to become the first vice presidential candidate? What year? Who was the first woman to run for President of the United States from a major political party? Put your list in a spreadsheet and sort by date.
22	Elephant Appreciation Day	Elephants are amazing animals and although they don't eat peanuts, it's true that they never forget. Elephants are part of the pachyderm family. They have advanced brains and can use tools. They can break a stick in half and swat flies. Elephants have been ill-treated by man but the treatment of elephants is improving. Find ten important math facts that you could present to your class about elephants. Create a feature story for a news broadcast. Write your story and record your voice reading your story along with illustrations, video and audio clips.
25	National Ask a Question Day	This day honors the birthday of Barbara Walters, a famous television interviewer. In her career, she interviewed world leaders and celebrities and authored the book *How to Talk with Practically Anybody about Practically Anything*. Put on your interviewer hat. Make a list of ten number related questions you would like to ask a favorite celebrity, your school principal or the mayor of your city.
26	Johnny Appleseed Day	Folk hero John Chapman, nicknamed Johnny Appleseed, was born in Massachusetts in 1774. The story of Johnny Appleseed spreading apple seeds wherever he went is a myth. He was an eccentric man who was a pioneer nurseryman mostly in North Central Ohio. He planted hundreds of thousands of seeds in anticipation of settlers. He was a generous man and an early conservationist. Today, the top nine varieties of Apples are grown in Washington State. Whether your preference is Red Delicious, Gala, Fuji, or Granny Smith, apples make great STEM projects. Apples can be observed, measured, weighed and cut into fractions.

29	ESP Day	Joseph Rhine studied extrasensory perception and coined the term ESP. He was born in Juniata, Pennsylvania on this day in 1895. Rhine wrote about telepathy, the possible communication of thoughts and ideas in ways other than the five senses. Is telepathy a stunt or science? Try a telepathy game with a friend. You will need a bell and a deck of cards. Ask a friend to turn over a card from a deck of cards hidden from your view. Your friend will ring a bell and will send the image of card's suit (hearts, diamonds, spades or clubs) to your brain "telepathically". Each time the bell rings, write down the suit. Compare your notes with the order of the deck. How many did you get right? Keep a checklist of how many you got right in a 52-card deck? What percentage of cards did you correctly identify? Some believe if you agree on an emotion prior to the experiment your number correct improves. For example, when you turn over a heart, think about love; with spades send the feelings of dislike; with clubs send fear; with diamonds, send pleasure. Try the experiment again. What percentage of cards did you correctly identify when you sent them with emotion? Did your ESP improve?
30	Chewing Gum Day	Gum chewers honor William Wrigley, Jr. who was born on this day in 1862. People have used gum for over 5,000 years. In the 1890s William began selling his father's scouring soap and baking powder in Chicago. Wrigley offered two free packages of gum with each can of baking powder. The gum proved to be more popular than the baking powder. In 1893 he introduced Juicy Fruit Gum. The company continues today with a variety of products. Try some chewing gum experiments. Design an experiment to test which brand has the longest lasting flavor by having several students chew a piece of gum at an even pace. Combine and display the data. Chewing gum gets smaller as it is chewed. How would you design an experiment to determine the decomposition rate?

September Overview

Hispanic Heritage Month
Math Lesson: Making Salsa
Poetry Lesson: One Today by Richard Blanco
Hispanic Heritage Month is set aside to recognize the contributions of Hispanic Americans. Students use their taste buds and measuring skills to create their own salsa recipe that will be written, copied and distributed to classmates. Blanco's inaugural poem captures the oneness that exists in America and students write about their collective and individual American experience.
NCTM Process Standard – Problem Solving: Apply and adapt a variety of appropriate strategies to solve problems.

Let's Celebrate Fall
Math Lesson: Leaf Length Investigation
Poetry Lesson: In Autumn by Winifred Marshall Gales
Fall begins with the occurrence of the autumn equinox in late September. In the math lesson, students collect and measure at least one hundred leaves from the same tree. They measure, record and compute the average length. Using Winifred Marshall Gales' poem as a model, students write about autumn leaves using personification and imagination.
NCTM Standard 5: Data and Probability, Gr 3 – 5B-3, 5B-4; Gr 4 – 5A-2; Gr 5 – 5A-2, 5A-4

Skyscraper Day
Math Lesson: Math Empire State Building Run-Up Race
Poetry Lesson: Skyscraper by Rachel Lyman Field
Skyscraper Day is a day set aside to appreciate magnificent tall buildings. In celebration, every year runners compete in an annual race in which they run up the 1576 interior stairs of the Empire State Building. Students write word problems based on a table of race results from previous years. In her poem, Rachel Lyman Field wonders how skyscrapers think and feel. Students personify and explore how their own skyscraper feels and thinks.
NCTM STANDARD 2: Algebra, Gr 3 – 2C-2; Gr 4 – 2C-2; Gr 5 – 2C-2; Gr 6 –2B-3
NCTM STANDARD 5: Data Analysis, Statistics, and Probability, Gr 6 – 5A-1

Grandparents Day
Math Lesson: Leaf Symmetry Cards
Poetry Lesson: Butterfly Laughter by Katherine Mansfield
National Grandparents Day is a day to honor our grandparents and special grand friends. In the math lesson, students collect and study fall leaves to learn about their symmetry. To conclude the lesson, they make leaf-print greeting cards from the symmetrical leaves. In the poetry lesson, students recall something funny or wise that one of their grandparents said to them.
NCTM Process Standard – Problem Solving: Apply and adapt a variety of appropriate strategies to solve problems.

Hispanic Heritage Month
Math Lesson: Salsa Measure by Measure

In this activity students use their measuring skills and their taste buds to construct their own salsa recipes. Salsa originated with the Incas. The combination of tomatoes, chilies and other spices can be traced to the Mayans, Aztecs and Incas. The Spaniards conquered Mexico in 1519-1521 and encountered tomatoes. In 1571, Alonso de Molina called the combination of ingredients salsa. In 1916, Charles E. Erath of New Orleans began manufacturing an extract of Louisiana peppers and created the Red Hot Creole Peppersauce. A year later, Salsa Brava was manufactured and sold by Victoria Foods in Los Angeles. Others soon followed. Although salsa is often tomato-based, modern salsas use a variety of ingredients. In 2013, more salsa than ketchup was sold in America, making it the nation's number one condiment.

MATERIALS
(for use in both basic recipe and student recipes)
- Tomatoes
- Red onions
- Limes
- Cilantro
- Salt and pepper
- Red wine vinegar
- Olive oil
- Assortment of extra vegetables: corn, peppers, black beans, green olives, chives
- Extra spices: cumin, red pepper flakes, garlic
- Extra fruit including: pineapples, mangos, bananas, avocados

PLAN
Begin with a class demonstration and tasting of the basic salsa recipe.

Basic Salsa Recipe
Ingredients:
- 2 medium tomatoes chopped
- ½ red onion chopped
- Juice of 1 lime
- ½ cup chopped cilantro
- ¼ teaspoon each of salt and pepper
- 1 tablespoon red wine vinegar
- 1 tablespoon olive oil

Directions:
- Combine and mix all ingredients.
- To enhance flavors allow the salsa sit for a few minutes.
- Taste with chips.

DO

- In groups, students devise their own salsas with or without the basic recipe ingredients choosing from a variety of fruits, spices and vegetables.
- They select ingredients from available supplies and tinker by slowly adding extra ingredients using measuring cups and spoons.
- They taste and record ingredients and measurements as they go along.
- They use their written records to create a salsa recipe.
- The finished salsas are placed on a tasting table accompanied by a bowl of chips so all students have a chance to taste.
- Recipes can be copied and distributed to the class.
- Extend the lesson by creating a salsa company.
    - Name your salsa and create a logo for use on your jar of salsa.
    - Using a spreadsheet, determine the amount of ingredients you will need to create a case of 24 bottles of eight-ounce salsa.
    - How much of each ingredient will you need?
    - What is the cost?
    - How much is the cost of the bottle?
    - What will your sales price be?
    - Are you competitive with other salsas available in the supermarket?

Hispanic Heritage Month
Poetry Lesson: One Today

In his inaugural poem, *One Today*, you can feel Richard Blanco's connection to his Spanish roots when he recalls his mother saying "Buenos dias" each morning and recalling his father "cutting sugarcane." Blanco was invited to write and read his poem at President Obama's 2013 inauguration. He captures the oneness that exists in America as people wake to "one sun" and sleep under "one moon" and face the future with "hope."

MATERIALS
- Richard Blanco Biography and excerpt from his poem *One Today*
- Desktop publishing software

PLAN
- Read and discuss Richard Blanco's biography and poem.
- Encourage responses to the following questions:
  - How do you know that this poem is one day long?
  - What makes us all the same in this poem?
  - Why is this poem an appropriate poem for a presidential inauguration?
  - What does Blanco mean when he writes "a new constellation/waiting for us to map it/together?"

DO
Getting Ready to Write
Discuss the following questions with students. Write answers on the board and have students add interesting descriptions.
- What common things would be under the one sun? What would be under your particular one sun? *For example: my grandmother waking me with a smile*
- What sounds would you hear that are familiar to all people in our country from the quietest things to the nosiest things? *For example: the sound of a cat's meow, the laugh of a mother, a fire engine rushing through the streets*
- What would be under the one moon that is under everyone's one moon? *For example: the sky turning dark,* or *the stars to stare at*
- What would be under your one moon? *For example: My grandfather reading the newspaper*

Writing the Poem
Students follow the steps below to write their poems.
- Students title their poems "One Today" and begin the first line of their poems with "Under one sun." Continue the stanza describing what is commonly under the sun and what is particularly under their sun. Students include what they see and hear.
- Begin the second stanza with "Under one moon." Continue the stanza describing what is commonly under the moon and what is under their moon.

Editing and Publishing
- Students read and edit poems with partners.
- Students write their poems in a poetry book or enter them in a word processing program. Have students illustrate their final masterpiece.

Richard Blanco Biography
February 16, 1968 -

Richard Blanco, whose parents were exiles from Cuba, was born in Madrid, Spain. Shortly after his birth his family moved to Miami and then to New York City. They eventually relocated back to Miami because of the large Cuban population there.

From a young age, Blanco was a creative child. His parents felt the need for him to have a secure career and wanted him to become a doctor, lawyer or engineer. He excelled in math and became an engineer.

After graduating college, he worked as an engineer. But his strong desire to write and strong identification with his Cuban community led him to author poetry and books about his personal history. He returned to college and earned a master's degree in fine arts and creative writing. Soon after graduation, he wrote a book of poetry that was published. Blanco didn't give up engineering when he became a poet. He worked part-time as a teacher in several universities.

Blanco feels there is a similarity between poetry and engineering. Poetry connects him on a psychological level with his home and identity and engineering connects him on a physical level with his home and identity.

Blanco became a traveler desiring to understand how people's environments give them a sense of belonging and identity. His personal experiences of belonging that he formed in his Cuban community and knowledge that he attained during his travels were to become the subjects of his poetry.

Blanco was invited to write and read his public poem *One Today* at President Obama's 2013 inauguration. He was the fifth poet, the first Latino, the first immigrant and the youngest poet at the age of 44 to recite a poem at an inauguration. His poem symbolizes his own journey and the journey of all Americans, each with their own identity, forming our diverse country.

One Today
by Richard Blanco

Richard Blanco's poem is available online. Search or go to the following website and find the poem to use with your class.

http://www.poemhunter.com/poem/one-today/

In Richard Blanco's Inaugural poem, *One Today,* we see a panoramic view of our country in the course of a single day from sunrise to sunset and from one sun to one moon. The poem begins in the morning with "each one yawning to life." Under the "one sun" he symbolizes the oneness of America. We all see under this sun the "pencil-yellow school buses" in the traffic and the "fruit stands" on the street.

Blanco introduces us to his own life under this one sun as he describes his hard working mother ringing up "groceries as my mother did/for twenty years, so I could write this poem." The poem continues with the many sounds in our country from "honking cabs" and "the symphony of footsteps" to the sounds of the "unexpected song bird on your clothes line" and the "squeaky playground swings." He writes about the personal hello he grew up with "buenos días" and the other hellos "in every language spoken into one wind carrying our lives." The poem ends in the evening when the moon rises, we head home and face the future.

Under one sun I wake up to see it rising from the east
The beginning of a brand new day
Chattering to the morning breeze
Wondering what the new day will bring
Looking up to the sky and cloud formations
Gazing up and losing myself in identifying the shapes And curves of the white, puffy, circling air
by David – 5th grade

Let's Celebrate Fall
Math Lesson: Leaf Length Investigation

Working in pairs or small groups, students use their math skills to measure the lengths of leaves they gather from an individual tree or plant. They use the leaves to compute the average length of the leaves.

MATERIALS
- Inch ruler
- Leaves
- Leaf Measurement Chart

PLAN
Students collect at least 100 leaves as follows:
- Leaves can be collected school and/or brought to school.
- Leaves should have simple shapes and should not be broken.

DO
- Using an inch ruler, students measure each leaf from top to bottom
- Record the measurements on the Leaf Measurement Chart, one at a time.
- When all leaves have been measured, the sums of each column are computed.
- The columns are added and divided by the total number of leaves to calculate the average leaf length.

Noa – 5th grade

Leaf Measurement Chart

Write each measurement to the nearest inch in a separate square.

Compute the sums of each column and record here:

Add Across for the Total Sum = _____

Compute the Average, Total Sum/100 = _____

Let's Celebrate Fall
Poetry Lesson: In Autumn

Winifred Marshall Gales' poem, *In Autumn*, is the perfect poem for fall. Students tap their imaginations while writing about their own images of autumn leaves. Gale celebrates "all gold and red" autumn leaves as they spread their "fairy carpet" on the street. She describes the sounds of the leaves as they "rustle 'neath our feet."

MATERIALS
- Winifred Marshall Gales Biography and her poem *In Autumn*
- Word processing or desktop publishing software or pencils, pens and paper

PLAN
- Read and discuss Winifred Marshall Gales biography and poem.
- Ask the following questions:
  - What do the leaves do that are magical?
  - What do the leaves do that are ordinary?
  - Where does Winifred Marshall Gales use personification?

DO
Getting Ready to Write
Ask students the following questions. As they give their responses, encourage discussion. Write answers on the board.
- What is the first image that comes to your mind when you think of autumn leaves? Encourage personification, magical actions, similes, and metaphors.
  For example: *dancing from the trees, twirling through the air*
- What magical and/or imaginary things can you think of that the leaves do?
  For example: *a brown and orange carpet blanketing the ground, turn into butterflies*
- What sounds do the leaves make when you step on them?

Writing the Poem
Using *In Autumn* as a model, students write their own poems. Encourage line breaks so that the poem looks like a poem and not like a story.
- Students title their poems "In Autumn" or "Autumn Leaves" or something similar.
- Suggest they begin their poems by using the first image that comes to mind describing where the leaves are and what they are doing.
- Students continue writing about the leaves in autumn using descriptive language.
- Encourage personification and magical actions.

Editing and Publishing
- Students read and edit poems with partners.
- Students write their poems in a poetry book or enter in a word processing program.
- Have students illustrate their final masterpieces.

Winifred Marshall Gales Biography
January 10, 1761 - June 26, 1839

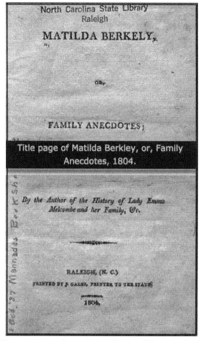
Title page of Matilda Berkley, or, Family Anecdotes, 1804.

Winifred Marshall Gales was born in England. She is well known as a novelist, memoirist, and poet. Her family was well educated. She was taught to read great works of literature. She wrote poems and stories at a very young age. At the age of seventeen she had a novel published.

Winifred married at the age of twenty-three. Her husband was a printer and published a newspaper. Both she and her husband wanted political reform in England. Through their newspaper they voiced the need for change, including better working conditions for adults and children. They wanted all men to have the right to vote, no matter their social class.

Because her husband's activities were against the ruling political system, he left England and went to Germany. After ten years of marriage, Winifred was left alone to take care of their children, their newspaper and their bookstore. Eventually she left England for Germany along with her children.

Later the family sailed across the Atlantic to live in Philadelphia and then on to North Carolina. It was there that she continued her life as a writer and wrote the book *Matilda Berkely*. She was the first resident of North Carolina to have a book published.

In North Carolina, she developed a reputation for generous hospitality and interesting conversation. An increasing population of people who did not believe in equal opportunities for all were moving to North Carolina. Winifred felt uncomfortable with people who held those views. She and her family packed up and moved to Washington, D.C. where she continued publishing her essays and poetry.

In Autumn
by Winifred Marshall Gales

They're coming down in showers,
The leaves all gold and red;
They're covering the little flowers,
And tucking them in bed
They've spread a fairy carpet
All up and down the street;
And when we skip along to school,
they rustle 'neath our feet.

Swirling through the air
Like a leaf shower
When the moon comes up
Leaves fall asleep
by Mateo – 4th grade

Skyscraper Day – September 3rd
Math Lesson: Empire State Building Run-Up Race

The Empire State Building, built in 1931, was the world's tallest building for over four decades. The building has a distinctive art deco style and National Historic Landmark status. Over 110 million people have visited the observation deck on the 86th floor. Every year since 1978, runners have competed in an annual race up 1576 interior stairs to the observation deck. Many of the invited participants complete the race to raise money for favorite charities. The race statistics for a selection of recent years appears on the Table of Winners Handout. The handout provides a wealth of information that groups of students will use to create word problems that demonstrate several mathematical functions.

MATERIALS
- Table of Winners Handout for each class member
- Board or Chart, markers, pencils and paper

PLAN
- Introduce skyscrapers. Discuss prior knowledge.
- Perhaps some students have visited the Empire State Building and can share experiences.
- Possibly share a few YouTube videos so students can visualize the building.
- Note that everyone can reach the observation deck on the 86th floor by elevator. However, the only time anyone is allowed to climb the 1576 stairs to the 86th floor is during the yearly Empire State Building Run-Up Race.
- Distribute the Table of Winners Handout to the class.
- Point out that some names are starred indicating when the race did not include all 86 floors. From 1991-1994, the top floors were closed for remodeling and the race ended on the 80th floor. In 2014, a snowstorm prevented the race from concluding on the observation deck.
- Begin by writing a few word problems on the board and have students use the handout to solve them. Some sample questions include:
    - The first man to win the race in 1978 was Gary Muhrke. The man to win the race in 2015 was Christian Riedl. What is the difference between their winning times?
    - What is the total sum of minutes run by Paul Crake?
    - How many times did someone complete the run in less than 10 minutes?

DO
- Divide the class into groups and have them use the Table of Winners Handout to write at least six word problems about the race. Encourage groups to create problems and solutions containing a variety of math functions.
- Have groups exchange problems with another group to solve and check their work.

Table of Winners Handout

Here is a partial table displaying information about the winners of the Empire State Run-Up Race. The complete list of winners can be found at: https://towerrunning.com/empire-state-building-run-up-all-winners.html

MEN	TIME	YEAR	WOMEN	TIME
Darren Wilson	10:36	2016	Suzy Walsham	12:19
Christian Riedl	10:16	2015	Suzy Walsham	12:30
Thorbjörn Ludvigsen**	10:06	2014	Suzy Walsham**	11:57
Mark Bourne	10:12	2013	Suzy Walsham	12:05
Thomas Dold	10:28	2012	Melissa Moon	12:39
Thomas Dold	10:10	2011	Alice McNamara	13:03
Thomas Dold	10:16	2010	Melissa Moon	13:13
Thomas Dold	10:07	2009	Suzy Walsham	13:27
Thomas Dold	10:08	2008	Suzy Walsham	12:44
Thomas Dold	10:25	2007	Suzy Walsham	13:12
Thomas Dold	10:19	2006	Andrea Mayr	11:23
Rudolf Reitberger	10:24	2005	Andrea Mayr	11:51
Rudolf Reitberger	10:37	2004	Andrea Mayr	12:08
Paul Crake	9:33	2003	Cindy Moll	13:06
Paul Crake	9:40	2002	Kerstin Harbich	12:46
Paul Crake	9:37	2001	Cindy Moll	12:45
Paul Crake	9:53	2000	Cindy Moll	12:51
Paul Crake	10:15	1999	Angela Sheean	13:23
Terry Purcell	10:49	1998	Cindy Moll	14:17
Kurt König	10:22	1997	Belinda Soszyn	12:32
Kurt König	10:44	1996	Belinda Soszyn	12:19
Kurt König	10:39	1995	Michelle Blessing	13:03
Darrin Eisman*	09:37	1994	Belinda Soszyn*	11:36
Geoff Case*	10:18	1993	Sue Case*	12:42
Geoff Case*	09:33	1992	J'ne Day-Lucore*	12:00
Geoff Case*	10:13	1991	Corliss Spencer*	11:32
Scott Elliot	10:47	1990	Suzanne Malaxos	12:27
Robin Rishworth	11:09	1989	Suzanne Malaxos	12:25
Craig Logan	11:29	1988	Janine Aiello	13:43

*   From 1991 to 1994 the race ended at the 80th floor due to construction
** Because of weather the race finished indoor at the 86th floor in 2014

Skyscraper Day
Poetry Lesson: Skyscrapers

Rachel Lyman Field's poem *Skyscrapers* is the perfect poem for National Skyscraper Day celebrated each year on the third of September. Field wonders how skyscrapers think and feel. She gives skyscrapers human qualities through her use of personification. As students write their poems, they personify and explore their own skyscraper's feelings and thoughts.

MATERIALS
- Rachel Lyman Field Biography and her poem *Skyscrapers*
- Word processing or desktop publishing software or pencil, pens and paper

PLAN
- Read and discuss Rachel Lyman Field's biography and poem.
- Discuss the poem with the following questions.
    - Discuss personification. Where does Field use personification?
    - How does she think the skyscrapers might feel?
    - What is the most interesting line of the poem and why?

DO
Getting Ready to Write
- During a brainstorming session, encourage students to think of words that describe what skyscrapers look like. *For example: magnificent, powerful, towering*
- Encourage students to use words that describe how skyscrapers feel. *For example: lonely, tired, scared, shy, humble*
- Students imagine themselves as skyscrapers as they explore the following questions. Encourage interesting language and the use of personification.
    - How do you feel as a skyscraper and why?
    - Where are you and what are you doing?
    - How do you feel about the clouds surrounding you?
    - How do you feel about the wind?
    - What do you see as you look around?
    - What do you think of the people making noise inside of you?
    - How do you feel on the weekends or in the evening when all is quiet?

Writing the Poem
Students write a poem in which they become a skyscraper using the personal pronouns like I, me or mine as they write. Encourage line breaks so that the poem looks like a poem and not like a story. Have students:
- Title their poems "Skyscraper."
- Begin their poems with where they are. For example: *Up high my head beyond the clouds*
- Continue writing the poem telling how you feel, what you see and what you are thinking.

Editing and Publishing
- Students read and edit poems with partners.
- Students draw a picture of a tall and thin skyscraper in the margins of their poem.

Rachel Lyman Field Biography
September 19, 1894 - March 15, 1942

Rachel Lyman Field was born in New York City but spent much of her childhood in Massachusetts. She didn't have many friends and spent time alone outdoors often in below zero weather. In the spring and summer, she observed animals and flowers and learned how they lived and grew. In school she was, in academic subjects, below her grade level not learning to read until the age of 10. But surprisingly, Rachel knew how to write. She excelled in acting, memorizing poems and writing.

Although she never did well in academic life, she did graduate from high school and was accepted to Radcliffe College because of her talents in the arts. It was not until college that Rachel began studying. She wrote children's plays. These plays were produced, published and distributed to schools all over the country.

Lyman illustrated twelve of her own books creating black and white cut outs as design elements on the pages. She also illustrated books by other authors. She won a Newbery Award and a National Book Award. Her most famous poem, *Something Told the Wild Geese,* was made into a song. She also wrote the English lyrics to *Maria*, which was used in Disney's film, *Fantasia*. Her poetry, written primarily for children, is enjoyed by adults as well. Field offers a deep and close observation of objects and nature as she observes and writes about her subjects with a unique perspective.

Skyscrapers
by Rachel Lyman Field

Do skyscrapers ever grow tired
Of holding themselves up high?
Do they ever shiver on frosty nights
With their tops against the sky?
Do they feel lonely sometimes
Because they have grown so tall?
Do they ever wish they could lie right down
And never get up at all?

Sometimes I just want to be alone
No clouds bumping into me
Watching things go by
I am a skyscraper in the sky
Watching things go by
by Lola – 4th grade

Grandparents Day – First Sunday after Labor Day
Math Lesson: Leaf Symmetry Cards

Math and art come together for Grandparents Day. Students collect a variety of fall leaves and discover which are the most symmetrical. They select their most interesting leaves to use in the creation of a painted leaf greeting card inscribed with a special message.

MATERIALS
- Variety of freshly gathered leaves
- Water-based paints in autumn colors like red, orange, etc.
- Paper plates, paint brushes, pencils, paper to cover work area
- 3" x 5" art paper in beige or other light fall colors
- 5" x 7" folded greeting card paper and envelopes

PLAN
- Take your class on a leaf-gathering walk around the neighborhood.
- When you return, select a symmetrical leaf to use during a class discussion about symmetry. Do the following:
  - Have a volunteer come up and fold the leaf to verify that the two sides match or are identical. If they are identical, the leaf has symmetry. If they are not identical, have a volunteer select another leaf from those gathered.
  - Open the symmetrical leaf. Define the fold line (line of reflection, mirror image), congruent sides and symmetrical shape. We call the sides congruent and define the shape as symmetrical.

DO
- Divide the class into small groups of five or six.
- Distribute a collection of leaves to each group.
- Have each group try the folding method above as well as the following method to find their most symmetrical leaves. Some students may wish to devise their own method.
  - Place the leaf on a piece of paper.
  - Trace around the leaf with a pencil. Flip the leaf and place it on the pencil outline. The more the flipped leaf and pencil outline match, the more symmetrical the leaf is.
  - Share your most symmetrical leaves with the class.
- Have each student pick a symmetrical leaf that has an interesting shape and lots of veins and follow the directions below:
  - Place paints, brushes and water on covered tables.
  - Put different colors of paint on a paper plate and use it as a palette.
  - Turn the selected leaf with its under-side facing up and paint its entire surface with a selection of the colors.
  - Blot the leaf on a paper towel or newsprint paper.
  - Press the leaf on the 3" x 5" art paper and remove to reveal a beautiful leaf print.
  - Repeat the process if a second print is desired. Let the leaf prints dry.
  - Glue the print onto a folded blank 5" x 7" greeting card.
  - Write a poem or a message on the inside of the card.

Grandparents Day
Poetry Lesson: Butterfly Laughter

In her poem, *Butterfly Laughter,* Katherine Mansfield recalls mornings with her grandmother and the memory of the bowls of porridge that had a "blue butterfly painted." Since the porridge covered the butterfly, it could only be seen when the porridge had been eaten. She recalls how her grandmother made her laugh when she would say: "Don't eat the butterfly." In this lesson, children recall something funny or wise that one of their grandparents said to them. What a perfect poem to honor a grandparent on Grandparents Day.

MATERIALS
- Katherine Mansfield Biography and her poem *Butterfly Laughter*
- Word processing or desktop publishing software or pencil, pens and paper

PLAN
- Read and discuss Katherine Mansfield's biography and poem.
- Discuss the poem with the following questions:
  - What meal do you think the children were eating?
  - What did the children need to do to reach the butterfly?
  - What made the children laugh and why?
  - Where does Mansfield use imagination in her poem?
  - How does the format of the poem make us know this is a poem?

DO
Getting Ready to Write
- During a brainstorming session, ask students the following questions:
  - What grandparent do they want to write about?
  - What funny or wise statement do they remember hearing from their grandparent? Where did this take place? What were they doing?
  - Draw a picture of the scene.
  - What details of the scene (including what they were doing) come into their mind when they recall what their grandparent said?
    For example: Walking on the cold dark street in New York

Writing the Poem
Students use a poetic format as they follow the steps below to write their poems.
They may want to title their poem "Remembering (Grandma or Grandpa)"
- Using their picture for inspiration, students write their poem with details and images they remember.
- Students include what was said by their grandparent.
- Students may wish to include what they recall thinking or doing at the time.

Editing and Publishing
- Students read and edit poems with partners.
- Students write their poem and draw a picture along with it on colored paper and present it to their grandparent on Grandparents Day.

Katherine Mansfield Biography
October 14, 1888 – January 9, 1923

Katherine Mansfield, most popular for her short stories, was born in Thornton, New Zealand into a prosperous family. Her father was a banker and her mother was from a prominent family. She had three sisters and a brother. When Katherine was five, she moved from her birthplace in Thornton to a village, Karori, New Zealand that she would always remember as the happiest time in her young life.

Katherine loved to write and had her first work published at the age of ten in her school newspaper. Even at this young age, her teachers recognized her rich imagination. She was also an accomplished cellist and dreamed of having a musical career, but her father would not allow this.

When she was fifteen, Katherine moved to London with her sisters where they all attended college. There she began writing for the school newspaper where she published five stories and became its editor.

After graduating, she returned to New Zealand with her sisters but was very unhappy there. Her desire was to live in London, being bored with the people and the environment of New Zealand. She moved back to London and spent most of her time writing.

Katherine was an unusual woman for the Edwardian period in which she lived. She was a free spirit much different from most of the women of her time. Her hairstyle was cut plainly like a Japanese doll unlike the pompadour, a very fancy style popular at that time.

In London she befriended some of the most well-known writers that respected and admired her talent. Some were also jealous of her. Katherine was married twice. Although her first marriage was very short, her second marriage was longer and successful.

Katherine Mansfield's life was the subject of a BBC miniseries, *A Picture of Katherine Mansfield* starring Vanessa Redgrave. New Zealand has honored her by naming high schools after her, as well as a park.

Butterfly Laughter
by Katherine Mansfield

In the middle of our porridge plates
There was a blue butterfly painted
And each morning we tried who should reach the butterfly first.
Then the Grandmother said: "Do not eat the poor butterfly."
That made us laugh.
Always she said it and always it started us laughing.
It seemed such a sweet little joke.
I was certain that one fine morning
The butterfly would fly out of our plates,
Laughing the teeniest laugh in the world,
And perch on the Grandmother's lap.

My grandma said
Don't be afraid of darkness
It's afraid of you.
by Vasilia – 4th grade

October Monthly Holidays

Adopt-a-Shelter Dog Month • American Magazine Month • Computer Learning Month • Consumer Information Month • Cookbook Month County Music Month • Crime Prevention Month • Dessert Month Energy Awareness Month • Family History Awareness Month • Fire Prevention Month • Mental Illness Awareness Month • National Bullying Prevention Month • National Clock Month • National Dollhouse and Miniature Month • National Roller Skating Month • National Stamp Collecting Month • National UNICEF Month • National Youth Against Tobacco Month • Pasta Month • Pizza Month • Popcorn Poppin' Month Spinach Lovers Month • Vegetarian Awareness Month

October Weekly Holidays

First Week of October
Albuquerque International Balloon Fiesta • Animal Welfare Week • Get Organized Week • Great Books Week • Kid's Goal Setting Week • Mental Illness Awareness Week Metric Week • National Carry a Tune Week National Chili Week • National Customer Service Week • National Hispanic Heritage Weeks (September 15 – October 15) • National Newspaper Week • National Walk Your Dog Week • No Salt Week Space Week

Second Week of October
Firefighters and Fire Prevention Week • National Chestnut Week • National Hispanic Heritage Weeks (September 15 – October 15) • National School Lunch Week • Pet Peeve Week • Teen Read Week • World Rainforest Week

Third Week of October
Character Counts Week • Free Speech Week • Getting the World to Beat a Path to Your Door Week • Make Your Mark Week • National Bulk Foods Week • National Chemistry Week • National Friends of Libraries Week National Health Education Week • National Kraut Sandwich Week National School Bus Safety Week • National Nuclear Science Week National Teen Driver Safety Week • National Wolf Awareness Week Pharmacy Week • Pickled Peppers Week • Safe Schools Week Save for Retirement Week

Fourth Week of October
Chicken Soup for the Soul Week • National Magic Week • National Red Ribbon Week • National Respiratory Care Week • World Population Awareness Week

October Moveable Holidays

World Habitat Day	first Monday
National Kale Day	first Wednesday
Walk to School Day	first Wednesday
Manufacturing Day	first Friday
Frugal Fun Day	first Saturday
Columbus Day Holiday	second Monday
Native American Day	second Monday
International Top Spinning Day	second Wednesday
Stop Bullying Day	second Wednesday
World Egg Day	second Friday
National Clean Your Virtual Desktop Day	third Monday
Take Your Parents to Lunch Day	third Wednesday
Sweetest Day	third Saturday
Make a Difference Day	fourth Saturday
Mother-in-Law Day	fourth Sunday

October Days for STEAM Makers and Poets

1 Model T Day
2 Charlie Brown and Snoopy Day
3 Emily Post Day
4 Sputnik Day
5 First Televised Presidential Address
6 The Jazz Singer Day
7 America's First Railroad Day
8 The Great Chicago Fire Day
9 Leif Ericson Day
10 The Pledge of Allegiance Day
11 Eleanor Roosevelt Day
12 Columbus Day
13 White House Day
14 e.e.cummings' Birthday
15 Global Handwashing Day
16 Dictionary Day
17 Black Poetry Day
18 Alaska Becomes a U.S. Territory Day
19 Lightning is Electricity Day
20 The 49th Parallel Day
21 The Light Bulb Day
22 First Wireless Message Day
23 TV Talk Show Host Day
24 United Nations Day
25 First U.S. Postcard Postmarked in 1870
26 National Pumpkin Day
27 Disneyland TV Show Premiered
28 Cotton Gin Day
29 Fanny Brice's Birthday
30 Bodybuilder's Day
31 National Magic Day

Integrating October Math Days

Science　　Technology　　Engineering　　Arts　　Math

Day		Make and Do
4	Sputnik Day	The Space Age began when the U.S.S.R. launched Sputnik, the first satellite on this day in 1957. Movies and television in the 1950s were full of space stories. It came as a big surprise that the Soviet Union launched the first satellite. The U.S. soon followed. Sputnik led directly to the creation of NASA and inspired a generation of engineers and scientists. For Sputnik Day, learn the order of the planets from the sun and calculate how much you would weigh on each planet. Start your research by visiting nineplanets.org. For planet lovers, find out why Pluto no longer qualifies as a planet.
7	America's First Railroad Day	The first railroad in the United States was completed on this day in 1826. Today, Amtrak carries over 31 million passengers a year. Learn how to read a train schedule. Go to Amtrak on-line and download a timetable at http://www.amtrak.com/train-schedules-timetables. For example, the Capitol Limited travels from Washington, D.C. to Chicago. Create ten quiz questions and answers using the schedule. For example, how many hours does it take to go from Washington, D.C. to Cleveland, Ohio? How many miles did you travel?

9	Leif Ericson Day	Viking explorer Leif Ericson landed in America on this day in 1000 A.D. He was the first of many explorers to visit the New World. Make an explorer spreadsheet with at least five explorers. You can use Excel, Google Sheets or Numbers. Include their names, the dates of their birth and death, the country they explored for, what they found, and one interesting fact about each explorer. What will your column headings be? Learn how to sort your chart in your spreadsheet program.
12	Columbus Day	Columbus set sail across the Atlantic with three small ships, the Santa Maria, the Pinta and the Niña. On this day in 1492, he went ashore in the Bahamas, claiming the land for Isabella and Ferdinand of Spain. He believed he had reached East Asia but he did not. An historically correct model of the Niña, Columbus' favorite ship, was built. Since 1991 the ship has become a sailing museum that continuously travels to ports for visitors to learn more about the history of Columbus and his ships. Find a map of the ports that the Niña will visit this year. Are any of the ports near where you live? Calculate your distance to the port using this website: www.thenina.com/the_original_nina.html.

16	Dictionary Day	Today is the birthday of Noah Webster, born in 1758. He was one of our nation's founding fathers. He was a lexicographer (one who writes, compiles and edits dictionaries) and today his name is synonymous with the word dictionary. Divide class into pairs and have a STEM dictionary challenge. Find three new words that are part of the language of Science, Technology, Engineering and Math. For example: a branch of science like astrophysics; technology buzzwords like blog; engineering words like bionics; and math words like trigonometry. Score 5 points for each unique word that you and your partner come up with and 3 points for each word that matches another team's words. How many points did you earn?
26	National Pumpkin Day	Pumpkins are native to North America and are part of the squash family. One and a half billion pounds of pumpkins are produced in the United States each year. For a great pumpkin math lesson, estimate the weight of several pumpkins. Think of a clever way to weigh a pumpkin. For example, try weighing yourself with and without a pumpkin to determine the weight of the pumpkin. Find out how much pumpkins cost per pound in your local newspaper market ads and create math word problems for your classmates to solve.

October Overview

Apple Month
Math Lesson: Apple Pie Graph
Poetry Lesson: The Old Apple-Tree by Paul Laurence Dunbar
October is known as Apple Month. In the math lesson your students create pie graphs displaying the frequency of weekly apple consumption. In the poetry lesson, students write poems filled with memories sparked by their experiences with apples.
NCTM STANDARD 5: Data Analysis and Probability, Gr 3 – 5A-2, 5A-3, 5A-4, Gr 4 – 5A-2, 5A-3, 5A-4; Gr 5 – 5A-3, 5A-4, 5A-5; Gr 6 –5A-5, 5A-6

United Nations Day
Math Lesson: Time Zones
Poetry Lesson: I Dream a World by Langston Hughes
We celebrate the founding of the United Nations with a week of activities. United Nations Day was established on October 24, 1948. Students use a map and atlas with time zones to create math problems related to timely activities around the world. In the poetry lesson students write their dreams of a united world.
NCTM STANDARD 4: Measurement, Gr 4 – 4B-11; Gr 5 – 4B-1; Gr 6 – 4B-14
NCTM STANDARD 1: Numbers and Operations, Gr 5 – 1C-9, 1C-10; Gr – 6 1A-4, 1A-5

Statue of Liberty Dedication Day
Math Lesson: Monumental Math
Poetry Lesson: The New Colossus by Emma Lazarus
The Statue of Liberty was a gift from the people of France to the people of the United States and was dedicated on October 28, 1886. To the immigrants who saw her as they came to America, she represented the promise of freedom and a good life. In the math lesson students use statue facts and measurements to create and compute math word problems. In the poetry lesson, students personify the Statue and write their thoughts and experiences.
NCTM STANDARD 4: Measurement, Gr 4 – 4B-11; Gr 5 – 4B-1; Gr 6 – 4B-14
NCTM STANDARD 1: Numbers and Operations, Gr 5 – 1C-9, 1C-10; Gr – 6 1A-4, 1A-5

Halloween
Math Lesson: Comparing Pumpkins
Poetry Lesson: Excerpt from The Raven by Edgar Allen Poe
Children enjoy dressing up in costumes, trick-or-treating and carving pumpkins. Students make predictions, analyze data, determine relationships and draw conclusions as they weight and measure pumpkins of different sizes and shapes. In the poetry lesson, students recall frightening nighttime sounds and create poems in the style of *The Raven*.
NCTM STANDARD 4: Measurement, Gr 3 – 4A-7; Gr 4 – 4A-6, 4A-7, 4B-6, 4B-8; Gr 5 – 4A-1, 4A-3; Gr 6 – 4A-1, 4A – 3

Apple Month
Math Lesson: Apple Pie Graph

Students work in groups demonstrating their knowledge of fractions and percentages. They create pie graphs that show the frequency of weekly apple eating by the members in the group. Students complete the information on the Apple Pie Graph Worksheet.

MATERIALS
- Apple Pie Worksheet
- Board or chart
- Marker

PLAN
- Tell students in honor of Apple Month they will be working with fractions and percentages to create pie graphs about their apple preferences eating habits.
- Demonstrate the creation of a circle graph. Write the following list on the board or chart:
  - Red
  - Yellow
  - Neither
- Have students vote on whether they prefer red apples, yellow apples or neither and write the responses.
- Tally the votes.
- Write total as a fraction demonstrating that the numerators are the number of votes for each and the denominators are the total votes.
- Divide the numerators by the denominators to find the percentage each represents.
- Draw a circle on the board and discuss how to show the results on a pie graph.

DO
- Distribute the Apple Pie Graph Worksheet.
- Tell the class they are going to create pie graphs to show the number of days class members eat apples.
- Conduct a class vote and record the student responses.
- Have students complete the worksheet to produce the pie charts.
- Encourage students to think of other ways to represent the data such as bar graphs and pictographs.

Apple Pie Graph Worksheet

How Many Days a Week Do We Eat Apples?

Number of Days	Number of Votes	Number of Votes in Fractions	Number of Votes in Percentages
Never			
1 time a week			
2 times a week			
3 or 4 times a week			
5 or 6 times a week			
Everyday			
Totals			

Directions for completing the chart:

Number of Votes
Calculate the total number of votes by adding them together and finding the sum. Add to the chart above.

Number of Votes in Fractions
From the votes in each category, write a fraction in the above chart. The numerator is the number of votes in each category and the denominator is the total number of votes. For example, in a group of five, if two group members ate apples once a week, the fraction would be 2/5. Record the fractions in the chart above.

Number of Votes in Percentages
Divide the denominator into the numerator of each fraction to determine the percentage each contributed towards the total number of votes. Record the percentages in the chart above.

Using the data, create a pie graph and key.

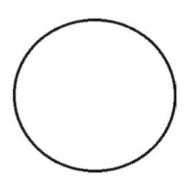

Apple Month
Poetry Lesson: The Old Apple-Tree

In his poem, *The Old Apple-Tree*, Paul Laurence Dunbar introduces us to his apple tree and to the wonderful memories attached to it when: "Once again I seem to see-- The verdant leaves an' branches/Of an old apple-tree." In this poetry lesson, students write poems filled with memories sparked by their experiences with apples.

MATERIALS
- Paul Laurence Dunbar Biography and excerpt from his poem *The Old Apple-Tree*
- Word processing or desktop publishing software or pencils, pens and paper

PLAN
- Read and discuss Paul Laurence Dunbar's biography with the class. Explain to students that Dunbar uses dialect in the poem. Discuss the meaning of dialect (a specific form of language particular to a region or social group).
- Tell students they are going to read a famous poem that Dunbar wrote. This poem describes an apple tree and the memories attached.
- Begin discussing the poem by asking students to share what they liked and disliked.
- Continue the discussion by asking the following questions:
  - Where does Dunbar use dialect?
  - Why, if this tree is considered "ugly" to some people, is it precious to him?
  - What words does Dunbar use to describe how the tree looked then and now?

DO
Getting Ready to Write
There are so many memories related to apples. Ask students what memories they have of apples, applesauce, apple pie, or any other food that has apples in it. Ask them if they ever had an apple related experience. Share some of your own experiences.

Writing the Poem
Students close their eyes and take a few moments to recall their memories of their apple experience and where it took place. After their memory meditation, students write their poems. Encourage line breaks so that the poem looks like a poem and not like a story.
- Students can title their poem the name of the apple product that holds the memory.
- Students begin their poems with "There's a memory keeps running in my head today."
- Begin the second line with where they were when they had their apple memory, using a verb that ends in *ing*. For example: *Sitting in the kitchen*
- Students continue writing about their memories using descriptive language.

Editing and Publishing
- Students read and edit poems with partners.
- Students draw an illustration of their memory.
- They present their poems by including them in a class book shaped like an apple or on an apple bulletin board.

Paul Laurence Dunbar Biography
June 27, 1872 - February 9, 1906

Paul Laurence Dunbar was born in Dayton, Ohio. Both his mother and father had been slaves. His mother was a freed slave. His father escaped from slavery and served as a soldier in the Civil War. Although his family was poor, his mother provided him with a rich education filled with her love of storytelling and songs. She even learned to read to help him with his schooling. Paul was six years old when he started school. He was already reading and writing poetry. He was a very successful student. In high school, he was part of the debate team, president of the literary society and editor of the school paper.

Dunbar was one of the first African-American poet to achieve fame as a writer. In much of his poems, short stories and novels, he wrote about the problems that faced his race. He was versatile and wrote not only in Standard English but also in dialect. Dunbar's work is known for its colorful language and conversational tone.

After his first book of poetry was published, both writers and critics saw his great talent. His popularity grew. When his second book of poetry was published, he was asked to do a reading in London. At the age of twenty-five, he had achieved fame both nationally and internationally. President Theodore Roosevelt honored him with a ceremonial sword.

Dunbar died at the age of thirty-three from tuberculosis. He produced internationally respected and renowned work and will never be forgotten. In 1975, a 10-cent postage stamp was issued in his honor.

Excerpt from The Old Apple-Tree
by Paul Laurence Dunbar

There's a memory keeps a-runnin'
Through my weary head to-night,
An' I see a picture dancin'
In the fire-flames' ruddy light;
'Tis the picture of an orchard
Wrapped in autumn's purple haze,
With the tender light about it
That I loved in other days.
An' a-standin' in a corner
Once again I seem to see
The verdant leaves an' branches
Of an old apple-tree.
You perhaps would call it ugly,
An' I don't know but it's so,
When you look the tree all over
Unadorned by memory's glow;
For its boughs are gnarled an' crooked,
An' its leaves are gettin' thin,
An' the apples of its bearin'
Would n't fill so large a bin
As they used to. But I tell you,
When it comes to pleasin' me,
It's the dearest in the orchard,—
Is that old apple-tree.

Laying in a field of apple blossoms
Memories of my mother appear in front of me
Laughing and singing together
by Maggie – 3rd grade

United Nations Day
Math Lesson: Time Zones

In this activity students work in pairs or groups and use a map or an atlas with time zones to design math problems related to timely activities around the world. After discussing the Security Council of the United Nations and its five permanent member countries, students work in groups to write math problems related to the time zones in cities of the five countries.

MATERIALS
- Atlases with time zones
- Pencils, paper

PLAN
- Discuss the following information about the Security Council of the United Nations.
    - The council has primary responsibility for maintaining the peace around the world.
    - The council has five permanent member countries: United States, Russian Federation, China, United Kingdom and France.
    - The council has ten temporary members representing all areas of the world who are elected for two-year terms.
    - A representative of each of its member countries must be present at all times at the United Nations Headquarters in New York City so that the Security Council is always available to meet when the need arises.
- Discuss time zones.
    - Tell students they will be working in groups to write math problems related to everyday activities in the time zones of different cities located in the five countries that are permanent members of the Security Council.
    - Students use an atlas with time zones to gather the information they need.
    - Examples of problems include:
        - When it is noon in Moscow, what time is it in Shanghai?
        - When people are having breakfast in Paris, what might the people in California be doing?
        - What is a good time to have a video conference call to a relative who lives in Liverpool, England, if you live in New York and want to reach your relative in the late afternoon?

DO
- Divide the class into small groups.
- Distribute an atlas with time zones to each group.
- Have groups create time zone problems along with an answer key.
- Have groups exchange problem sets and solve each other's time zone problems.

United Nations Day
Poetry Lesson: I Dream a World

What better way to sum up the ideals for which the United Nations was founded than with the poem *I Dream a World* by Langston Hughes? Hughes writes about a world "where love will bless the earth and peace its paths adorn." Throughout his poem, he expresses his dreams of harmony, equality and freedom: "I dream a world where all/Will know sweet freedom's way." In this lesson, students write their dreams of a united world filled with peace.

MATERIALS
- Langston Hughes Biography and his poem *I Dream a World*
- Word processing or desktop publishing software or pencils, pens, and paper

PLAN
- Read and discuss Langston Hughes's biography and poem.
- Discuss the poem with the following questions:
  - What kind of world does Hughes dream about?
  - In this kind of world is war possible? Why or why not?
  - Where does he use a simile?
  - Where does Hughes use personification?
  - How does the last line of the poem add to its power?

DO
Getting Ready to Write
Ask students to describe a united world where there is peace, love and freedom. Record their responses on the board.

For example: *where all guns are thrown away, where flags of all nations wave side by side*

Writing the Poem
- Ask students to title their poem *I Dream a World*.
- Students begin by repeating the title.
- Continue poem with descriptions of their perfect united world using line breaks after each description.
- Students may end their poem with "Of such I dream, my world."

Editing and Publishing
- Students read a stanza of their poem to the class.
- Students write their poems in a poetry book or enter them in a word processing program.
- Students illustrate their final masterpiece.
- Extend the lesson by putting together some of the best lines from each poem to create a class anthology.

Langston Hughes Biography
February 1, 1902 – May 22, 1967

Langston Hughes was raised by his grandmother. He began writing poetry in grammar school. He was elected class poet and from that moment he knew that was what he wanted to do. He achieved recognition as an African American poet.

When growing up, he encountered prejudice because he was Black. His grandmother always had confidence in his ability to succeed and he did. From the time he was very young, she recounted stories about hard-working slaves and the heroes who set them free.

His grandmother encouraged Langston to always hold on to his dreams. Although the life of a slave was difficult, many were able to hold onto their dreams despite their life circumstances.

After his grandmother died, Hughes went to live with his mother and his stepfather who was from a very politically active family. Langston became involved in politics and continued to be a social activist throughout his life. He toured the Southern and Southwestern United States, doing readings at universities. Hughes continually called for an end to racism and segregation in America. He didn't feel that Blacks should be second class Americans. He never allowed himself to be in that position and did not believe that anyone of any race should be.

Hughes encouraged Black children to have pride in themselves. His poetry encouraged children to hold on to their dreams. He knew the emptiness of a life without dreams.

I Dream a World
by Langston Hughes

The poem is available online. Search or go to the following website and find the poem. It is ready to print and copy.

http://allpoetry.com/I-Dream-A-World

Langston Hughes in his poem *I Dream A World* describes a united perfect world where peace exists and all: "Will know sweet freedom's way" and "Whatever race you be/Will share the bounties of the earth." The last line of the poem reinforces his desire for peace: "Of such I dream, my world!"

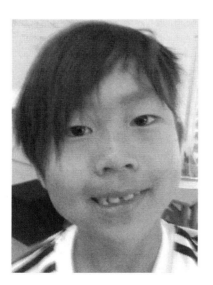

I dream a world where no man fights
And freedom comes to all man
by Casey – 3rd grade

Statue of Liberty Dedication Day
Math Lesson: Monumental Math

The Statue of Liberty was a gift from the people of France to the people of the United States in 1886. To the immigrants who first saw her when they entered the United States for the first time, she represented the promise of freedom and a good life. In this math lesson, students use the facts and measurements on the Monumental Math Worksheet to first answer sample questions as a class group and then work in small groups to create math word problems.

MATERIALS
- Monumental Math Worksheet
- Poster-size picture of the Statue of Liberty
- Pencils, paper

PLAN
- During a class discussion students tell what they know about the Statue of Liberty.
- Encourage students who have visited the Statue and Ellis Island to share their experience.
- Display a poster-size picture of the Statue of Liberty.
- Distribute the Monument Math Worksheet.
- Discuss the facts and measurements on the table.
- Have the class refer to the facts and measurements on the worksheet to answer the questions at the bottom of the page.

DO
- Divide the class into small groups.
- Have each group use the facts and measurements on the worksheet to design problems of their own. Students with Internet access could add more measurement information and use the data to create their group problems.
- Each group's problems need to include a minimum of six problems and include a minimum of:
  - Two problems based on length and width
  - Two problems based on weight
  - One problem based on time
  - One problem based on money
- During a whole class session, each group presents their word problems while the remainder of the class members use the data on the worksheet to solve them.

Monumental Math Worksheet

Use the facts and measurements below to answer the questions at the bottom of the page and to create questions of your own in a small group setting.

Information	Data
Ground to the tip of torch	305'1" high
Pedestal	154' high
Torch	298' above the ground
Mouth	3' wide
Length of right arm	42' long
Eyes	2'6" across
Steps in the Statue to the torch	187
Steps in the pedestal	171
Ticket to access the Statue of Liberty Crown and the ferry to both Liberty Island and Ellis Island	Adult Price: $28.00 Child (4-12): $19.00 Senior (62+): $24.00
Date the Statue was presented to the U.S. minister to France in Paris.	July 4, 1884
Date the Statue arrived in New York Harbor	June 17, 1885
Date the Statue was dedicated	October 28, 1886

1. Use the measurement in feet from the ground to the tip of the torch and the measurement in feet from the ground to the torch to find the height of the torch.

2. Compute the cost of tickets for two adults, three children ages eight, ten and thirteen and one grandparent (62+) for tickets to access the Statue of Liberty Crown and ferry to both Liberty Island and Ellis Island.

3. Write a question of your own using the above data.

Statue of Liberty Dedication Day
Poetry Lesson: The New Colossus

The words from the sonnet *The New Colossus* by Emma Lazarus were engraved and mounted on the Statue of Liberty. The title itself expresses the meaning of the poem. The word colossus means a statue that is larger than life. The word new means that this colossus is "Not like the brazen giant of Greek fame" but rather a symbol of liberty. She welcomes the exiles as she stands at "the air-bridged harbor that twin cities frame" and cries "with silent lips" to "give me your tired, your poor, your huddled masses yearning to breathe free." Students imagine themselves as The Statue of Liberty and think of what she has seen, thoughts she has had about the exiles and words she might speak today.

MATERIALS
- Emma Lazarus Biography and her poem *The New Colossus*
- Pictures of The Statue of Liberty
- Word processing or desktop publishing software or pencils, pens and paper

PLAN
- Read and discuss Emma Lazarus' biography and poem.
- Ask the following questions:
    - What is the meaning of the title *The New Colossus*?
    - What makes The Statue of Liberty different from statues of Greek times?
    - Why do you think The Statue of Liberty is a female rather than a male?
    - Why is she called "Mother of Exiles?"
    - Where does Emma Lazarus use personification?
    - Why are her lips "silent?" To whom is she speaking?

DO
Getting Ready to Write
Discuss class experiences and knowledge about the Statue of Liberty. Who has seen it? What does the torch represent? How do they think the people looked as they walked off the ship that brought them to our country? From what countries did they come?

Writing the Poem
Using *The New Colossus* as a model, students write poems of their own. They become The Statue of Liberty and write in the first person. Encourage line breaks so that the poem looks like a poem and not like a story.
- Students can title their poem "The Statue of Liberty."
- Suggest they begin their poems with the words: "With silent lips."
- Writing in the first, continue with what the statue says she stands for and what she has experienced.
- For example: *I am here welcoming you to freedom*

Editing and Publishing
- Students read and edit poems with partners.
- Students draw pictures of The Statue of Liberty and write their words near their drawing.

Emma Lazarus Biography
July 22, 1849 – November 19, 1887

Emma Lazarus was born in New York and grew up in a wealthy Jewish family. As a child, she was very shy and didn't make many friends. She stayed close to her family, so close in fact that she never attended school. Instead she had tutors who taught her many foreign languages.

In the society in which she lived, it was unacceptable for women to become writers or to participate in the literary world. Emma was alone in her world of books. Although she always showed poetic talent, her poetry became stronger and more powerful as she began hearing about the persecution of Jews occurring in Europe. She wrote poetry and prose about these persecutions in both Jewish and non-Jewish magazines. She wrote that until all people were free, no one was safe.

While visiting Jewish immigrants who arrived on Ward's Island from Russia, she thought about how horrible it must have been for them to live in a country where they couldn't be free. Lazarus was among a few great poets asked to write a poem about The Statue of Liberty, a gift from the people of France to the United States. Lazarus liked the name of the statue, "Liberty Enlightening the World," and the sculptor's idea of liberty as a woman with a torch upheld to the sky. She sat down and wrote a sonnet that came to her very easily written to the exiles everywhere. Her words inscribed on it were her idea of what America should be.

For the last six years of her life, she became a Jewish leader. When she died, she became more than a literary figure. She became known as a spokesperson of liberty for all people.

The New Colossus
by Emma Lazurus

Not like the brazen giant of Greek fame,
With conquering limbs astride from land to land;
Here at our sea-washed, sunset gates shall stand
A mighty woman with a torch, whose flame
Is the imprisoned lightning, and her name
Mother of Exiles. From her beacon-hand
Glows world-wide welcome; her mild eyes command
The air-bridged harbor that twin cities frame.
"Keep ancient lands, your storied pomp!" cries she
With silent lips. "Give me your tired, your poor,
Your huddled masses yearning to breathe free,
The wretched refuse of your teeming shore.
Send these, the homeless, tempest-tost to me,
I lift my lamp beside the golden door!"

Halloween
Math Lesson: Comparing Pumpkins

Students make predictions, analyze data, determine relationships and draw conclusions as they work in groups to weigh and measure three pumpkins of different sizes and shapes. Select three pumpkins: one tall and thin; one short and fat; and the last one round and well-proportioned.

MATERIALS
- Three pumpkins of different shapes and sizes for each group: tall/thin; short/fat, and round/well proportioned.
- Scale – shared for weighing
- Tape measures
- Child-safe serrated knives
- Plates and paper towels
- Computer (optional to create the table)
- Pencil and paper
- Table covers

PLAN
- Cover tables to prepare for messy pumpkin carving.
- Have students collect and bring several pumpkins of various sizes and shapes to class.
- Divide the class into small groups.
- Distribute tape measures, serrated knives, plates and paper towels to each group.

DO
The group members record their results as they do the following:
- Pick up the pumpkins one at a time. Estimate the weight of each pumpkin. Estimate which one is the heaviest. Use a scale to compare student estimates to the actual weight.
- Estimate the circumference of each pumpkin and use a tape measure to compare estimates to the actual measurement.
- Count the ribs on each pumpkin. Determine what the relationship is between the size (height, width, and so on) and the number of ribs on each pumpkin.
- Predict which of the pumpkins will have the most seeds and the least seeds.
- Hollow out the tallest and shortest pumpkins and count the seeds in each pumpkin.
- Based on the seed count of the previous two pumpkins, predict the number of seeds the round pumpkin has.
- Hollow out the last pumpkin and count the seeds to compare student estimates to the actual seed count.
- Make a computer or hand-drawn table illustrating the ratio of seeds to the circumference of each pumpkin.

Halloween
Poetry Lesson: Excerpt from The Raven

The mysterious life of Edgar Allen Poe and the chilling tale in his narrative poem *The Raven* make for a great Halloween lesson. Poe wrote *The Raven* after the death of his wife. The poem tells a story about a stately bird that visited and spoke to him. Poe recalls the frightening sounds that he heard that night which filled him "with fantastic terrors never felt before." Poe uses repetition in stanzas two, three and four to add intensity to his writing.

MATERIALS
- Edgar Allen Poe Biography and excerpt from *The Raven*
- Word processing or desktop publishing software or pencils, pens and paper

PLAN
- Share a brief summary of *The Raven*.

    The poem begins with a man sitting alone one wintry dark night. He is almost dozing off as he thinks about his wife who had died. Suddenly he is frightened by a knock at his door. Half asleep, and not sure whether he is still dreaming, he answers the door in the darkness. To calm his fears, he tells himself the knocking is some visitor tapping at his bedroom door.

    When he opens the door, no one is there. He hears a tap at the window. He opens the window and lets in a stately raven. The raven perches on a sculpture in his room. The man begins to talk to the bird about his sadness at the loss of his wife. He discusses ways to overcome his sadness with the raven, but the ebony bird repeatedly says, "nevermore, nevermore." He gets angry at the bird and tries to get the bird out of his house. At the end of the poem the raven is still perched on the sculpture forever reminding the man of his sorrow.

- Read and discuss Edgar Allen Poe's biography and poem.
- Explain that *The Raven* is a narrative poem (a form of poetry that tells a story).
- Ask students:
    - Who the narrator is in this poem.
    - What was the narrator doing in the beginning of the poem?
    - Why is the narrator sad?
    - In what month did the story take place?
    - Why did Poe select a winter month for his story?
- Have students look at the repetition in the poem.
    - What does the repetition add to the poem?

DO
Getting Ready to Write
Record student responses on the board.
- Think of scary sounds you have heard. What were they?
- Where were you?
- What did you think the sound was?

Writing the Poem
Using *The Raven* as a model, students write narrative poems.
- Students begin their poem with the sound they heard at night when they were alone. Keep repeating the sound throughout the poem.
  For example: *rat tat tat* on my bedroom door.
- Continue the poem by describing all they can remember when they heard the sound.
  - Where they were
  - What they were doing
  - How they were feeling
  - What it reminded them of
- End the poem with the repeating sound.

Editing and Publishing
- Students read their poems aloud in their scariest voices to a partner.
- Students perform their poems with sound effects.
- Students write their poems in a poetry book or enter in a word processing program.
- Have students illustrate their final masterpiece.

The raven perches on a bust of Pallas Athena, a symbol of wisdom meant to imply the narrator is a scholar. Illustration by Édouard Manet for Stéphane Mallarmé's translation, *Le Corbeau* (1875).

Edgar Allen Poe Biography
January 19, 1809 – October 7, 1849

Edgar Allen Poe led a mysterious life. He is known as the creator of the modern detective story. Biographers wrote about his life from tales passed on from generation to generation. His life has also been pieced together by found notes, letters, photographs, and news articles. He was one of the great writers of the 19th century.

Edgar Allen Poe was born in 1809 in Boston, Massachusetts. His parents were both in the theatre. His mother and father both died when Poe was very young. He was raised by a wealthy merchant who gave Poe the advantages of a good education. He went to West Point for a while but was expelled due to bad behavior. Most of Poe's working life was spent as a journalist.

By the time he was twenty, Poe was recognized as a literary talent. When Poe was twenty-seven, he married his cousin who was almost fourteen years old. She died eleven years after they were married. He missed her very much. *The Raven*, Poe's most famous poem, is about the loneliness he felt after his wife's death.

Poe was an editor and a reviewer. But his name will always be remembered for his poetry, fiction, and essays. He created two forms of literature, the modern detective story and science fiction. Poe died at the age of forty, the circumstances surrounding his death are as mysterious as he was.

Excerpt from The Raven
by Edgar Allen Poe

Once upon a midnight dreary, while I pondered, weak and weary,
Over many a quaint and curious volume of forgotten lore,
While I nodded, nearly napping, suddenly there came a tapping,
As of some one gently rapping, rapping at my chamber door.
"'Tis some visitor," I muttered, "tapping at my chamber door-
Only this, and nothing more."
Ah, distinctly I remember it was in the bleak December,
And each separate dying ember wrought its ghost upon the floor.
Eagerly I wished the morrow;- vainly I had sought to borrow
From my books surcease of sorrow- sorrow for the lost Lenore-
For the rare and radiant maiden whom the angels name Lenore-
Nameless here for evermore.

And the silken sad uncertain rustling of each purple curtain
Thrilled me- filled me with fantastic terrors never felt before;
So that now, to still the beating of my heart, I stood repeating,
"'Tis some visitor entreating entrance at my chamber door-
Some late visitor entreating entrance at my chamber door;-
This it is, and nothing more."

Presently my soul grew stronger; hesitating then no longer,
"Sir," said I, "or Madam, truly your forgiveness I implore;
But the fact is I was napping, and so gently you came rapping,
And so faintly you came tapping, tapping at my chamber door,
That I scarce was sure I heard you"- here I opened wide the door;-
Darkness there, and nothing more.

Open here I flung the shutter, when, with many a flirt and flutter,
In there stepped a stately Raven of the saintly days of yore;
Not the least obeisance made he; not a minute stopped or stayed he;
But, with mien of lord or lady, perched above my chamber door—
Perched upon a bust of Pallas just above my chamber door—
Perched, and sat, and nothing more.

And the Raven, never flitting, still is sitting, still is sitting
On the pallid bust of Pallas just above my chamber door;
And his eyes have all the seeming of a demon's that is dreaming,
And the lamp-light o'er him streaming throws his shadow on the floor;
And my soul from out that shadow that lies floating on the floor
Shall be lifted—nevermore!

November Monthly Holidays

Adopt A Senior Pet Month • Adopt A Turkey Month • America Recycles Month • Aviation History Month • Banana Pudding Lovers Month • Child Safety and Protection Month • Family Literacy Month • Family Stories Month • Great American Smokeout Month • Good Nutrition Month • Historic Bridge Awareness Month • International Creative Child and Adult Month • Movember • National Candle Month • National Diabetes Month • National Fragrance Month • National Peanut Butter Lovers Month • National Pepper Month • National Raisin Bread Month • Native American Heritage Month • Picture Book Month • Sweet Potato Awareness Month • World Vegan Month

November Weekly Holidays

First Week of November
National Card and Letter Writing Week • National Fig Week • World Communication Week

Second Week of November
American Education Week • Give Wildlife a Brake Week • International Week of Science and Peace (UN) • National Split Pea Soup Week • National Young Readers Week • Pursuit of Happiness Week

Third Week of November
American Education Week • Better Conversation Week • Fraud Awareness Week • Geography Awareness Week • • National Family Week • National Geography Awareness Week • World Kindness Week

Fourth Week of November
Make Up Your Own Week Week • National Game and Puzzle Week • National Leftover Awareness Week • Thanksgiving Week

November Moveable Holidays

Fountain Pen Day .... first Friday

Digital Scrapbooking Day .... first Saturday

Sadie Hawkins Day .... first Saturday

Election Day .... first Tuesday after the first Monday

Great American Smoke Out .... Thursday before Thanksgiving

Guinness World Record Day .... third Saturday

Thanksgiving .... last Thursday

Macy's Thanksgiving Parade .... last Thursday on Thanksgiving Day

Christmas Shopping Season Begins .... Friday after Thanksgiving

Buy Nothing Day .... Friday after Thanksgiving

Cyber Monday .... Monday after Thanksgiving

International Computer Security Day .... last workday

November Days for STEAM Makers and Poets

1	National Vinegar Day
2	Look for Circles Day
3	National Sandwich Day
4	Use Your Common Sense Day
5	Guy Fawkes Night
6	Saxophone Day
7	Notary Public Day
8	X-Ray Day
9	Chaos Never Dies Day
10	Sesame Street Day
11	Origami Day
12	Rodin's Birthday
13	World Kindness Day
14	World Diabetes Day
15	America Recycles Day
16	Button Day
17	Homemade Bread Day
18	GIS Geographic Information Systems Day
19	American Made Matters Day
20	Universal Children's Day and World Children's Day
21	World Hello Day
22	Alascattalo Day
23	Fibonacci Day
24	Celebrate Your Unique Talent Day
25	Blasé Day
26	National Cake Day
27	Pins and Needles Day
28	Red Planet Day
29	Square Dance Day
30	Computer Security Day

Integrating November Math Days

Science — Technology — Engineering — Arts — Math

Day		Make and Do
1	National Vinegar Day	Vinegar and oil don't mix, but vinegar, kids and science do. Today make an egg bounce! You will need one hard-boiled egg, white vinegar and a large jar. Cover the egg with vinegar and wait three days. Rinse the shell off the egg with tap water. Does the egg feel rubbery? How high can you bounce the egg? Measure the height. Why does this work? (Hint: vinegar is an acid that reacts with the calcium carbonate of the eggshell).
2	Look For Circles Day	A circle is a shape that is made by drawing a curve so that points are always the same distance from the center. Circles are all around. How many circles can you find in your classroom? Take pictures of circles that you find in your neighborhood and make a book of circles.
10	Sesame Street Day	Can you tell me how to get to Sesame Street? Sesame Street debuted on November 10, 1969 and as a pioneering children's television show, it has taught kids from over 120 countries. Many segments incorporate puppets and animation. Make a sock puppet and have the puppet teach a fellow classmate a math lesson for example, counting by threes, dividing treats, or telling time.

11	Origami Day	Get folding! The Chinese invented paper around 105 A.D. Paper was brought by monks to Japan in the sixth century. Origami folding patterns have been handed down from generation to generation. Create a zoo filled with origami animals as a class project. You will find many origami websites to help get you started.
16	Button Day	Sponsored by the National Button Society, button collectors since 1938 have recognized this day. Snipping buttons from old clothes and saving them in a jar or a tin was a popular hobby. Button Society websites can be found for many states. Check them out and learn the history of button collecting. For Button Day, make up your own button game. Try stacking, sorting, categorizing or sliding them across the floor. Create the game, write the directions and package your creation.
17	Homemade Bread Day	Learning to bake bread is fun, be it black bread, bagels or brioche. Bread is one of the oldest foods in recorded history. Most bread recipes require yeast, a microscopic fungus. You can find easy bread recipes and get started with baking two loaves of bread from a package of dry yeast and 7 cups of flour, along with small amounts of water, sugar, salt and canola oil. Research different methods and write out the directions for your baking day.
23	Fibonacci Day	The Fibonacci sequence is a pattern of counting where each number is the sum of the previous two. This system is widely used in computer data storage and can be seen in nature. These numbers were first written about by Leonardo of Pisa. Create a Fibonacci sequence of numbers, for example: 1, 1, 2, 3, 5, 8, and so on. Can you find dates in the year that display a Fibonacci sequence? For example: 5, 8, 13.

24	Celebrate Your Unique Talent Day	We all have our own special talents. Some of us sing, tell a good joke or perform magic tricks. Others have unique talents. Do you know people who can wiggle their ears, twitch their nose, roll their tongue or raise one eyebrow? Plan and organize a class talent show of traditional and unique talents. Create several graphs and charts that graphically display your talented class.
28	Red Planet Day	Mars, the fourth planet in our solar system is known as the red planet. This day commemorates the launch of the Mariner 4 Spacecraft in 1964. The 228-day mission flew within 6,118 miles of Mars. Divide into groups and find at least twenty facts about Mars. For example, Mars is often visible to the naked eye and it rotates around the sun every 687 days. Design a trivia game using your found facts. Play your game as a group and share each group's game with the class.

November Overview

National Aviation Month
Math Lesson: Cruising Altitude Rule of Thumb
Poetry Lesson: High Flight, by John Gillespie Magee, Jr.
National Aviation Month celebrates the achievements and contributions of men and women who were aviation pioneers. Students calculate the cruising altitude of a flight by applying an established rule of thumb used by pilots. In his poem, Magee captured the thrill of flight. Students write a poem imagining the emotions they might feel when flying their own plane.
NCTM STANDARD 4: Measurement, Gr 3 – 4A-7, 4B-4, 4B-5; Gr 4 – 4A-6; Gr 5 – 4A-10, 4A-11; Gr 6 – 4A-13, 4A-14; NCTM STANDARD 5: Data Analysis and Probability, Gr 3 – 5A-2; Gr 4 – 5A-2, 5A-3; Gr 5 –5A-2, 5A-3, 5A-4

Native American Heritage Month
Math Lesson: Throw Sticks Game
Poetry Lesson: The Thanksgivings translated by Harriet Maxwell Converse
This month-long celebration provides students with an opportunity to learn about the traditions and ancestry of Native Americans. Students learn and play a throw sticks game as they practice many math skills. The featured poem is a traditional Iroquois prayer of gratitude that helps students explore the gifts of nature as they write their own poems.
NCTM STANDARD 5: Data Analysis and Probability, Gr 3 – 5D-1, 5D-2, 5D-3; Gr 4 – 5D-1, 5D-2; Gr 5 – 5D-5

Veteran's Day
Math Lesson: Honoring the Numbers
Poetry Lesson: In Flanders Fields by John McCrae
Veterans Day is held on November 11th on the anniversary of the end of World War I. This national holiday honors all US veterans who served their country during war or peacetime. Students interpret chart statistics to develop graphing and word problem skills. John McCrae's poem *In Flanders Fields* serves as the springboard for student poems about freedom.
NCTM STANDARD 5: Data Analysis and Probability, Gr 3 – 5A-3, 5B-1, 5B-2, 5C-2; Gr 4 – 5A-3, 5A-4, 5A-5 5C-4; Gr 5 – 5A-4; Gr 6 – 5A5

Thanksgiving Day
Math Lesson: Traveling to Medford
Poetry Lesson: Thanksgiving Day by Lydia Maria Child
The fourth Thursday of November is our national holiday for giving thanks for the harvest of the preceding year. Families and friends gather for a traditional meal. In this math lesson, students plan a journey to the historic house visited by Lydia Maria Child. Students write poems with repetitive phrases in the style of her *Thanksgiving Day* poem.
NCTM Process Standard – Problem Solving: Apply and adapt a variety of appropriate strategies to solve problems.

National Aviation Month
Math Lesson: Cruising Altitude Rule of Thumb

Math is a vital part of aviation. Sometimes pilots rely on established rules of thumb to perform calculations in flight. In this lesson, students find the distances in miles between different cities and towns in the United States on a map, on a globe, and on the Internet to calculate the best cruising altitude for a plane flight of that distance.

MATERIALS
- Internet access
- United States map with miles per inch scale
- Globe
- Ruler
- String
- Pencil and paper
- Distance and Altitude Chart

PLAN
- Share with students that airplane pilots determine the best cruising altitudes for their planes to fly by calculating 10 percent of the trip's mileage and multiplying that number by 1000.
- Divide the students into small groups of two or three and distribute maps with mileage keys to each group.

DO
- Using the map as reference, students choose at least six routes of various distances to measure.
- They measure the routes and use the inch key to determine distances.
- Groups write the map distances in the Map Column on the DIstance and Altitude Chart.
- Next, measure the same routes on a globe. Use a piece of yarn and stretch it firmly between both places. Place the yarn on a ruler and measure the distance.
- Determine the size of your globe and use the following key to calculate global mileage:
    - A 9-inch globe is 880 miles per inch.
    - A 10-inch globe is 660 miles per inch.
    - A 16-inch globe is 500 miles per inch.
- Students write the map distances in the Global Column on the Distance and Altitude Chart.
- Students search the Internet to find the distances of the same routes on their list. One possible site to use is:
  http://www.math.com/everyone/calculators/online_calculators.htm.
- They write the mileage on the Internet column of the Distance and Altitude Chart.
- Have students use an average of the miles calculated on the map, globe and Internet to determine the cruising altitude for each flight.

Distance and Altitude Chart

From	To	Map Miles	Global Miles	Internet Miles	Average Miles	Cruising Altitude

National Aviation Month
Poetry Lesson: High Flight

The poem, *High Flight* by John Gillespie Magee, Jr. is a perfect match for National Aviation Month. After reading his poem one can sense the thrill experienced by the heroes who discovered new flying techniques and felt the exhilaration of flying through the air. This poem became one of the world's most well-known poems about flight and expresses the emotions being in the sky above the clouds. From the beginning of the poem, we enter the world of flight with words that soar as he "slipped the surly bonds of Earth/And danced the skies on laughter-silvered wings." In this lesson, students write about something they have experienced that gives them a thrill just as Magee experienced in flying.

MATERIALS
- John Gillespie Magee, Jr. Biography and his poem *High Flight*
- Word processing or desktop publishing software or pencils, pens and paper

PLAN
- Read and discuss John Gillespie Magee, Jr.'s biography and poem.
- Discuss the poem with the following questions:
    - How does the reader know that Magee loves flying?
    - What verbs, nouns and adjectives capture the spirit of flying?

DO
Getting Ready to Write
- Ask students the following questions. As they gives their responses, encourage discussion. Write answers on the board.
    - What one experience do students remember that gives them the deep feelings that are expressed in *High Flight*? It may be an experience that they could have had more than one time such as *reading a book, baking a cake,* or *running down a mountain trail.*
    - Where were they when they had this experience?
    - What phrases would they use to convey the feelings of excitement, the pleasure, even fear that they remember and the beauty that they saw or felt during this experience?
- Suggest students refer to the poem for verbs, nouns, and adjectives to help them respond.

Writing the Poem
Using *High Flight* as a model, have students write poems of their own.
- Students begin their poems with "Oh, I have."
- Have them continue their poems, writing where they were, what they saw and how they felt that made this experience unforgettable. Encourage using the most powerful descriptive language that they can.

Editing and Publishing
- Students read and edit poems with partners.
- Students write their poems in a poetry book, or enter in a word processing program and illustrate their final masterpiece.

John Gillespie Magee, Jr. Biography
June 9, 1922 – December 11, 1941

John Gillespie Magee, Jr. was born in Shanghai, China where both of his parents were missionaries, his father arriving in China from the United States and his mother from England. He had three younger brothers. When he was nine years old, he moved to England with his mother. He loved writing poetry and won a much-valued poetry prize in public school.

When Magee was seventeen his family moved to the United States. While in high school, he had his one and only book of poems published. He was accepted to Yale University on scholarship, but instead enlisted as an American volunteer in the Royal Canadian Air Force to fight the Nazis. Magee knew the value of freedom. He knew he had to do his part. He graduated as a pilot and then went to England for combat duty in July of 1941.

Magee tested a new model of a plane that was able to fly at an altitude of 30,000 feet. He loved this new height and wrote his famous poem *High Flight* because of the thrill he experienced so high in the sky. He sent the poem on the back of a letter that he wrote to his parents. In the note he wrote, "I am enclosing a verse I wrote the other day. It started at 30,000 feet, and was finished soon after I landed." Sadly, at the age of 19, his plane collided with another plane during practice maneuvers and he crashed to his death.

John's parents wrote a letter to the Royal Canadian Air Force, ending with these last two lines. "We are thinking that this [poem] may have been a greater contribution than anything he may have done in the way of fighting. We will be forever proud of him."

High Flight
by John Gillespie Magee, Jr.

Oh! I have slipped the surly bonds of Earth
And danced the skies on laughter-silvered wings;
Sunward I've climbed, and joined the tumbling mirth
of sun-split clouds, — and done a hundred things
You have not dreamed of — wheeled and soared and swung
High in the sunlit silence. Hov'ring there,
I've chased the shouting wind along, and flung
My eager craft through footless halls of air. . . .

Up, up the long, delirious burning blue
I've topped the wind-swept heights with easy grace
Where never lark, or ever eagle flew —
And, while with silent, lifting mind I've trod
The high untrespassed sanctity of space,
Put out my hand, and touched the face of God.

I have jumped in a split so high
I took the clouds
And shined as bright as the sun
by Tatiana – 4th grade

Native American Heritage Month Math Lesson: Throw Sticks Game

Apache women played the Throw Sticks game in winter when the farming months were over. They also played the game in their free time throughout the year. The game is played in a circle. As student groups learn and play this game they hone their probability, patterns, relationships and place value skills.

MATERIALS
- Tongue depressors for each student
- Colored markers
- Stones – 40 per group
- Place markers such as feathers or shells – 2 per group
- Board or chart

PLAN
Tell students they are going to play a circle game that is often played by Native American Apache women. Divide the class into small groups and have group members follow the directions below to get the game ready for play:
- Each group member decorates one side of a tongue depressor in a Native American design. They leave the other side blank. These sticks will be used as dice for each game.
- The group members place 40 stones around a circle in groups of 10.
- They place two markers on opposite sides of the circle.

DO
Distribute the Score Chart and the Throw Record Chart to each group.
- Two students in each group are chosen to be players in the game as the rest of the group calculates the points, and tallies each throw on the record.
- The first two players sit on opposite sides of the circle next to one of the markers.
- The players take turns throwing the three sticks down the center of the circle.
- The results of each throw are recorded on the Tally Chart.
- The players move the markers around the stones according to the points received on the sticks. Each stone counts as one point. See point chart below.
- If a player's marker lands or goes past his/her opponent's marker, the player whose marker was landed on or passed over has to go back to the starting point.
- The first player to take his/her marker all the way around the circle, passing all 40 stones, wins.
- At the end of each game two new group members become players and the players join the others to continue scoring and record keeping.
- When all group members have had a chance to play, tallies are totaled on the Record Chart.
- Combine the tallies of all the groups when all the games have been played.
- The class discusses the combined frequencies of each type of throw to discuss theoretical probabilities by asking a series of questions. For example, is a throw with three sticks decorated more likely than a throw with two sticks decorated? Is a throw with no sticks decorated more likely than a throw with three sticks decorated?

Throw Sticks Game Score Chart

3 blank sides up	10 points
2 blank sides up, 1 painted side up	1 point
1 blank side up, 2 painted sides up	3 points
3 painted sides up	5 points

Record Chart

Throws	Tally Marks	Frequency For all games
3 blank sides up		
2 blank sides up		
1 blank sides up		
3 painted sides up		

Native American Heritage Month
Poetry Lesson: The Thanksgivings

The Thanksgivings is a traditional Iroquois prayer of gratitude translated by Harriet Maxwell Converse. One of their religious traditions is giving daily thanks to the Great Spirit whom they feel is responsible for all creation.

MATERIALS
- Harriet Maxwell Converse Biography and her translation of *The Thanksgivings*
- Word processing or desktop publishing software or pencil, pens and paper

PLAN
- Read and discuss Harriet Maxwell Converse's biography and poem.

DO
Getting Ready to Write
- During a brainstorming session, ask students the following questions and discussion points. As the class gives their responses, list them on the board or on a chart.
  - Ask students to thank one of the following: the Great Spirit, Mother Nature, or any nature mythological figure.
  - For what would they give thanks?
    For example, *the trees, the sky, etc.*
  - What reason would they give thanks?

Writing the Poem
- Students title their poem "My Thanksgivings."
- Have them begin each line with "I thank *(whomever they give thanks to)*."
- Continue the line with *(for whatever in nature they are thanking)*.
- Remind them to describe each object they thank with interesting adjectives and strong verbs in their description.
- Encourage line breaks so that the poem looks like a poem and not like a story.

Editing and Publishing
- Have students read and edit poems with partners.
- Students can write their poems in a poetry book, or enter them in a word processing program and illustrate their final masterpiece.

Harriet Maxwell Converse Biography
1836 - 1903

Harriet Maxwell was born in 1836 in Elmira, New York. Her father and grandfather were Indian Traders and well respected and liked by the Seneca Nation. At a very young age her mother died and she was reared by an aunt.

At twenty-five she married a popular wealthy musician. Along with an inheritance from her father, they travelled to many countries in Europe and throughout the United States.

When Converse was not traveling, she spent much of her time writing. She became a published poet. She inherited from her father and grandfather an interest in the Native American culture. She wanted to know more about their culture and began researching and writing about the Six Nations, a group of six tribes that composed the Iroquois League. These tribes are considered to be the oldest living participatory democracy. As part of her research she traveled to reservations collecting objects such as wampum belts. She wrote articles defending the Native American Indian rights to their own citizenship and to their property.

Harriet Maxwell Converse was a well-known and respected poet, but more than her stature as a poet was the honor bestowed upon her by the Six Nations when they gave her the name of chief, the first white woman to bear that name.

The Thanksgivings
Translated by Harriet Maxwell Converse
from a traditional Iroquois prayer

We who are here present thank the Great Spirit that we are here
      to praise Him.
We thank Him that He has created men and women, and ordered
      that these beings shall always be living to multiply the earth.
We thank Him for making the earth and giving these beings its products
      to live on.
We thank Him for the water that comes out of the earth and runs
      for our lands.
We thank Him for all the animals on the earth.
We thank Him for certain timbers that grow and have fluids coming
      from them for us all.
We thank Him for the branches of the trees that grow shadows
      for our shelter.
We thank Him for the beings that come from the west, the thunder
      and lightning that water the earth.
We thank Him for the light which we call our oldest brother, the sun
      that works for our good.
We thank Him for all the fruits that grow on the trees and vines.
We thank Him for his goodness in making the forests, and thank
      all its trees.
We thank Him for the darkness that gives us rest, and for the kind Being
      of the darkness that gives us light, the moon.
We thank Him for the bright spots in the skies that give us signs,
      the stars.
We give Him thanks for our supporters, who had charge of our harvests.
We give thanks that the voice of the Great Spirit can still be heard
      through the words of Ga-ne-o-di-o.
We thank the Great Spirit that we have the privilege of this pleasant
      occasion.
We give thanks for the persons who can sing the Great Spirit's music,
      and hope they will be privileged to continue in his faith.
We thank the Great Spirit for all the persons who perform the ceremonies
      on this occasion.

Veterans Day
Math Lesson: Honoring the Numbers

The tradition of paying tribute to the American men and women – living or dead – who have served our country both in peacetime and in war is a long one. The holiday began as Armistice Day one year after the armistice was signed to temporarily end World War I on the 11th hour of the 11th day of the 11th month in 1918. Armistice Day became known as the legal holiday of Veterans Day in 1954 to honor all who have served in every branch of the military. Students use the list of the number of veterans who have served in each war since the American Revolution to create graphs and word problems.

MATERIALS
- United States War Veterans Handout
- Graph paper
- Computer, printer and spreadsheet program (optional)
- Pencil and paper

PLAN
- Discuss Veteran's Day.
- Distribute and discuss the United States War Veterans Handout.
- Below are some possible discussion questions:
  - In which war did the greatest number serve?
  - In which war did the smallest number serve?
  - What were the shortest and longest wars?
  - How long has the current US Global War on Terrorism lasted to date?

DO
- Divide the class into small groups.
- Have groups use the data in the chart to do three of the following:
  - Enter the numbers in a spreadsheet program and create a line graph showing the total number of veterans who served in each war.
  - Use graph paper and create a bar graph to compare the number of veterans who served in each war.
  - Create five word problems and an answer sheet using the dates the wars were fought.
  - Create five word problems and an answer sheet using the numbers who served.
  - Create ten multiple choice math problems and an answer sheet using both dates fought and number served statistics.
- Have groups share their work with the class.

United States War Veterans Handout

War	Date	Number Served
American Revolution	1775-1783	217,000
War of 1812	1812-1815	286,730
Indian Wars	1817-1898	106,000
Mexican War	1846-1848	78,718
Civil War (number includes Union/Confederate)	1861-1865	3,26,3363
Spanish-American War	1898-1902	306,760
World War I	1917-1918	4,734,99
World War II	1940-1945	16,112,566
Vietnam War	1964-1975	8,744,000
Desert Shield/Desert Storm	1990-1991	2,322,000
U.S. Global War on Terrorism	2001 -	2,000,000+

Veterans Day
Poetry Lesson: In Flanders Fields

In the poem written by John McCrae, *In Flanders Fields*, the voices of fallen heroes are heard telling us they too "lived, felt dawn, saw sunset glow/Loved and were loved."

They ask us to fight our enemies and "take up quarrel with the foe" when freedom is being threatened so they can sleep peacefully. McCrae writes about the torch that symbolizes the freedom for which they fought. The soldiers ask us "to hold it high" so that they and the freedom they died for will always be remembered. In this lesson, students speak to the dead soldiers telling them they will be remembered each time freedom is experienced in their own lives.

MATERIALS
- John McCrae Biography and his poem *In Flanders Fields*
- Word processing or desktop publishing software or pencil, pens and paper
- Optional animated video clip of *In Flanders Field* from *What Have We Learned Charlie Brown?* (1983)

PLAN
- Read and discuss John McCrae's biography and poem.
- Discuss the poem with the following questions:
    - Who is speaking?
    - What do the speakers want us to do?
    - What does "the torch" symbolize?
- This may be an opportune time to show a video clip of Linus reciting *In Flanders Field* from *What Have We Learned, Charlie Brown? (1983)*. You can find it on YouTube.

DO
Getting Ready to Write
- Ask students what freedoms they experience in their lives.
  For example: *being able to attend school, speak their own mind*
- What symbols have they seen?
  For example: *an eagle soaring through the blue sky*

Writing the Poem
Students title their poem "I Will Remember."
Encourage line breaks so that the poem looks like a poem not like a story.
- They begin their poem with "I promise to remember you."
- Continue with their own experiences involving freedom, beginning each idea with the word "when."

Editing and Publishing
- Students read and edit poems with partners.
- Students can create a banner with a quote from their poem.
- Hold a class parade.

John McCrae Biography
November 30, 1872 - January 28, 1918

John McCrae was born in Canada. His father was a Lieutenant Colonel in the Canadian military. Both his parents were Scottish immigrants. From a very early age, he was interested in the military and joined the Canadian militia when he was seventeen. He was also creative and enjoyed writing poetry and drawing.

McCrae received a scholarship to the University of Toronto to study medicine. It was there that his first poems were published. He became a doctor and had his own medical practice. When Canada entered World War I, he enlisted in the military. He was appointed a surgeon and a major in the Canadian artillery.

In Flander Fields has become one of the most popular poems about World War I and is known internationally. There are many stories about why John McCrae wrote the poem *In Flanders Fields*. One well-known story is that he wrote it while in the Belgium trenches during a battle in which a friend of his died. Another story is that he wrote it the day after the funeral of this friend. After writing the poem, it was misplaced, had no name and was published anonymously. Not too long after the publication, McCrae was named as its author.

The Canadian government placed a memorial to John McCrae with his poem inscribed at the war site in Belgium. McCrae would be proud that his poem gives hope to future generations and encourages them to carry the torch for freedom.

In Flanders Fields
by John McCrae

In Flanders fields the poppies blow
Between the crosses, row on row,
That mark our place; and in the sky
The larks, still bravely singing, fly
Scarce heard amid the guns below.

We are the dead; short days ago
We lived, felt dawn, saw sunset glow,
Loved and were loved, and now we lie
In Flanders fields.

Take up our quarrel with the foe!
To you from failing hands we throw
The torch; be yours to hold it high!
If ye break faith with us who die
We shall not sleep, though poppies grow
In Flanders fields.

I will remember you
When I see the colors red, white and blue
On the American flag waving
When I see the eagle in the sky flying high
Boldly
I will remember you
by Jan – 4th grade

Thanksgiving Day
Math Lesson: Traveling to Medford

The house Lydia Maria Child was visiting in her poem *The Thanksgiving* was first built as a small farmhouse in the early 1800s. Later in the century, Paul Curtis, a local shipbuilder, bought and enlarged the original farmhouse. The house was added to the National Register of Historic Places in 1975 and was purchased and restored by Tufts University. It is currently known as the Paul Curtis house and is located in Medford, Massachusetts, at 114 South Street on the banks of the Mystic River. In this lesson students plan a Thanksgiving trip to the Medford house.

MATERIALS
- Internet capable devices and Internet access
- Word processing and spreadsheet software
- Atlases and road maps
- Calculators one per student - optional

PLAN
- During a class discussion, students share driving trips they have taken with their families.
- Write down the destinations they have visited.
- Using atlases and/or an online navigation system such as Google Maps or MapQuest, find the distance from the classroom to the places they visited.
- Have the student whose family took the farthest trip share the following information:
    - How long did it take to get to their destination?
    - Did they stop overnight on the way? If so, where?
    - What did they do for meals?
- Allow other students to share details about their trips.

DO
- Divide the class into groups of four or five students.
- Distribute the Traveling to Medford Handout.
- Review the information on the handout with the class.
- Decide whether the class needs calculators to complete the calculations. If so, distribute calculators.
- Allow two days for the groups to complete their itineraries.
- Have the groups present their itineraries to the class.

Traveling to Medford Handout

- Imagine that you will be going "over the river and through the wood" to visit the grandparents in the poem *Thanksgiving Day*.

- The house is located at 114 South Street in Medford, Massachusetts.

- Your family [choose the largest family in your group] will be traveling together by car.

- You must plan all the details and expenses for your trip by doing the following:

    - Estimate the distance to the house from your home.
    - Use travel sites on the Internet such as Kayak, Expedia and Priceline to find the cost of rental cars. Select the model and make to find the miles per gallon of the car you plan to rent. A compact car will get better gas mileage, but may not be roomy enough for your family and their luggage. You may need a full-size car or a mini-van, but they will use more gas.
    - Estimate the round-trip cost of gas for the trip by dividing the distance by the miles per gallon. Multiply the answer by the current cost of gas near you to get your total gas cost. You can search the Internet to find the current cost of gas near you.
    - If the length of the trip warrants overnight stays, use travel sights such as those listed above to find the best places to stay and the best prices. Calculate the cost of lodging for the entire round trip journey.
    - Create a food budget for the trip. Estimate the food cost for the journey. Include snacks, drinks and restaurant meals.
    - Create an itinerary in a word processing program. Use a spreadsheet to display an itemized list of expenses along with a total cost for the entire trip.

Thanksgiving Day
Poetry Lesson: Thanksgiving Day

In her poem *Thanksgiving Day,* Lydia Maria Child expresses the family's excitement about a Thanksgiving journey as they travel "over the river, and through the wood, to grandfather's house" where they will celebrate Thanksgiving. One can feel the eagerness as they anticipate visiting their grandparents, eating a delicious meal and having fun. The poem is familiar as a song called "The New-England Boy's Song about Thanksgiving Day." In this lesson, students write poems about their Thanksgiving Day journeys.

MATERIALS
- Lydia Maria Child Biography and her poem *Thanksgiving Day*
- Word processing or desktop publishing software or pencil, pens and paper

PLAN
- Read and discuss Lydia Maria Child's biography and poem.
- Discuss the poem with the following questions:
    - How do you know that this is not a modern day Thanksgiving journey?
    - What repetitive phrase does Child use in the poem?
    - What images does Child use to make this an exciting journey for the family?
    - What awaits the family when they reach their grandparent's house?

DO
Getting Ready to Write
Students write a poem about a Thanksgiving journey they have taken or plan on taking.
- What repetitive phrase could replace "over the river, and through the wood."
- Discuss the places they have seen, or plan on seeing or experiencing while traveling to a close relative or friend's house on Thanksgiving.
- What verbs, nouns and adjectives could they use that expresses excitement about their journey?
- What do they think awaits them at their destination?
    For example: *my grandmother giving me a warm hug* or *the tasty food at the table*

Writing the Poem
Using Child's poem as a model, have students write their poems.
- Suggest they begin the first stanza with their repetitive phrase and include to whose house they are going.
- Continue the first stanza with what they might see and/or experience on their journey. What makes this an exciting journey?
- Continue each new stanza with their repetitive phrase and continue to complete the poem.

Editing and Publishing
- Have students read and edit poems with partners.
- Students can present their poems to the class.
- The poem is also popular as a song. Singing the lyrics would be a fun activity.

Lydia Maria Child Biography
February 11, 1802 – October 20, 1880

Lydia Maria Child was born in Massachusetts. She was educated in local schools where she studied to become a teacher. Child's parents were wealthy and part of the Boston upper class society. They worried that Lydia would marry and have no money. Their worries came true. Her husband, although an attorney and a graduate of Harvard, could not make a living. And so in order to support them, she began writing to make money to survive.

Child wrote novels and also published in a magazine for children called "The Child's Magazine." She wrote popular articles on how to be a good and frugal housewife. With her writing, they were able to get by.

Child became an abolitionist supporting the freedom of African American slaves. She was not the kind of woman to be verbally outspoken about her views, but she supported the cause of civil rights by editing a book written by an ex-slave. She used her own money to publish *The Freedman's Book* which contained biographies she wrote about slaves and short stories and poems written by abolitionists, slaves and freed slaves. In the preface of the book she wrote: "I have prepared this book expressly for you (recently freed African Americans) with the hope that those of you who can read will read it aloud to others, and that all of you will derive fresh strength and courage from this true record of what colored men have accomplished, under great disadvantages." She did this out of the goodness of her heart, never being paid for her labor or her materials.

Upon her death at the age of seventy-eight, she had written more than two dozen books. She was a novelist, journalist and teacher but what she has been remembered for most is a poem written in 1844, *The Thanksgiving,* about her memories of a Thanksgiving journey to her grandparent's home. Her grandparent's house still stands in Massachusetts near the Mystic River referred to in the poem.

Thanksgiving Day
by Lydia Maria Child

Over the river, and through the wood,
    To grandfather's house we go;
        The horse knows the way
        To carry the sleigh
Through the white and drifted snow.

Over the river, and through the wood,
    To grandfather's house away!
        We would not stop
        For doll or top,
For 't is Thanksgiving day.

Over the river, and through the wood—
    Oh, how the wind does blow!
        It stings the toes
        And bites the nose
As over the ground we go.

Over the river, and through the wood,
    To have a first-rate play.
        Hear the bells ring
        "Ting-a-ling-ding",
Hurrah for Thanksgiving Day!

Over the river, and through the wood
    Trot fast, my dapple-gray!
        Spring over the ground,
        Like a hunting-hound!
For this is Thanksgiving Day.

Over the river, and through the wood,
    And straight through the barn-yard gate.
        We seem to go
        Extremely slow,—
It is so hard to wait!
Over the river and through the wood—
    Now grandmother's cap I spy!
        Hurrah for the fun!
        Is the pudding done?
Hurrah for the pumpkin-pie!

December Monthly Holidays

Art and Architecture Books Month • Bingo's Birthday Month • Hi Neighbor Month • Made in America Month • National Impaired Driving Prevention Month • National Stress-Free Family Holiday Month • Read a New Book Month • Safe Toys and Gifts Month • Universal Human Rights Month

December Weekly Holidays

First Week of December
Christmas Tree Week • Cookie Cutter Week

Second Week of December
Civil Rights Week • Human Rights Week

Third Week of December
Gluten-free Baking Week • Las Posadas • Tell Someone They're Doing a Good Job Week

Fourth Week of December
Kwanzaa begins on December 26 • It's About Time Week
Orange Bowl Week

December Moveable Holidays

Apple Pie Day	Thursday after first Tuesday
Army and Navy Union Day	second Saturday
Klopfeinachte	three Thursdays before Christmas
Election Day	first Tuesday after the first Monday
Underdog Day	third Friday

December Days for STEAM Makers and Poets

1. Rosa Parks Day
2. National Mutt Day
3. Make a Gift Day
4. National Cookie Day
5. International Volunteer Day
6. St. Nicholas Day
7. Pearl Harbor Remembrance Day
8. National Brownie Day
9. Christmas Card Day
10. Nobel Prize Day
11. UNICEF's Birthday
12. Gingerbread House Day
13. Ban a Silly Superstition Day
14. Monkey Day
15. Bill of Rights Day
16. National Chocolate Covered Anything Day
17. Wright Brother's Day
18. Pantomime Day
19. National Hard Candy Day
20. Louisiana Purchase Day
21. Crossword Puzzle Day
22. International Arbor Day
23. Roots Day
24. Christmas Eve Broadcast
25. A'Phabet Day or No "L" Day
26. Boxing Day
27. Visit the Zoo Day
28. Pledge of Allegiance Day
29. Tick Tock Day
30. Bicarbonate of Soda Day
31. New Year's Eve

Integrating December Math Days

 Science   Technology   Engineering   Arts   Math

	Day	Make and Do
4	National Cookie Day	Holiday season is definitely cookie season. Who doesn't like cookies? For those of you who like to bake cookies, learn why baking cookies is both an art and a science. What is the science behind baking cookies? For example, recipes with more butter give you thinner and crisper cookies and if you use baking powder rather than baking soda you get softer cookies. Melted butter and bread flour makes a chewier cookie. Why is this so? Search the web for a favorite cookie recipe for the best cookie ever. Word process the recipe onto a 4 x 6 recipe card. Using a spreadsheet, make a shopping list with prices for each ingredient and the amount needed as stated in the recipe. How much of each ingredient and what would be the cost for 10 dozen cookies? How about 100 dozen?
17	Wright Brother's Day	American brothers, Orville and Wilbur took to the air on this day in 1903, ushering in the age of flying machines. Their imaginations were sparked by a childhood toy helicopter. In honor of the innovative brothers, make a few different paper helicopters. You will find templates on the web. What design works best? Decide which design spins the longest or falls to the ground the slowest. Time your flights. Create a graph showing the amount of time the designs stay in the air.

19	National Hard Candy Day	How do you make hard candy? Find a basic recipe and adapt it with your own special ingredients. Write out your recipe. How many pieces of candy will it make? How much of each ingredient will you need? How much more of each ingredient will you need to make enough hard candy for everyone in your class to have three pieces?
20	Louisiana Purchase Day	The Louisiana Purchase was completed on this day in 1803. How much did it cost? What could you purchase with that amount of money today? Using a spreadsheet, make a list of what you would purchase and total your list. Figure out the sales tax for your city and state and include that cost as well. How close to the purchase price can you get?
21	Crossword Puzzle Day	Are you a cruciverbalist, a person who is skillful in creating or solving crossword puzzles? Arthur Wynne's puzzle was the first crossword puzzle published in a New York Sunday newspaper on this day in 1913. Other newspapers discovered this pastime and crosswords became featured in almost all American newspapers. Create a mathematics crossword puzzle. Make a list of math words. Build your puzzle using an online crossword puzzle builder. One site, Instant Online Crossword Puzzle Maker, is found at http://www.puzzle-maker.com/CW/. See if you can find another crossword puzzle generator and create the same puzzle a second time. Which puzzle do you like best and why?
26	Boxing Day	Boxing Day follows Christmas Day and in England and other British Commonwealth countries, tradespeople and servants received a gift known as a Christmas Box. This practice may date back to the Middle Ages. Examine a box to determine its height, width and depth. Determine the number of cubic units the box will hold. Compare the sizes of several boxes.

December Overview

National Write a Letter to a Friend Month
Math Lesson: Writing in Code
Poetry Lesson: O! why was I born with a different face? by William Blake

We celebrate this month by encouraging children to focus on the art of handwritten letter writing. In this thematic unit, students practice the art of written correspondence with letters that include secret-coded messages. Students write a letter poem that reflects upon a unique aspect of themselves in the style of William Blake.
NCTM Process Standard – Problem Solving: Apply and adapt a variety of appropriate strategies to solve problems.

Winter
Math Lesson: Marshmallow Geometry
Poetry Lesson: Winter Haikus by Matsuo Basho

Winter is the coldest of the four seasons in the Northern Hemisphere. It evokes images of rain, snow and freezing weather. In this lesson, students use marshmallows to emulate snowballs and build three dimensional structures with toothpicks. Students identify the vertices, edges and faces of the structures. Students write their own winter seventeen syllable, three line Haikus describing winter.
NCTM Standard 3: Geometry, Gr –3, 3A-all; Gr – 4, 3A-5, 3A-6; Gr – 5, 3A-1, 3A-2; Gr – 6, 3A-1, 3A-2, 3A-3, 3A-5

December Holidays
Math Lesson: Shopping for Holiday Parties
Poetry Lesson: little tree by e. e. cummings

When we think of December, we think of holidays. All around the world, this is the month for celebrating Christmas, Chanukah, Kwanzaa, Las Posadas, St. Lucia Day, New Year's Eve and more. Students practice math skills as they plan a holiday party. Students write about a symbol of a December holiday in the style of e.e.cummings.
NCTM Standard 4: Measurement, Grade – 3, 4B6; Grade – 4, 4B-2; Grade – 5, 4B-6

New Year's Eve
Math Lesson: Minute to Win It
Poetry Lesson: A Song for New Year's Eve by William Cullen Bryant

On New Year's Eve in 1907, the first crystal ball was dropped in New York's Times Square. Students work in small groups to try to finish a math-based Minute to Win It game in sixty seconds or less. Bryant writes about the previous year and its trials and tribulations. Students write poems in which they reflect back and look forward to the year ahead.
NCTM Process Standard – Problem Solving: Apply and adapt a variety of appropriate strategies to solve problems.

National Write a Letter to a Friend Month
Math Lesson: Writing in Code

We text, we tweet, we chat, we Facebook and we email. In this digital age it is easy to forget the joy and pleasure of receiving a handwritten letter via snail mail. It is no surprise that December is "Write a Letter to a Friend Month." During the holiday season many families compose special letters for friends and family near and far. December 7 is designated as National Letter Writing Day.

To celebrate National Write a Letter to a Friend Month students are encouraged to focus on the art of hand-written letter writing. In this lesson, they write and read letters handwritten in secret numeric code and craft their own. Math skills are honed as students crack the codes and figure out the meaning of secret messages. Mathematicians were some of the most famous cryptologists in history.

One famous cryptologist was mathematician Alan Mathison Turing. He is known as the creator of modern computing. He played a crucial part in the Allied victory in the Second World War by cracking the Enigma code. German armed forces used a type of enciphering machine to send secure messages. The system changed daily making the task of breaking the code very difficult. Turing created a machine known as the Bombe that was able to read the coded messages of the Nazis.

MATERIALS
- Break the Code Worksheet
- My Secret Message Worksheet
- Board or chart
- Papers and pencils

PLAN
- Begin a class discussion by asking students to talk about letters they have written and received in snail mail.
- Tell them that they are going to write a letter in which they will include some secrets they wish to tell to a classmate. In order to keep the secret for the recipient's eyes only, they will write in secret code.
- Have the class talk about what they already know about secret codes.
- Tell them they are going to learn how to use letters and numbers to create secret codes for their message.

DO
- Distribute and discuss the Break the Code Worksheet.
- Discuss both types of number and letter codes on the worksheet.
- Students work individually or in pairs to decode each message.
- Once the codes are broken, they write secret messages of their own to include in a handwritten letter.
- Students write the letter and deliver it to a fellow classmate.

Break the Code Worksheet

A	B	C	D	E	F	G	H	I	J	K	L	M	N	O	P	Q	R	S	T	U	V	W	X	Y	Z
1	2	3	4	5	6	7	8	9	10	11	12	13	14	15	16	17	18	19	20	21	22	23	24	25	26

__ __ __ __   __ __ __ __
13   1   11   5   7 15 15   4

__ __ __ __ __ __ __ __ __ __ __ __
3   18 25 16 20 15 12 15   7   9 19 20 29

My Secret Information

1	O	3	4	5	I	7	8	9	10
11	12	13	D	15	16	17	18	19	C
21	T	23	24	25	26	27	28	29	30
31	32	33	34	K	36	37	38	39	40
41	42	43	44	45	46	47	S	49	L
51	52	53	E	55	56	57	58	59	60
61	62	63	64	65	66	67	68	N	70
71	R	73	74	75	76	A	78	79	80
81	82	83	84	85	86	87	88	89	90
91	92	93	94	95	96	97	98	99	V

__   __   __   __   __   __   __   __   __   __
3+3 24x2 25-3 3+3 2x25 5x10 100÷2 1x1 100 27+27

__   __   __   __   __   __   __   __   __   __   __
68+4 1+1 10x2 5x7   11x7 60+9 7x3 8x9 12÷6 100÷2 10x5

My Secret Message Worksheet

Create secret codes in the spaces in which you hide some secret information about yourself. Enclose your codes in a handwritten friendly letter.

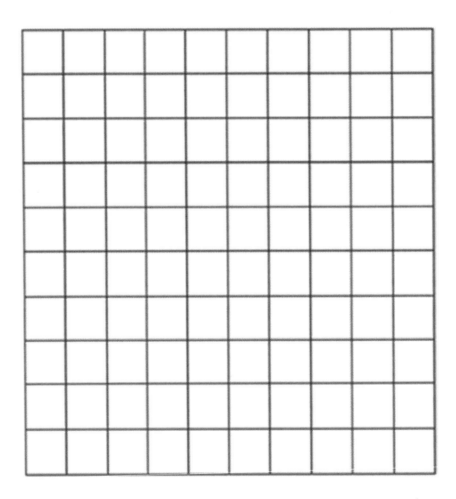

National Write a Friend Month
Poetry Lesson:
O! why was I born with a different face?

In his letter poem to Thomas Butts *O! why was I born with a different face?* William Blake expresses honestly and poetically that he is feeling like an outsider when he writes "why was I not born like the rest of my race?" He also feels he can't do anything right "when I speak, I offend;/then I'm silent & passive & lose every friend." He conveys his distrust of himself as an artist "my verse I dishonour, my pictures despise." His letter reads like a poem because of its rhymes, line breaks and powerful intense poetic descriptions.

MATERIALS
- William Blake Biography and his poem *Oh! why was I born with a different face*
- Desktop publishing software
- Colored paper, pencils, crayons and other art supplies
- Envelopes (optional)

PLAN
- Read and discuss William Blake biography and poem.
- Encourage responses to the following questions:
    - What makes Blake's letter to his friend sound like a poem rather than a letter?
    - What does he mean when he writes "why was I not born like the rest of my race?"
    - What does he write that makes us know that he is not feeling good about himself?
    - When does he feel that people envy him?
    - When does he feel they despise him?

DO
Getting Ready to Write
Discuss the following questions with students:
- Why would you want to share your feelings about yourself?
- If you shared your feelings about yourself with a friend in a letter, how do you think it would make you feel?
- If you were to share something about yourself that you do not like what would it be? For example: *curly hair* or *straight hair*
- What details would you write about this part of yourself that you do not like? For example: *my freckles, my big feet, my curly hair*

Writing the Poem
Students write at least a four line poem by following the steps below.
- Title poems "To [the receipient of their letter]."
- Begin the first line of your poem with "Why was I born with [an aspect about yourself you do not like]?"
- Continue the poem describing what you don't like about this part of yourself.
- Each description should be on its own line and use descriptive language.
- If you want to rhyme, feel free to do so.

Editing and Publishing
- Students handwrite or print their letter poems on construction paper or other writing paper.
- Decorate the paper using colored pencils or crayons.
- Students could fold and enclose their poems in decorated envelopes and mail them to their friends.

Why was I born with so many freckles?
Jack – 4th grade

William Blake Biography
November 28, 1757 – August 12, 1827

William Blake was born in England. His parents were not wealthy but always supported his genius. When he was only four years old, he began to have visions. In one, he saw a tree filled with angels who sang and waved their wings in the branches. These visions were to become the subjects of his drawings and poetry throughout his life.

William's love of drawing and writing began at a very young age. Although he never attended school, he learned to read from his mother. When he was ten, his father, recognizing his artistic talent, sent him to drawing school. There he learned to develop his skills by copying prints. His teacher at the school sent him to Westminster Abbey, a famous church in London. At the Abbey, he spent his time sketching the statues. These statues were a major influence on his drawings. At about age fourteen, he started writing poetry and combining his writing with his drawing.

As he walked along the streets of London, he saw children being mistreated and working very long hours in city factories. In his visions, he saw a different world. He saw angels dancing around the sun that shined over London and children laughing on clouds. He wrote about the innocence of children. Much of his artistic energy was used to bring about a change in the way people treated children.

His life of writing and working on engravings was interrupted for a brief time when one evening a drunken soldier came into Blake's garden. A fight started and Blake overcome with anger said some negative things about the king and his soldiers. The soldier and one of his friends communicated and exaggerated what Blake had said and he was tried for high treason. At trial, he was acquitted when his attorney and many of his neighbors attested to Blake's fine character. The trial must have been a difficult experience for Blake and he expressed his feelings in a letter poem to his friend *O! why was I born with a different face?* He truly was born with a different way of seeing his world.

[To Thomas Butts]: O! why was I born with a different face?
by William Blake

"Oh! why was I born with a different face?
Why was I not born like the rest of my race?
When I look, each one starts! when I speak, I offend;
Then I'm silent and passive and lose every friend.

Then my verse I dishonour, my pictures despise,
My person degrade & my temper chastise;
And the pen is my terror, the pencil my shame;
All my talents I bury, and dead is my fame.

I am either too low or too highly prized;
When elate I'm envy'd, when meek I'm despis'd"

Winter
Math Lesson: Marshmallow Geometry

Winter is the coldest of the four seasons in the Northern Hemisphere. It evokes images of rain, snow and freezing weather. In this lesson, students use marshmallows to emulate snowballs and build three dimensional structures with toothpicks. Students identify the vertices, edges and faces of the structures.

MATERIALS
- Large and mini marshmallows
- Toothpicks
- Geometry 3D Shapes Handout
- Silver glitter and water

PLAN
- Discuss the difference between two and three-dimensional geometric figures. Emphasize how a two-dimensional figure has only length and width while a three-dimensional figure has thickness and volume.
- Distribute mini-marshmallows and toothpicks to every two students and have them create a square cuboid (cube).
- Tell them since this is a winter project they are using the marshmallows to represent snowballs.
- Have students identify the faces (spaces created between the mini marshmallows and toothpicks), the edges (toothpick line segments) and vertices (mini-marshmallow points where the edges meet).
- Student pairs count the 6 faces, 8 vertices, and 12 edges of their cube.

DO
- Distribute the Geometric 3D Shape Handout.
- Discuss each of the nine geometric shape pictures on the handout.
- Talk about the main difference between pyramids, which have two bases, and prisms, which have only one base.
- Demonstrate how easy it is to add sparkle to the snowy marshmallows. Students place each marshmallow on the end of a toothpick, dip them in a dish filled with water and then into a dish containing silver glitter.
- Divide the class into small groups.
- Distribute both large-sized and mini-marshmallows to each group. Have students pick at least three more of the nine objects to create in their groups. They must select at least one geometric shape from each row, skipping the square cuboid.
- Each group presents their products to their classmates. They point out the number of faces, vertices and edges of their shapes they have created.
- Create a classroom display of the 3D shapes.

Geometric 3D Shapes Handout

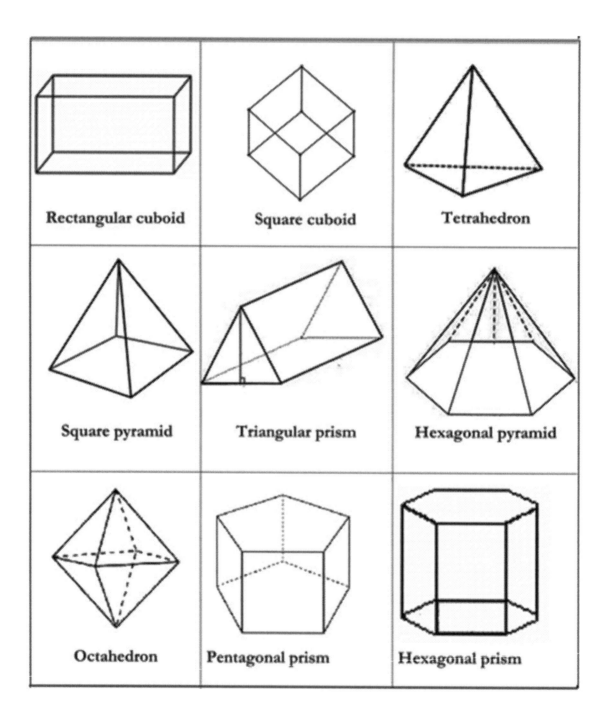

Winter
Poetry Lesson: Winter Haikus

In Basho's winter haikus, he captures the stillness, cold and beauty of this season in diverse images: clouds that promise snow; the wind's sound; chrysanthemums and more. Through observation that is close to meditation, he brilliantly takes a moment and makes it last forever.

MATERIALS
- Matsuo Basho Biography and a selection of winter haikus
- Pencil, paper, word processing and/or desktop publishing software
- Chart or smart board

PLAN
Read and discuss Matsuo Basho's biography and the selection of winter haikus.
- Review the structure of the haiku that typically has three lines with five syllables in the first, seven syllables in the second and five in the third.
- Explain that Basho's poetry often loses the 5-7-5 pattern of haiku during the translation from Japanese to English.
- Tell students that each haiku is a scene about a moment in nature. Ask which is their favorite scene and why.
- Discuss the words Basho uses to capture the season and feeling of winter.

DO
Getting Ready to Write
Discuss with students the following questions:
- What nouns, verbs, adjectives and adverbs does winter bring to mind?
- What colors do you see and sounds do you hear when you think about winter?

- Chart responses.
- Have students refer to the words listed in writing a whole class haiku.
- Guide them through the process through editing and revising while creating a poem that has the haiku structure and conveys the feeling of winter.

Writing the Poem
- Students write their own winter poems using the haiku structure.
- Remind them to focus on the smallest details of a larger scene.

Editing and Publishing
- Students first read to themselves to check the 5-7-5 syllable structure.
- The poems by students are perfectly suited for a class anthology.
- Create and distribute the anthologies to the students and have a class read-around.

Matsuo Basho Biography
1644 - 1694

Matsuo Basho was born in Ueno, a small city in Japan. Japan had a society that consisted of classes. Basho was a Samurai. Unlike those in lower classes, Samurais were allowed to own their own land and receive an education. Basho was educated and learned Japanese and Chinese classics. When he was twelve, he began writing haiku, a form of Japanese poetry. At age twenty-two, he had haikus published in anthologies and he began to teach haiku. His haikus were written in a plain language and about ordinary subjects. In his haikus, the seasons would often appear in either the first or third line of his three-line poems. He thought that poetry should be written about experiences with nature because nature held the highest meaning in life. Through nature, he expressed the emotions he felt.

Often, in his travels, after he would reach the top of a hill, or when he would pause to take a rest, he would stop and look around. Basho saw beautiful energy flow around him – the golden sun bathing a valley or blooming trees by the path. He would also find the same beauty in much smaller things – tiny purse weed flowers under a bush or honeybees busy collecting nectar from flowers. This intense feeling of total awareness that often lasts just for a short moment Basho made permanent by describing it in his poems. By the time he was thirty-four, Basho was considered a great poet and had several men studying with him.

Eventually Basho retired from the literary world. He shaved his head, became a Zen monk and moved to a small and extremely quiet area of Edo. He studied Chinese poetry and meditated. A fire destroyed much of Edo, and Basho's house burned to the ground. After the fire, Basho became disinterested in earthly possessions and began travelling. After three years of travel he returned to Edo. Basho no longer wanted to be involved with the literary world and thought of giving up the writing and teaching of poetry. Because of his love and dedication to both he continued writing and teaching until he died. He was dedicated to improving haiku and was responsible for making it one of the greatest forms of poetry in the literary world.

Winter Haikus
by Matsuo Basho

Even that old horse
is something to see
this snow-covered morning
    ...

Hello! Light the fire!
I'll bring inside
a lovely bright ball of snow
    ...

Crossing half the sky,
on my way to the capital,
big clouds promise snow
    ...

Winter garden,
the moon thinned to a thread,
insects singing.
    ...

Winter seclusion –
sitting propped against
The same worn post
    ...

Winter solitude--
In a world of one color
the sound of wind.
    ...

When the winter chrysanthemums go,
there's nothing to write about
but radishes.
    ...

First snow
falling
on the half-finished bridge.
    ...

The winter leeks
Have been washed white –
How cold it is!

December Holidays
Math Lesson: Shopping for Holiday Parties

In this activity, students work with a partner to go shopping on the Internet to purchase party items for a holiday party of twenty people. Their spending limit will be $200. They will be responsible for purchasing all the items they need for their party.

MATERIALS
- Internet access
- Paper and pencils
- Whiteboard or chart paper

PLAN
- During a class discussion, have students talk about holiday parties.
- Tell them they are going to work with a partner to plan a party.
- Their party will need to include items from the following categories: party essentials, decorations, accessories and food and beverages.
- As they name items, list them on a board or chart under the suggested categories.

DO
Working in pairs, students decide on a holiday party theme and do the following:
- Using pencil and paper, students make a list of items they wish to purchase from the following categories:
  1. Party essentials (invitations, plates, napkins, cutlery, drinking cups, etc.)
  2. Decorations
  3. Accessories (party favors, games, etc.)
  4. Food and beverages
- Students purchase all essential items on their list.
- Using the search engine of their choice, students explore a few party and grocery sites before selecting the ones they will use.
- To create a balance sheet, students divide a paper into thirds. They write the following headings, one on top of each column: Item, Price, Balance.
- Students begin by writing $200.00 on the first line in the balance column.
- Next, students write the name of the first item they wish to purchase and its price on the second line under the appropriate column heading.
- Students subtract the cost of the item in dollars and cents from the $200 budget and write the new balance.
- Students continue to shop until they reach or are close to a zero balance.
- When students are finished they can check their work in one of two ways:
  - Exchange papers and check each other's calculations.
  - Open a spreadsheet, create three columns, write the headings for each column and enter the data from their worksheet to check their bookkeeping.

December Holidays
Poetry Lesson: little tree

What better way to think about the December holidays than with the poem *little tree* by e. e. Cummings? In this poem, Cummings speaks to a symbol of Christmas, a tree. Children will think about the different winter holidays through the symbols that represent each.

MATERIALS
- e. e. cummings Biography and his poem *little tree*.
- Pencil, paper, word processing and/or desktop publishing software
- Chart or smart board

PLAN
Read and discuss the biography of e. e. cummings and his poem *little tree*.
- Cummings did not use punctuation or capitalization except for the words "Christmas" and "Noel." In this poem, Cummings only capitalized words referring to God including Noel, a French word meaning Christ's birthday.
- Discuss personification. Where does Cummings use personification?
- Call attention to his use of arms rather than branches and fingers rather than twigs.

DO
Getting Ready to Write
- During a brainstorming session, use the following discussion points and questions. As the class gives their responses, list them on the board or on a chart.
  - The "little tree" is a symbol for one of the December holidays, Christmas. What other holidays are in December?
  - What symbols are there for each of these holidays?
- Write a sample poem with the class using a December holiday symbol. Replace the title *little tree* with a symbol representing that holiday. Give the symbol human feelings and human form. Prompt the students to include the symbol's past, present and future.

Writing the Poem
- Students write a poem to a symbol, as if they are speaking to it, using personification.
- Remind them that they refer to their symbol with "you" as the pronoun.
- Refer to the poem and the board examples for ideas. Their symbol can be used as the title.

Editing and Publishing
- Students read and edit poems with partners.
- Students write their poems in a poetry book or enter them in a word processing program and illustrate their poetic works.

e. e. cummings Biography
September 3, 1894 – October 14, 1962

Edward Estlin Cummings (known as e.e. cummings) was born in Cambridge, Massachusetts in 1894. His father was a minister. Cummings received a B.A. degree at Harvard in 1915 and a M.A. in 1916.

After Cummings graduated from Harvard, he went to France as a volunteer during World War I. In France, he was suspected of being an enemy and was put into a French detention center for three months. He eventually wrote a book about the people whom he met in this camp. He respected their ability to keep their spirits high in such a horrible environment.

After the war, Cummings lived in Paris and began painting and writing. It was there that he had his first book of poetry published. He was one of the most original of modern poets, dropping most punctuation and capitalization.

Many of his poems were about people who tried to ruin the natural world and about people who were opposed to freedom. He made friends with the poor and wrote poems honoring them. He admired above all else the freedom that children express. In his writing, he never lost that freedom. He writes with a childlike wonder and humor.

Cummings was a modern-day Robin Hood who loved the poor. He was humorous, affectionate, and tough. Instead of carrying a bow and arrow to fight the everyday wrongs that he saw in society, he used words.

little tree
e. e. cummings

The poem is available online. Search or go to the following website and find the poem. Print, copy, and share with your class.

http://www.poetryfoundation.org/poem/176724

The poem *little tree* is perfect for children because it is easily understood. Cummings uses personification in almost every line of the poem. He questions "little tree," by asking it "who found you in the green forest/and were you very sorry to come away?" To him, the "little tree" is sad and throughout the poem he comforts it by saying "i will kiss your cool bark/ and hug you safe and tight." Even its ornaments become alive and human as he writes that they have been sleeping in a box and "dreaming of being taken out and allowed to shine." The tree's branches are arms and its twigs are fingers as he tells the tree "to put up your little arms" and "every finger shall have its ring" so it can be dressed with decorations.

Matthew – 4th grade   Vasilisa – 4th grade

New Year's Eve:
Math Lesson: Minute to Win It

On New Year's Eve in New York City, millions of people gather in Times Square to watch the New Year's Ball take its sixty-second drop to illuminate the final minute of the year. What started in New York City has been copied around the country. Each part of the country puts its own stamp on the tradition. The city of Atlanta, Georgia drops a giant peach and Miami, Florida drops Mr. Neon, a giant orange. Instead of dropping an object, the city of Seattle, Washington raises the elevator to the Space Needle; when the elevator reaches the top at exactly midnight a fireworks display illuminates the sky.

This lesson focuses on the one-minute time frame. Students discuss experiences they have had in the sixty seconds before midnight on New Years Eve. They do exercises to evaluate their ability to judge how long a minute feels. Students work in small groups to try to finish a math-based Minute to Win It game in sixty seconds or less. After trying out a teacher-designed game, the groups work together to create math-focused Minute to Win It games.

MATERIALS
- A Minute to Win It planning sheet
- Commonly found objects for game play. The following list includes some suggested commonly found objects that could be gathered for use in game play:
  - Stopwatches
  - Scissors
  - Popsicle sticks
  - Markers
  - Dice
  - Decks of cards
  - Clothes pins
  - Ping pong balls
  - Paper or plastic cups
  - Paper plates
  - Hershey Kisses
  - Small candies (like M&M's)
  - Straws
  - Poster board
  - Bowl
  - Tweezers

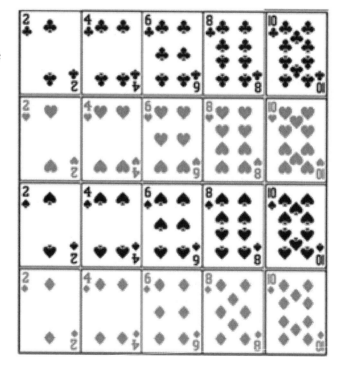

330

PLAN

- Discuss the famous New Year's Eve Ball Drop in New York City. Have students who have witnessed the ball drop in person and those who have watched it on television share their experiences. Expand the discussion to include other New Years Eve countdowns.
- Have everyone stand and turn toward the back of the room.
- Tell them you are going to set a stopwatch for sixty seconds.
- When they think a minute has passed, have them quietly face the front of the room.
- At the end of the minute, students evaluate how close they came to judging the length of a minute.
- Divide the class into small groups and have each group repeat the above activity using stopwatches to time each other. Allow time for them to take several turns to make them better able to judge the length of a minute.
- Distribute a deck of cards to each group. Tell them their challenge is to pull the even numbers from the deck to make a new deck with all even numbers. This can be modified depending on math level to all numbers divisible by 2, divisible by 3, and so on. Have them place the cards in each group in numerical order. For example, one stack would include the 2, 4, 6, 8 and 10 of hearts. The spades, diamonds and clubs would be placed in the same order.
- Have the groups discuss whether this game was possible in a minute or whether they had had too much time left over.

DO

Have each group create A Minute to Win It Math Challenge for the class by doing the following:

- Complete the A Minute to Win It planning sheet.
- Gather supplies.
- Try the challenge using stopwatches to time each other and adjust the activity if it seems too easy or too difficult to complete in one minute.
- Present their challenge to the class and select volunteers to try to complete their challenge in a minute.

A Minute to Win It!

Materials

Game Directions

New Year's Eve
Poetry Lesson: A Song for New Year's Eve

In his poem *A Song for New Year's Eve,* William Cullen Bryant speaks to the passing year and to his friends asking them both to stay just "one little hour, and then away." In this hour, he also asks his friends to look back at the passing year "While yet he was our guest/How cheerfully the week was spent!"

MATERIALS
- William Cullen Bryant Biography and his poem *A Song for New Year's Eve*
- Word processing or desktop publishing software or pencils, pens and paper

PLAN
- Read and discuss William Cullen Bryant's biography and poem.
- Ask the following questions:
    - To whom was Bryant speaking?
    - How did Bryant feel about the old year leaving and why did he feel that way?
    - Where does Bryant use personification when writing about the passing year?

DO
Getting Ready to Write
Ask students the following questions. As the class gives their responses, encourage discussion.
- How do you feel about your old year leaving? Why?
- Personify the New Year. What would you say to the passing year?

Writing the Poem
Using *A Song for New Year's Eve* as a model, have students write poems of their own.
- Students write poems by addressing the passing year with either "stay" for the things they liked or "away" for the things they didn't.
- Students begin each stanza with either "stay" or "away."
- Students continue their poems telling the New Year what they liked or disliked about it using personification as much as possible.

Editing and Publishing
- Students read and edit poems with partners.
- Students write their poems in a poetry book, or enter them in a word processing program and illustrate their final masterpiece.

William Cullen Bryant Biography
November 3, 1794 - June 12, 1878

William Cullen Bryant was born in Massachusetts. His mother's family came to America on the Mayflower. His father was a physician who strongly influenced William.

William learned poetry at a young age in his father's large library. One poet who had a great deal of influence on him was William Wordsworth. His father encouraged William's writing and at times even sent William's poems to magazines for publication without his knowledge. At the age of ten, William had his first poem published. At thirteen his first book was published.

Although his first love was poetry, the life of a poet was not practical for him. With the encouragement of his father he became a lawyer. Eventually he left law and moved his family to New York City. There he began his career in journalism. As editor-in-chief of the Evening Post, one of the nation's most respected newspapers, he wrote articles that defended Abraham Lincoln, human rights, free trade and the abolition of slavery. Although he was also known as a poet and critic, he felt that he didn't have enough time to devote to his writing because he traveled frequently and was busy in his work as a journalist.

He didn't publish many poems in his lifetime, but he was very popular due to his writing as a journalist and his many public speeches. Bryant was one of the founders of the Republican Party, and at one time he considered running for President of the United States.

A Song for New Year's Eve
by William Cullen Bryant

Stay yet, my friends, a moment stay,
Stay till the good old year,
So long companion of our way,
Shakes hands, and leaves us here.
Oh stay, oh stay,
One little hour, and then away.

The year, whose hopes were high and strong,
Has now no hopes to wake;
Yet one hour more of jest and song
For his familiar sake.
Oh stay, oh stay,
One mirthful hour, and then away.

The kindly year, his liberal hands
Have lavished all his store.
And shall we turn from where he stands,
Because he gives no more?
Oh stay, oh stay,
One grateful hour, and then away.

Days brightly came and calmly went,
While yet he was our guest;
How cheerfully the week was spent!
How sweet the seventh day's rest!
Oh stay, oh stay,
One golden hour, and then away.

Dear friends were with us, some who sleep
Beneath the coffin-lid:
What pleasant memories we keep
Of all they said and did!
Oh stay, oh stay,
One tender hour, and then away.

Even while we sing, he smiles his last,
And leaves our sphere behind.
The good old year is with the past;
Oh be the new as kind!
Oh stay, oh stay,
One parting strain, and then away.

About Us

GARY CARNOW has been a classroom teacher, administrator, author and educational consultant. Dr. Carnow specializes in administrative and instructional technologies, grants and funding procurement, instructional program development, emerging technologies, makerspaces and 3D printing. He has consulted for major hardware and software computer companies and has written extensively for Tech&Learning magazine. He was one of the first educators to provide content for AOL and the Scholastic Network. Beverly and Gary have written educational materials together for over twenty-five years.

BEVERLY ELLMAN is an educator who has enjoyed wearing many different hats. She has been a classroom teacher, an author of educational publications and an educational product developer. She has enjoyed watching the enthusiasm, energy, and creativity sparked in students as they experience learning and master STEM content. She has co-taught several classes which combined poetry and multimedia through UCLA extension with Joyce Koff. In addition, Joyce and Beverly have worked together presenting educational workshops to various elementary and middle school teachers.

JOYCE KOFF is a poet and a teacher. Her work has been published in numerous poetry journals and she has taught in elementary and middle schools in her self-created program. Joyce makes the reading, understanding and writing of poetry accessible to all students and these methods are applied in this book. Joyce has also conducted classes at UCLA demonstrating to teachers how valuable and rewarding the teaching of hands-on poetry can be. As the resident poet at Coeur d'Alene Elementary School in Venice, California, she taught poetry for over 25 years and was part of the art's team that was awarded the prestigious Los Angeles Music Center's Bravo Award.

SIAN BOWMAN has never lost the giddy excitement she experienced as child when drawing and painting. After graduating from Aberystwyth University with a Masters in Fine Art, specializing in children's book illustration, she started freelancing as an illustrator. She is in her element working on picture books and educational books for children. She finds inspiration for her characters in walking her wonderful, cheeky whippet, Jet, through the countryside of Mid Wales, where her imagination can wander. You can learn more about Sian at sianbowman.com.

Made in the USA
Columbia, SC
04 July 2022